CAMBRIDGE STUDIES IN EARLY MODERN HISTORY

Editors

J. H. ELLIOTT   OLWEN HUFTON
H. G. KOENIGSBERGER

The Princes of Orange

CAMBRIDGE STUDIES IN EARLY MODERN HISTORY

*Edited by Professor J. H. Elliott, The Institute for Advanced Study, Princeton,
Professor Olwen Hufton, University of Reading, and Professor H. G. Koenigsberger, King's
College, London*

The idea of an "early modern" period of European history from the fifteenth to the late eighteenth century is now widely accepted among historians. The purpose of the Cambridge Studies in Early Modern History is to publish monographs and studies which will illuminate the character of the period as a whole, and in particular focus attention on a dominant theme within it, the interplay of continuity and change as they are represented by the continuity of medieval ideas, political and social organization, and by the impact of new ideas, new methods and new demands on the traditional structures.

The Princes of Orange

The Stadholders in the Dutch Republic

HERBERT H. ROWEN

Emeritus Professor, Rutgers University

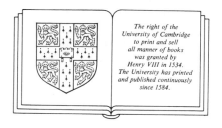

*The right of the
University of Cambridge
to print and sell
all manner of books
was granted by
Henry VIII in 1534.
The University has printed
and published continuously
since 1584.*

CAMBRIDGE UNIVERSITY PRESS

Cambridge

New York   Port Chester   Melbourne   Sydney

Published by the Press Syndicate of the University of Cambridge
The Pitt Building, Trumpington Street, Cambridge CB2 1RP
40 West 20th Street, New York, NY 10011, USA
10 Stamford Road, Oakleigh, Melbourne 3166, Australia

First published 1988
First paperback edition 1990

Printed in Great Britain at the University Press, Cambridge

British Library cataloguing in publication data
Rowen, Herbert H.
The princes of orange: the stadholders in
the Dutch Republic. (Cambridge studies
in early modern history).
1. Netherlands–Politics and government
–1648–1795
I. Title
354.492′0009   JN5745

Library of Congress cataloguing in publication data
Rowen, Herbert Harvey.
The princes of Orange.
(Cambridge studies in early modern history)
Bibliography
Includes index.
1. Netherlands–Politics and government–1556–1648.
2. Netherlands–Politics and government–1648–1795.
3. Netherlands–Kings and rulers–History.
4. Orange-Nassau, House of.   I. Title.   II. Series.
DJ158.R693   1988   949.2′04   87–18323

ISBN 0 521 34525 1 hardback
ISBN 0 521 39653 0 paperback

CS

To the memory of
Jan den Tex and Jan Poelhekke

Contents

Illustrations

Preface

Political history has usually been studied in two separate ways. One is to look at events, the working out of actual politics; included in this approach is the biography of individual statesmen. The other is to examine institutions, the formal structures and explicit rules that hold sway over the long run. These two approaches have most often been treated as mutually exclusive contraries, and those historians who have been effective in one have seldom been so in the other. Yet, lost in the vast middle ground between them, touching on both but distinct from either, is another kind of political history, the study of informal institutions, which we might also describe as the interplay of events and institutions. The stadholderate in the Dutch Republic was such an institution, embodying formal, informal and (to use the neologism of the *Annales* historians) *événementiel* aspects.

Like the Republic of the United Provinces as a whole, the stadholderate was an improvisation that lasted more than two centuries (with two long breaks). Again as with the Republic, it was difficult for contemporaries to fit it into the standard categories of political analysis. Modern political theory does little better, for its slots are carved for different situations. The usual solution has been to describe the stadholdership in terms of monarchy, as crippled and incomplete kingship. Although the present book is an effort to break out of this pattern, candor requires that the author at once inform the reader that he himself has used this approach, citing with certainty of its aptness Thomas Jefferson's description of William V as "half-king."[1] Indeed, this study was begun in the confident expectation that it would be an elaboration of this approach.

It was not long afterwards that I began to be uneasy about the value of the description of the stadholderate as quasi-monarchy. For one thing, my study of the proprietary aspect of the French monarchy of the *Ancien Régime*, culminating in the book *The King's State: Proprietary Dynasticism in Early Modern France*,[2] had been conducted as the analysis of what I call above an "informal institution." When I looked at the stadholderate in the

---

1 See below, ch. 11, p. 226.   2 New Brunswick, NJ, 1980.

same way, what I discovered produced anomalies (to use Thomas Kuhn's formulation) that did not go away when I examined the problem more closely, but became worse. For another thing, my studies of the French monarchy had made me aware of the importance of distinguishing between monarchy and kingship. They are not different words for the same thing, stylistically convenient synonyms; they describe different things. Monarchy is best used as a precise word for the Aristotelian concept of the rule of one person; kingship, for a historically evolved kind of political status and power. To speak of absolute monarchy is to commit a tautology; to speak of an absolute king is not. Put in another way, an absolute king is indeed a monarch; a constitutional king (or equivalent crowned head under another title) is not.

As my investigations continued, I more and more saw the stadholderate as an institution *sui generis*: it was, as I put it in the title of my Clark Library seminar paper of 1982, "neither fish nor fowl."[3] It turned out, too, that significant episodes in the history of the Dutch Republic emerged in a new light. I was able to escape the chronic anachronism of Dutch historians who saw the stadholdership as the embryonic form of the modern Dutch monarchy (or, in the more precise terminology that I insist upon above, "kingship"). I have long been averse to backwards causality in history, believing it more productive to find results than to seek origins, and I was, I think, rewarded in this case by achieving a fuller understanding of the novelty as well as the continuity of the Dutch state that re-emerged in independence in 1813–15.

This work had its inception six years ago in a conversation with Jan Poelhekke at the Catholic University of Nijmegen, and his death last year is a loss I feel all the more because he had no opportunity to read this book, even in draft form. My research was supported by a senior followship from the National Endowment for the Humanities and a grant-in-aid from the American Philosophical Society, as well as by the Research Council of Rutgers University : to all, heart-felt thanks. I have discussed my ideas with colleagues in this country and Europe, and my thanks go to all of them, but I must single out Andrew Lossky as the warmest of friends and the most penetrating and encouraging of critics. A different kind of gratitude is due to two friends, David Lester and Rudolph Bell, whose urgings to go the way of the word processor I did not accept for too long. It has made the completion of this work far easier than I ever anticipated. The illustrations were selected for me by my friend and colleague, J. W. Schulte Nordholt, who knows the full meaning of *quid pro quo*. All the

---

3 "Neither Fish nor Fowl: The Stadholderate in the Dutch Republic," in: Herbert H. Rowen and Andrew Lossky, *Political Ideas and Institutions in the Dutch Republic: Papers presented at a Clark Library Seminar, 27 March 1982* (Los Angeles, 1985), 1–31.

customary remarks upon the contributions of spouses are still true, however trite, of my wife Mildred: Thank you for forty-six years and what has
been possible in them.

Rocky Hill, New Jersey
November, 1986

Prologue: lieutenants of the crown

Like the Dutch Republic itself, the stadholderate was an improvisation. Both were old structures adapted to new needs and a new situation, the product of the peculiar course of the Revolt of the Low Countries. The Republic of the United Provinces of the Netherlands was a rump remnant of the "Burgundian state," as historians call the assemblage of lands under the rule of the French dukes of Burgundy since the late fourteenth century.[1] But it was more than a rump; it had become a new nation, a new state, in which the stadholderate changed character.

The core of "Burgundy" was neither the duchy of Burgundy within France itself nor the adjacent "Free County" (Franche-Comté) of the same name within the Empire, but the seventeen[2] provinces that straddled the delta of the merged Rhine, Maas (Meuse) and Schelde (Scheldt) Rivers as they flowed into the North Sea. They had never formed a unified state in the modern sense, such as France and England had already become, but were little more than a congeries of lands acquired by the Burgundian dukes beginning in the late fourteenth century and by their heirs, the Habsburgs of Austria and Spain, in the first half of the sixteenth. Their unity consisted essentially in shared rulership and the single policy which their resources served.[3] Because the revenues of the dukes, fed by the fabulous industry, trade and agriculture of the Low Countries, were immense, the "Burgundian state" was one of the great powers of the fifteenth century. Sharing in the costs and consequences of the ducal wars, the provinces began to see, however faintly, that they had common interests, even if only to resist the bellicose policies of the dukes for which they had to pay and to urge use of Burgundian power for their own special advantage. At the same time, the

---

1 See A. G. Jongkees, "Vorming van de Bourgondische staat," in: *Algemene Geschiedenis der Nederlanden* (2nd edn, 15 vols.; Haarlem, 1977–83), III, 191.
2 The number was conventional. Several of the "seventeen" were not provinces at all but titles held by Charles V in the Low Countries.
3 Richard Vaughan (*Philip the Bold: The Formation of the Burgundian State* [Cambridge, Mass, 1962], 237–38; *John the Fearless: The Growth of Burgundian Power* [New York, 1966], 287–89) emphasizes that the Burgundian state was already a "political entity," although not one territorially or juridically.

dukes gradually set various central organs over the provincial institutions to make them serve the Burgundian purposes more effectively. The result was the emergence of a significant sense of common fate and the formation of common administrative structures that were two of the most important elements in the embryonic nationhood[4] of the Netherlands.[5]

After 1430 the dukes became more "Netherlandish" (to use the term to include the French as well as the Dutch-speaking provinces)[6] than Burgundian, and their usual residence was at Brussels, the capital of Brabant. They were therefore able to exercise their governance in the Low Countries either directly or through lieutenants (in Dutch *stadhouders*, the term which has come over into English as "stadholders"). These lieutenants were identical with the "governors" in France, who were the military and political leaders in the provinces on behalf of and under the authority of the royal crown.[7] They fell between the two poles of governmental power, at the one end the intensifying administrative centralization of the dukes and at the other the persistent local self-governance of towns and noblemen; indeed, the primary task of the stadholders was to connect the two poles into a single system of effective rule. They had no fixity of office, however; although usually notables from within the province or at least the Low Countries as a whole, they commanded the duke's troops as captains-general and executed his instructions.[8]

A significant innovation came late in the fifteenth century, after the death of Duchess Mary, when her widower, Maximilian of Habsburg, governed the Netherlands on behalf of their son, Duke Philip the Handsome. Frequently absent from the country because of his duties as King of the Romans (elected successor to the Imperial throne) and Austrian archduke, Maximilian named Duke Albert of Saxony as his stadholder-general in the Netherlands.[9] Philip came of age in 1493 and governed in

---

4 Jongkees, 101–92, 196–98; Leo Delfos, *Die Anfänge der Utrechter Union, 1577–1587: Ein Beitrag zur Geschichte der niederländischen Erhebung, insbesondere zu deren Verfassungsgeschichte* (Berlin, 1941; reprint edn, Vaduz, 1965), 19; J. J. Poelhekke, *Frederik Hendrik, Prins van Oranje: Een Biografisch Drieluik* (Zutphen, 1978), 23; P. Geyl, *Geschiedenis van de Nederlandse Stam* (reprint edn; 6 vols.; Amsterdam, 1961–62), I, 145.
5 The names "Netherlands" and "Low Countries" were already losing their strictly geographic denotation and becoming the designation of a particular territory.
6 See Geyl, *Geschiedenis*, I, 139, which, however, in accordance with the author's "Great Netherlands" principle, emphasizes the Dutch–Flemish (*Diets*) character of the Burgundian state – not of the dukes themselves – at the expense of its French element.
7 See Robert R. Harding, *Anatomy of a Power Elite: The Provincial Governors of Early Modern France* (New Haven and London, 1978).
8 Paul Rosenfeld, "The Provincial Governors from the Minority of Charles V to the Revolt," *Anciens Pays et Assemblées d'états*, 17 (1959), 16.
9 For the conflict-filled rule of Maximilian in the Netherlands, see Helmut Georg Koenigsberger, "Fürst und Generalstaaten: Maximilian I. in den Niederlanden (1477–1493)," *Historische Zeitschrift*, 242 (1986), 557–79.

person. However, his marriage to the Spanish infanta Joanna, who became the heiress to the Castillian and Aragonese thrones in 1498, led him to make two journeys to Spain in 1501 and 1506. On both occasions he named lieutenants-general to govern in the Netherlands during his absence. He did not return from his second trip, dying in Spain in 1506. He was succeeded as lord of the Low Countries by his six-year-old son Charles, the most famed of all Habsburgs as King Charles I of Spain (1516), Emperor Charles V (1519) and head of the House of Austria. During his minority the governorship-general was in the hands of his aunt Margaret of Austria, dowager duchess of Savoy, and even after he came of age in 1515 Charles, who returned to his native Netherlands only infrequently, continued her in her office until her death in 1530. During this period, therefore, the provincial stadholders were themselves beholden to governors-general.[10]

It was during the last half-century of the rule of Charles V that the stadholdership was consolidated in the form that would be adapted and transformed during the Revolt. We need pay little attention to the governorship-general, for the stadholderate under the Dutch Republic did not develop out of that office but out of the provincial stadholdership. The powers of the governors-general were universal, save always the superior authority of Charles, who however gave his full confidence to the Regents, Margaret of Austria and her successor, Mary of Hungary, as full-fledged members of the House of Habsburg.[11]

The powers of the provincial governors were more carefully circumscribed. The stadholders were always appointed by the ruling prince himself, although on the advice of the Regent. They were recruited from the high noble clans that had served the Burgundians well, but their fidelity had been bought by munificent rewards and was hardly selfless.[12] Mary of Hungary in particular saw the peril that lay in the nobles' desire to pass on the office of provincial stadholder to heirs, for then they would be tempted to see themselves no longer as just exalted servants but as having powers in their own right.[13]

Governors exercised virtually all the rights of the ruling prince within their provinces. For the inhabitants, they were the government above the

---

10 P. J. Blok, *Geschiedenis van het Nederlandsche Volk* (8 vols.; Groningen, 1892–1908), I, 547–48, 563–64.
11 Blok, *Geschiedenis*, I, 548–49; N. Japikse, *De Geschiedenis van het Huis van Oranje-Nassau* (2 vols.; The Hague, 1937–38), I, 45.
12 Blok, *Geschiedenis*, I, 563–64; Rosenfeld, 4–5, 16–17, 25; H. G. Koenigsberger, "Orange, Granvelle and Philip II," *Bijdragen en Mededelingen betreffende de Geschiedenis der Nederlanden* (hereafter abbreviated as *BMGN*), 9 (1984), 575–76 (this article is reprinted in the author's *Politicians and Virtuosi: Essays in Early Modern Europe*, London and Ronceverte, West Virginia, 1985, 97–119).
13 Rosenfeld, 10, 35, 37.

local authorities. Two elements – military command and influence over election of members of some town governments – were crucial for the eventual development of the republican stadholdership. Much of the stadholders' prestige and effective power came from the fact that the professional armed force in the provinces was in their hands as captains-general. Almost equally important was the right of appointment to municipal offices within the provinces during the annual election called the *wetsverzetting* ("renewal of the government"),[14] for it limited the ability of the dominant cliques within the towns to govern on their own, without the effective control of the officials at Brussels. Only Friesland and Gelderland, the most recently acquired of the provinces, retained by special pledge of the Emperor the right to elect their own municipal officers, not merely to propose their names to the stadholder.[15] However, in the provinces of Holland, Zeeland and Flanders, even this limited right was taken away from Regent Mary, who also forbade the stadholders in office to nominate their successors, lest they come to consider their posts as in practice hereditary.[16]

The range and depth of the stadholders' powers can be seen with precise definition in the instructions given to the Prince of Orange, William I, when Philip II, who succeeded his father Charles V in 1555, named him stadholder of the counties of Holland and Zeeland and the land of Utrecht as well as certain other adjacent territories in 1559. His tasks were defined both broadly and specifically. On the one hand the instructions maintained Philip's "rights, highness and lordship," and on the other protected the rights of his subjects and safeguarded them against all "oppression" (*foulles et oppressions*). William was to seek the "welfare" of the provinces. He would provide justice to all who sought it and enforce the sentences of the courts. He would continue in the customary way to appoint burgomasters and members of the town councils. He would provide for the watch in the towns and garrisons in the fortresses, and call the States into session when needed. Overall, he was to do "everything and anything" that "a good and faithful governor-general can and should do."[17] Although these instructions gave the general tone of the powers entrusted to the

14 The word *wet* means literally "law," and the aldermen and burgomasters were "*de heren van de wet*," "the lords of the law." The term *wetsverzetting* at this time meant the normal election, but under the Republic it came to mean dismissals and appointments out of the ordinary course.

15 Rosenfeld, 23, 44–46; Blok, *Geschiedenis*, I, 566.

16 H. de Schepper, "De burgerlijke overheden en hun permanente kaders," in: *Algemene Geschiedenis*, V, 337.

17 Commission as governor and lieutenant-general of the counties of Holland and Zeeland, the land of Utrecht, West Friesland, Voorne, Den Briel, and lands adjacent and annexed to these counties, given by Philip II to William of Orange, 9 Aug. 1559, M. Gachard, ed., *Correspondance de Guillaume le Taciturne, Prince d'Orange* (6 vols.; Brussels, Leipzig, Ghent, 1850–66), I, 487–88.

stadholders in the other provinces and to different stadholders over the years, they varied considerably in detail and were not always as precise.[18]

Whatever difficulties occurred in the relations between the provincial stadholders on the one hand and the Emperor Charles V and the Habsburg governors-general on the other, they were still only ripples on the surface during his reign. A fundamental harmony of interests was carefully cultivated by the Emperor, and it was displayed for all to see in the final act of his rule when, during his abdication at Brussels in 1555, he gave his speech of farewell resting upon the shoulder of the young Prince William of Orange. Charles had received his first education in politics in the Netherlands, the land of his birth, and he understood its situation throughout his life, even though he spent more and more of his years in other realms under his scepter. For their part, the stadholders always had more to gain in Charles's service than they could hope to win by baronial opposition to him; the complaints by Mary of Hungary about their ambitions were aroused not by incipient rebellion but by their effort to carve out for themselves the greatest possible range of action, the greatest independence of judgment, within a collaboration that neither side ever called into question in principle. Furthermore, although both the rulers at Brussels and the stadholders sought to limit and inhibit the restless self-assertiveness of the towns, in particular notoriously rebellious Ghent, they did not attempt to abolish the provincial States or the States-General, without which the collection of taxes would have been far more difficult and laborious. The central councils established in Brussels were not intended to replace the States and even less the autonomous municipal governments, but to make them more amenable to the needs of the crown.

In this complex and inherently ambiguous relationship, the stadholders played an essential role. They were on the spot, the eyes, ears and the enforcing arms of the Emperor. Whatever the advances of centralized and bureaucratic government in Brussels, it remained much too thin to be able to govern the provinces directly. It rested upon the work of the stadholders in place. The stadholders for their part acquired a familiarity with local conditions – the interests involved, the persons in contention, the peculiarities of institutions and the traditions to which the people held – that could seldom be matched in Brussels. A stadholder with the abililty to project himself imaginatively into other people's predicaments might therefore find himself in the position of seeing the situation from below as well as from above.

The tensions of the relations between the ruler and the stadholders, already evident during the regency of Mary of Hungary, became more

18 Schepper, 337.

difficult after the accession of Philip II. Born and raised in Spain, Philip lacked his father's easy familiarity with the Low Countries. He took quite literally the injunctions of political theorists on the totality of his sovereign powers, subject always to the higher sovereignty of God, which he accepted with equal literalness. In Spain Philip tempered his absolutism with a ready skill in governing with the grandees and the States assemblies (Cortes), but he resented having to do so in the Netherlands. A key difference was that there the great nobles dominated the Council of State, in which members of the Order of the Golden Fleece had a seat by right. They benefited, too, by the continued strength of the States assemblies, of which they were leading and influential members. In 1576, William was to recall that Philip had expressed to him in so many words his distaste for the arrogance of the States, and hinted that it rested upon the support given them by unnamed persons.[19]

Another important difference concerned the size and character of the administrative apparatus available to Philip in Spain and in the Netherlands. It was highly developed in Spain and was essentially an emanation of the central government; in the Low Countries, on the contrary, it was much less advanced, with the few central agencies, however important, set over rather than taking the place of local and provincial governments, which retained a very large measure of continuing autonomy. When Philip attempted to diminish the role of the Council of State as the principal advisory body for the new governor-general, his half-sister Margaret of Parma, there was no adequate apparatus in place through which she could govern, even with the skillful guidance of Antoine Perrenot, a churchman from Franche-Comté who was elevated to the cardinalate under the title of Granvelle.

The immediate issue that brought on the clash[20] between Granvelle and the grandees – the Spanish term nicely expresses the status of the highest nobility in the Netherlands – was the reorganization of the bishoprics in the Low Countries, which Philip II had obtained from the papacy in 1559. It was not so much the undoubted rationality of the reorganization – creating an adequate number of bishoprics and withdrawing them from the jurisdiction of archbishops in Germany and France – that drew the fire of the nobles as that they had to pay the price of the change. The reorganization, by assigning the wealthiest abbeys to the new bishops to supplement their revenues, both took away moneys that ordinarily went to noble families and at the same time gave the bishops the representation in the provincial States that historically belonged to the abbots. In addition, there

19 William I to the States General, no date (Nov. 1576), William I, *Correspondance*, III, 146–47.
20 For this conflict, see H. G. Koenigsberger, "Orange, Granvelle and Philip II," 573–95.

was some unhappiness among the nobles at the prospect that the reorganized Catholic Church would be in a position to enforce the inquisition against heretics on which Philip had set his mind. A tradition of Erasmian toleration (however it be defined, its consequence was a detestation of burning bodies to save souls) was strong among the nobility, as among many classes of the population. The final blow to the grandees was the withdrawal of the king's confidence from them in favor of the Regent, Margaret of Parma, and especially of her advisor, Granvelle, who was totally Philip's servant. Although the great nobles were still granted key military and political offices, notably the stadholderships, their feeling of exclusion from rights to which they were entitled was not assuaged, all the more because Margaret and Granvelle considered that the post of stadholder undermined the Regent's authority.[21]

The opposition of the grandees coalesced in 1562 with the formation of a league aimed at the overthrow of Granvelle's ascendancy and their refusal in 1563 to attend meetings of the Council of State so long as he was present. The king conceded to them for the moment by transferring the cardinal to Spain the next year. Although the transformation of peaceful political resistance into outright civil war was to take several years, so that the beginning of the Revolt of the Low Countries cannot be precisely dated, it is fair to say that this strike of the grandees was either the start of the Revolt or was a Pre-Revolt (to follow the usage of the French historians who call the events of 1787–9 in France the "Pre-Revolution"). Although this resistance was in a way a replay of the baronial rebellions of earlier centuries, it was unusual in that it was the very class that had supported the crown most effectively during the Burgundian rule that now took up the challenge to the Burgundian heir who reigned as the Habsburg king in Spain.

21 Horst Lademacher, *Die Stellung des Prinzen von Oranien als Statthalter in den Niederlanden van 1572 bis 1584: Ein Beitrag zur Verfassungsgeschichte der Niederlande* (Bonn, 1958), 40.

William I: from courtier to rebel

At first glance William I, Prince of Orange and Count of Nassau, as the ranking nobleman in the country,[1] might well have seemed the least likely person[2] to lead the revolt that broke out in the Netherlands in 1566.[3] Born 25 April 1533, he had been sent as a boy from his birthplace in Germany to take up the inheritance of his cousin, René of Chalon. René had been the first to combine the sovereignty of the tiny principality of Orange, an enclave in southern France, with the vast wealth and the leading military and political role of the counts of Nassau in the Low Countries. Growing to manhood, William adapted to the plush luxuriance of his new life at the Brussels court of Charles V,[4] but retained in his relations with persons of all classes an earthiness that had been characteristic of the first ten years of his life in the Nassau castle at Dillenburg. Although even before the Emperor's abdication Charles's son Philip seems to have resented the confidence and affection that his father bestowed upon the Prince of Orange, it was not until the four years of Philip's residence in the Netherlands ended with his departure for his native Spain in 1559 that the king clearly came to

---

1 See H. F. K. van Nierop, "De adel in de 16de-eeuwse Nederlanden," *Spiegel Historiael*, 19 (1984), 163–68, and *Van ridders tot regenten: De Hollandse adel in de zestiende en de eerste helft van de zeventiende eeuw* (Dieren, Gelderland, 1984) for an overview of the nobility in this period.

2 This characterization is implicit in K. W. Swart, "Wat bewoog Willem van Oranje de strijd tegen de Spaanse overheersing aan te binden?," *BMGN*, 99 (1984), 554. For a brief presentation of William as the noble leader of the Revolt, see S. Groenveld, "Ter Inleiding: Willem van Oranje. Een hoog edelman in opstand," *Spiegel Historiael*, 19 (1984), 158–62.

3 The best modern account of the revolt is Geoffrey Parker, *The Dutch Revolt* (revised edn, 1979). Despite the title, it views the events from the perspective of the Low Countries as a whole, Dutch–Flemish and French–Walloon speakers both. Parker treats as actually three successive revolts what in modern times is usually called "the Revolt of the Low Countries" in the singular. Kossmann and Mellink agree that the singular is inaccurate, pointing to contemporary descriptions of "The Wars (or: The Civil Wars) in the Netherlands," but they place even more stress upon its complex and contradictory characteristics (E. H. Kossmann and A. F. Mellink, eds., *Texts concerning the Revolt of the Netherlands* [Cambridge, 1974], "Introduction," 1–2).

4 P. Janssens, "Willem van Oranje aan het Brussels Hof 1549–1559," *Spiegel Historiael*, 19 (1984), 174–81.

GVILELM. D.G. PRINC. AUR. COM. NASS. etc. VICEC. ANTV. et. VES. BARO BREDAE, et. GUB. HOL. SEL. UT.

William I, 1533–1584

look upon William with a suspicious eye. Yet, respect for his importance and influence prompted Philip to name William to the Council of State and to the Order of the Golden Fleece,[5] and upon quitting the country to appoint him stadholder for Holland, Zeeland and Utrecht, like two counts of Nassau, Henry III and René of Chalon, before him.[6]

There was good reason for Philip's distrust. The Prince of Orange was a faithful subject of his king, to be sure, but he did not see himself or his fellow grandees as no more than exalted instruments of the royal will. He took as his second wife[7] Anna of Saxony, the daughter of Maurice of Saxony, a notorious foe of Charles V, despite the dissuasions of Granvelle and Philip II, thereby calling into doubt the sincerity or at least the fervor of the Catholicism he had adopted on coming to court to take up René's inheritance.[8] Furthermore, William's Catholicism was in the Erasmian tradition, wide in its acceptance of doctrinal variation and hostile to the imposition of faiths by force. It was a commitment that he adhered to even as he changed his church membership; it may even have been, as one historian suggests, the fundamental cause of his conflict with Philip.[9]

Orange was proud of his high rank and jealous to preserve the right to take a leading part in the king's government that he believed his rank gave him. He had practical experience of government both as stadholder and as a member of the Council of State, the highest of the central councils instituted by Charles V.[10] He was neither a republican, believing in government without a crowned head of state,[11] nor a democrat, for whom rule ought to rest in the "people." But he was not an upholder of absolute monarchy either, one who imposed no limit other than divine law and ultimate divine judgment upon the power of the king.[12] He was a constitutional conservative, accepting the established traditions in the Low Countries, where for centuries the dukes and counts had governed with the participation of States assemblies in conformity with hallowed practice and

---

5 M. E. J. Baelde, "De Orde van het Gulden Vlies," *Spiegel Historiael*, 19 (1984), 169–73.
6 P. J. Blok, *Willem de Eerste, Prins van Oranje* (2 vols.; Amsterdam, 1919–20), I, 6, 9, 49.
7 For a brief account of William's wives, see Hilde de Ridder-Symoens, "Vrouwen rond Willem van Oranje," *Spiegel Historiael*, 19 (1984), 181–86.
8 Parker, 51.
9 Swart, "Wat bewoog," 554–55. M. E. H. N. Mout ("Het intellectuele milieu van Willem van Oranje," *BMGN*, 99 (1984), 596, 605–13) calls this view of William's attitude into doubt, referring to his "reputed (*vermeende*) Erasmianism."
10 See Kossmann and Mellink, "Introduction," 6–7, where the traditional view of the nobility's "lack of administrative capacity" is rejected.
11 He used the word *république* in accordance with contemporary custom as a synonym for a state, any country in the political sense. See William I to States General, end November 1576, William I, *Correspondance*, III, 153.
12 A. A. van Schelven, *Willem van Oranje: Een boek ter gedachtenis van idealen en teleurstellingen* (4th edn; Amsterdam, 1948), 61.

with respect for the power and the wealth of the towns.[13] His politics was that of a practical man, not that of a deep thinker; but he knew what ideas he wanted his ghost writers to present.[14]

In one respect William was unique among the provincial governors – as a sovereign prince in Orange, he enjoyed juridical equality with the king of Spain himself. William proudly reminded Elector August of Saxony, his uncle by marriage, that he held Orange as "my own free property," not as a fief of anyone else, neither the Pope nor the king of Spain or France.[15] In terms of real strength, of course, it was an equality of the elephant and the mouse as both mammals. William's wealth and resources lay, too, in the Low Countries and Germany, and large as they were, they were little compared to those of the king of Spain. But they were the basis of his honor and reputation, and this drove him forward as much as his distaste for religious persecution.[16]

Until 1565 William, like Philip himself, sought to avoid the extremity of direct confrontation toward which they seemed headed. It was this caution in expressing his full feelings that apparently led Granvelle to dub him *le taciturne*, the "close-mouthed," which was turned into Dutch as *de Zwijger* and into English as the identical "the Silent," although neither term was quite accurate for the voluble and often eloquent Prince of Orange. He took the lead in a virtual strike of the highest nobility – a refusal to come to meetings of the Council of State and a threat to resign – unless Granvelle was removed and their own voice in the determination of policy and the distribution of patronage became decisive.[17] They won when Regent Margaret persuaded Philip to concede Granvelle's withdrawal in 1564. William stood aside, however, when a band of lesser nobles, among them his own brother, Count John of Nassau, formed a league, the "Compromise"[18] of December 1565, aimed at open resistance to enforcement of the Inquisi-

---

13 Kossmann and Mellink, "Introduction," 5–6.
14 Mout, 599, 614–25. See also H. F. K. van Nierop, "Willem van Oranje als hoog edelman: patronage in de Habsburgse Nederlanden?," *BMGN*, 99 (1984), 651–76, for a fuller discussion of William's status and role as a high nobleman.
15 William I to Elector August I of Saxony, 16 April 1564, *Archives ou correspondance inédite de la Maison d'Orange-Nasssau*, eds. F. Groen van Prinsterer *et al.* (21 vols.; Leiden and Utrecht, 1835–1915) (hereafter abbreviated as *Archives*), 1e Série, I, 232. On the concept of political power as "property," see footnote 54 below.
16 Swart, "Wat bewoog," 568–72. Swart's position here would seem to be in conflict with that cited in note 5 above.
17 Koenigsberger ("Fürst und Generalstaaten," pp. 577–78) states this with some hesitation, emphasizing that "Orange's precise political objectives in this period are notoriously difficult to penetrate." His statement, repeated on p. 583, seems persuasive to me.
18 The term here means "confederation." See "Avis du Prince d'Orange," c. Oct. 1576, *Archives*, 1e Sér., V, 436. For the text of the Compromise, see Kossmann and Mellink, 59–62, or Herbert H. Rowen, ed., *The Low Countries in Early Modern Times: A Documentary History* (New York, 1972), 29–33.

tion. He continued his cautious policy the next year, when events came to a head. The restlessness of the population under the whip of crop failures, high grain prices and loss of employment fed the fires of revolt. At the higher level of society, a petition opposed to the Inquisition[19] was presented to the Regent in April 1566; the sneering comment of one of Margaret's advisors that the petitioners were just a band of beggars (*gueux* in French) was turned around, and the name "Beggars" became one of pride in resistance. The Calvinists began to preach openly in the countryside, and the denunciations of the "hedge preachers"[20] were followed in August by a wave of "image breaking" in the churches ("iconoclasm," as it is often called in English) that spread from Flanders up to the northernmost provinces. Margaret bent even further under the threats, but in Spain the wrathful Philip II prepared the restoration of his authority and the punishment of the offenders.

Margaret sent Orange into Holland and Utrecht to halt the turbulence with armed force, which he did, but she was displeased when he called the States of Holland to meet him at Schoonhoven and agreed with them upon a compromise that permitted Calvinist preaching outside of churches and cities – that is, hedge-preaching – where this had been previously tolerated, provided that the church buildings themselves were returned to the Catholics; but she had to go along, although urging him to seek a settlement more favorable to the Catholics.[21] He was not a rebel, at least not yet and not in his own mind.[22]

It was the consequences of the "iconoclasm," a movement which he had reproved, that carried Orange over the ridge between passive and active opposition. Philip II, who had already decided to crush the heretics and bring the refractory nobles to terms, responded to the "iconoclasm" by sending the duke of Alva (as the Dutch continue to spell his name; the Spaniards now use the form "Alba") to the Low Countries with a highly trained army to impose obedience,[23] and the "Iron Duke" made little distinction between unhappy recalcitrance and outright rebellion. Even before Alva's arrival in August 1567, William decided not to entrust his personal safety to the fierce Spaniard's judgment, and unlike several of his companions among the grandees who stayed on in the Netherlands, confi-

19 The text of the Petition of 5 April 1566, in Kossmann and Mellink, 62–65.
20 Phyllis Mack Crew, *Calvinist Preaching and Iconoclasm in the Netherlands 1544–1569* (Cambridge, 1978).
21 William I at Utrecht to Margaret of Parma, 15 Nov., Margaret to William, 5 Dec., Dec. [?], 19 Jan. 1566/67, Margaret to Philip II, 18 Dec. 1566, William I, *Correspondance*, 11, 268, 295, 309, 335, 400.
22 Swart, "Wat bewoog," 558–61.
23 See Parker, 84–90, 99–102. For Alva's career in the Netherlands, see William S. Maltby, *Alba: A Biography of Fernando Alvarez de Toledo, Third Duke of Alba, 1507–1582* (Berkeley, Los Angeles and London, 1983), chs. 6–11.

dent in their privileges as members of the Golden Fleece, he withdrew into Germany to the ancestral castles in Nassau. His flight was a retreat as well from Dutch politics into the position of a sad observer of the tragedy he saw descending upon the Low Countries which he could not prevent.[24] To Philip's call, transmitted through Margaret, to take a new oath of loyalty, he responded in April by resigning his stadholderships, although in language that maintained the air of proper deference.[25] It was, he emphasized the next year in a letter to Emperor Maximilian II, a "free" resignation "to avoid all suspicions."[26] To take his place, a South Netherlands nobleman, the Count of Bossu, was named to the stadholdership in Holland and Utrecht.

The seizure of his estates in the Low Countries and Franche-Comté and the summons to face trial before Alva's "Council of Troubles" destroyed William's hope of a personal settlement, while the harshness of Alva's rule shattered his hope of a settlement between the king and his subjects. Yet it was not until the Spring of 1568 that William came out openly as the leader of the armed resistance against Alva's government in the Low Countries. During the next five years, William launched three desperate campaigns with hired soldiery from Germany, but failed to win support from the frightened population in the Low Countries or from the German princes, with the exception of his own close family, the Nassaus.[27] Alva, a general immensely more skilled than the Prince of Orange, easily defeated the invaders.

Only on the North Sea and in the English Channel did privateers, the feared "Sea Beggars," carrying letters of marque from William as Prince of Orange, gain continued successes against Spanish (and sometimes neutral) shipping. William made no claim of authority to issue these licenses to prey upon an enemy on the basis of his former position as stadholder, but only as sovereign Prince of Orange (which did not even lie upon the sea but only upon a river that flows into the Mediterranean!). The letters of marque were vital to the Sea Beggars not because they offered any hope of leniency from the Spaniards if caught, but because they provided Queen Elizabeth of England with some ground for permitting the wild rovers to use her ports as bases. They repeatedly disregarded, however, the sieve-like boundary between privateering (with the Spaniards and the Netherlanders faithful to Philip as their victims) and piracy (with anyone, not least Englishmen, plundered at will). Finally the exasperated Elizabeth ordered them out of her harbors in 1572.

24 Swart, "Wat bewoog," 556–58, 561–64.
25 William I at Dillenburg to Philip II, Apr. 1657, *Archives*, 1e Sér., III, 64–65.
26 William I at Dillenburg to Maximilian II, 12 Aug. 1568, William I, *Correspondance*, III, 11.
27 Swart, "Wat bewoog" 562; Volker Press, "Wilhelm von Oranien, die deutschen Reichsstände und der niederländische Aufstand," *BMGN*, 99 (1984), 677–707.

The situation changed with a swiftness and suddenness that no one had anticipated. The flotilla of Sea Beggars put out to sea. All harbors were closed to them, and they roamed across the North Sea facing the prospect of extinction. In desperation they put in at the little port of Den Briel, (Brill, as the English called it), at the southwestern tip of the province of Holland, where they knew they had some friends. On landing on 1 April, they discovered that all the Spanish troops had been withdrawn to oppose an invasion by one of William of Orange's brothers far to the southeast, and they seized the town. Then, one after another, Dutch towns similarly stripped of their Spanish garrisons fell into the hands of the Beggars and their associates.

The course of the rebellion was utterly altered. The invasions from Germany and France upon which William had counted had all failed, but in October, instead of returning to his native land to attempt still another campaign from the east, he fled westward to Holland "to find my grave there."[28] He found instead a land in the grip of the rebels. Unless they gained an effective leader, however, they were doomed to be crushed when the implacable Spanish regiments returned. It was only half a year after his flight to Holland that William, a Lutheran for the first decade of his life and then a Catholic, although one with Erasmian attitudes, and now again "a sort of Lutheran," formally became a Calvinist.[29] Even then, his relation to the Reformed church remained always ambivalent: he was at heart a Christian without strong commitment to any particular variety of his faith, an Erasmian in his distaste for religious intolerance and oppression, and without hatred for Catholics as such. Yet he knew that the Calvinists were implacable foes of Spanish rule, and although only a minority in the country, ready to impose their faith upon the people. They were indispensable if troublesome allies.[30]

As a national movement, the rebellion was already ambivalent and even self-contradictory. On the one hand, it had begun as an effort of the forces of resistance of the Netherlands as a whole against the domination of a ruler who was above all a Spaniard, a foreigner, and no one represented that common interest of the Low Countries better than the German-born Prince of Orange. This "nationalism" was fostered by Orange's propaganda from 1568 onwards.[31] It was the high nobility, of which he was the outstanding member, which, because its interests were distributed widely over the provinces, was least bound to the interests of any single province, or

28 William I at Zwolle to Count John of Nassau, 18 Oct. 1572, *Archives*, 1e Sér., IV, 4.
29 Kossmann and Mellink, "Introduction," 15. Parker's description of William at this time as "a Lutheran" is too point-blank (*The Dutch Revolt*, 147). For a brief survey of the relations between William I and the Calvinists, see J. Decavele, "De edelman Oranje en de Calvinisten," *Spiegel Historiael*, 19 (1984), 201–6.
30 Swart, "Wat bewoog," 564–66.   31 *Ibid.*, 566–68.

any town within them.[32] On the other hand, the down-to-earth interests being defended against the centralizing Burgundian–Spanish rule were specifically provincial and local. This particularism had been carried over into the conduct of the rebellion, with each province, and within it each town, trying to protect its security and prosperity as best it could on its own.

Recognition of the peril of trying to go it alone, a growing sense that the shared struggle required a common policy and common measures, led the government of Dordrecht to call a meeting of the States of Holland on 19 July. Dordrecht, as the oldest town in Holland and the first in precedence, had acted on the suggestion of William of Orange, who sent as his personal representative Philip van Marnix, lord of St Aldegonde. The meeting marked the beginning of the transformation of the rebellion from a movement of armed protest and resistance seeking to change the ruler's policies and the personnel of his government, into a revolution against the monarch himself. It was in embryo the creation of an alternative government, a new source of political authority.[33] It had become necessary because William had drained his resources from Germany to the bottom, and without financial aid from the States, as Marnix told them, he would not be able to continue his struggle on their behalf.

Marnix carried with him an instruction drawn up on 13 July. Its very first article asked the States to give unconditional recognition of his position as "the general governor and lieutenant of the king over Holland, Zeeland, Friesland [actually the district called 'West Friesland' on the southwest shore of the Zuider Zee, which had long been part of the province of Holland] and the bishopric [actually the province, not the diocese] of Utrecht as he was heretofore, with the legal and proper commission of his Royal Majesty."[34] They did so formally the next day, on the grounds that he had never been dismissed "in accordance with the privileges of the Land." As "a foremost member of the General States," he would act as "protector and head" of the Netherlands "in the absence of his Royal Majesty." Not that they were ready to bow to Philip's commands if he returned to the Low Countries in person; on the contrary, they promised not to enter into any agreement with the king or any of his representatives without William's "advice, consent and authorization."[35]

---

32 Lademacher, 22; S. Groenveld, "Natie en nationaal gevoel in de zestiende-eeuwse Nederlanden," in: *Scrinium en Scriptura: Opstellen, aangeboden aan J. R. van der Gouw* (Groningen, 1980), 378–79.

33 The complex story of the relations between William I and the creation of a new "States government" is succinctly told by K. W. Swart, "Oranje en de opkomst van het Statenbewind," *Spiegel Historiael*, 19 (1984), 195–200.

34 Instruction of William I for Marnix de St Aldegonde, July 1572, in Kossmann and Mellink, 98–101.

35 Blok, *Willem de Eerste*. II, 11–12; Lademacher, 41.

The assertion that William was still stadholder because he had not been dismissed in the requisite manner after his resignation in 1567 was a legal nicety that would not hold water. Bossu's appointment had assumed Orange's departure, and neither appointment nor dismissal of a stadholder required prior approval of the provincial States.[36] The action of the States solved, however, an embarrassing difficulty facing them and the Prince. Unwilling to paint themselves as innovating revolutionaries, they had to find an adequate basis for their authority.[37] The States of Holland could go on functioning as they did before, extending their powers as the necessity arose; but William thus far had led the rebellion upon the basis of vague claims of social and political eminence. The States of Holland indeed did not *elect* him the stadholder of the province, which had always been the exclusive right of the count; they simply *acknowledged* and *accepted* him as continuing in that role. But, although maintaining that William was still stadholder was a trick with words, the claim that the Prince represented the "true" interests of Philip as Count of Holland and could continue to act on his behalf, even though Philip had been led astray by evil advisors, was not patent nonsense in an era when representation did not necessarily mean designation or election but could be merely acting on behalf of someone else.[38]

Orange, like the rebellious States, adhered to the formality that the revolt was not directed against Philip II himself but against his evil advisors, and specifically the duke.[39] It is customary to call this distinction a "legal fiction," but there was no question that Philip was the legitimate lord in the Low Countries, and neither Orange nor any of his fellow-rebels was spurred on by any ideological glorification of revolution.[40] Years would pass before William and the other rebels would finally call Philip a "tyrant" – one who used his power to oppress his subjects – and until then the aim of the revolt was to expel the Spaniards who served Philip, not to overthrow the ruler himself.

36 A. C. J. de Vrankrijker, *De Motiveering van onzen Opstand: De theorieën van het verzet der Nederlandsche opstandelingen tegen Spanje in de jaren 1565–1581* (Nijmegen/Utrecht, 1933; reprint edn, Utrecht, 1979), 88.
37 I. Schöffer, "De Opstand in de Nederlanden, 1566–1609," in: J. A. Bornewasser *et al.*, eds., *Winkler Prins Geschiedenis der Nederlanden* (3 vols.; Amsterdam and Brussels, 1977), II, 86; Kossmann and Mellink, "Introduction," 19–20, 22–23, "A kind admonition to the States of Brabant, Flanders etc on their supplication handed to Don Luis de Requesens, 1574," 117–19.
38 See A. Kluit, *Historie der Hollandsche Staatsregering, tot aan het jaar 1795* (5 vols.; Amsterdam, 1802–5), I, 56, for an effective statement of this subtle difference. See also Jan Wagenaar, *Vaderlandsche Historie, vervattende de geschiedenissen der nu Vereenigde Nederlanden, inzonderheid die van Holland, van de vroegste tyden af* (21 vols.; Amsterdam, 1790–96), I, "Voorrede," xxxix–xli.
39 See in particular Orange's "Warning to the Inhabitants and Subjects of the Netherlands," 1 Sept. 1568, Kossmann and Mellink, 84–86.
40 Kossmann and Mellink, "Introduction," 1–2.

The Prince of Orange and the States of Holland certainly thought of their actions as preserving and restoring the constitutional situation, but in the eyes of the established ruler armed resistance to his authority was rebellion, not legitimate self-defense – not at least, until the rebels had thrown off his rule. If the rebellion were to be successful, however, it would have to win on the battlefield and create a new government. But the conservative conceptions of these reluctant revolutionaries meant that the new regime would be as much like the old one as they could make it, that it would be its continuation wherever possible, and where not, it would be built upon the old institutions – the long-established local and provincial governments – modified to fit the new needs and purged of those still loyal to the king. It would be more than a decade and a half, filled with the travails and uncertainties of civil war, before the new regime would take firm shape.

Under this emerging new government William of Orange continued to play the same viceregal role as before the revolt, only with enhanced status and powers. He was now more than the servant of the ruler, for he shared government[41] with the States of Holland (and with the States of the other provinces that also acknowledged him as their stadholder). He described the government in his own words as consisting of "myself and the States" (*moy et les estats*).[42] But his position was nonetheless greatly altered, for the States shifted their role from that of granting revenues to the ruler toward becoming themselves the source of authority, the sovereigns of the land; but this change remained vague during the period of William's stadholdership. Indeed, even while the States more and more assumed the position of ultimate authority, the leadership role of the Prince became steadily larger.

The mutual dependence of States and Prince–stadholder nonetheless remained virtually total.[43] He could not do without the funds needed by the rebel – we might now say, the revolutionary – army, which only the States could provide him; and the States needed his leadership in the conception and execution of policy, a task they had never performed in the past.[44] In 1572 there was still in the actions of the States of Holland and the Prince a recognition that their relationship was not only that of stadholder (in the viceregal sense) and representative assembly, but also that he was leading the rebellion *de jure suo*, "by his own right."[45] He declined to assert himself as a new sovereign by taking for himself the king's title as Count of Holland.[46] If the sovereignty, indeed, were to be wrested from

---

41 Japikse's phrase is precise: he was "*mede-regerend*, co-governor." Japikse, *Geschiedenis*, I, 100.
42 William I to Philip de Marnix, 28 Nov. 1573, William I, *Correspondance*, III, 88.
43 Lademacher, 54.   44 Kluit, I, 78.   45 Lademacher, 55.
46 Blok, *Willem de Eerste*, II, 21, 23.

Philip, he felt, it should be given to a foreign prince able to give the rebellious provinces the military and financial assistance that they needed, and William's own first preference was for Elizabeth of England.[47] It was the practical success of the revolt that concerned him, not its immediate or even its eventual constitutional form. He governed with and for the States because that was the only way to win.[48]

During 1573 and 1574 the essential daily work of government was in the hands of the Prince, who worked with the advice and assistance of three councils. Yet the ambiguities that continued in the relationship between Orange and the States strained their mutual good will. Finally, on 24 October, 1574, he offered to give up his governorship entirely to the States, noting especially difficulties over financial matters; he made the offer not out of unwillingness to help them, he said, but in the hope of improvement. The offer put the States up against the wall. As they debated it, their need for him as governor became ever clearer. They therefore responded on 24 November "in all humbleness" with a request that he stay on as stadholder, exercising the "superintendence, authority (*overigheydt*) and government under the name of Governor or Regent," and they would "confer" upon him "absolute power, authority (*authoriteyt*) and sovereign command (*souverain bevel*) for the direction of all matters of the common country without exception." The last phrase was not as encompassing as it seemed; it applied really just to matters of general policy, for taxation, replacement of members of the municipal governments and the principal officials, including members of the Court of Holland and the Chamber of Accounts, would be made upon their nomination and with their approval. He accepted the next day, since an adequate sum for the troops was also granted.[49] Great as these powers were, they were no longer "acknowledged," as William's stadholdership had been in 1572, but were "conferred" by the States of Holland. By using the formula "head and highest authority," they began altering the character of the title "stadholder" which he retained.[50]

All the while the military situation remained filled with perils. The fall of Haarlem on 12 July 1573, after a siege of seven months, was almost a death blow to the rebellion. With Amsterdam still in the hands of a government loyal to Philip II, the province of Holland, which by this time had become the principal base of the revolt, was split into two parts. Worse was averted

---

47 *Ibid.*, 23–25.
48 Van Schelven, 213; K. W. Swart, "Willem de Zwijger," in: C. A. Tamse, ed., *Nassau en Oranje in de Nederlandsche Geschiedenis* (Alphen aan den Rijn, 1979), 62.
49 J. P. Arend, *Algemeene Geschiedenis des Vaderlands, van de vroegste tijden tot op heden* (15 vols.; Amsterdam, 1840–82), II, part 5, 408–10; Blok, *Willem de Eerste*, II, 48; Lademacher, 56–57.
50 Lademacher, 68–70.

18

the next year when Leiden held off a Spanish siege, and henceforth, amid the fluctuating fortunes of war, the consolidation of Holland and Zeeland as the heart of the revolt continued steadily.

William arranged a "Union" between the two provinces, not a merger but an agreement to work together under his leadership as stadholder and captain-general. His proposal was accepted on 11 July 1575. It defined his position more precisely as "sovereign and supreme head" (*souverein ende overhooft*) for the duration of the war. States, magistrates, burgher guards and citizenry would all take an oath of obedience to him. In Holland the three councilors would be replaced by a "provincial council" (*landraad*) of eighteen members. The council was established in August, but Orange was not happy with it because it was not given full power to make decisions without going back to the full assembly, and it was abolished in October. Instead he relied upon a permanent committee of the States of Holland. Zeeland took similar measures on its own. In both provinces, it was clear, the States wanted the leadership and the guidance of the Prince, but without putting ultimate power in his hands.[51]

The next year, as the civil war flared up again, Holland and Zeeland, responding to an appeal by William, made a "Closer Union" (*Nadere Unie*) at Delft in April. The Prince was again recognized as "sovereign and supreme head" for the duration of the insurgency against the "Spanish tyranny." He was given the right to convene the States in both provinces and "complete authority and power" in military matters. He would also be the administrator of justice together with the Court of Holland, whose members he would appoint, and he would have the right of pardon. Most important of all, he would have the right to appoint magistrates in the cities if necessary, provided that this was done with the approval of a majority of the town council. In general it was his stated duty to preserve the privileges of the towns, to protect the authority of the regents (the Dutch word *regenten* meant members of the governing bodies), and finally, to maintain the Reformed religion to the exclusion of the exercise of all others, although freedom of conscience was permitted to individuals. Magistrates, burgher guards and the citizenry would take an oath of loyalty, obedience and submission to him, and he would take an oath to maintain the privileges.[52]

The Union of Delft continued the process of adaptation of the old political institutions to the new political needs. The essential characteristics of the dual government of States-with-stadholder were clearly set forth, yet the ambiguity of such a regime was also present. The Prince might be called a "sovereign," but the powers granted to him did not make him a

51 Blok, *Willem de Eerste*, II, 55–56; Blok, *Geschiedenis*, II, 108; Lademacher, 60–64.
52 Blok, *William de Eerste*, II, 56–57; Wagenaar, VII, 94.

supreme ruler; when he had been stadholder in the name of Philip II, he had exercised virtually identical authority. To the extent that he acted on behalf of the States, he tacitly recognized them as sovereigns in the stead of the king–count.

In March 1576 the death of Requesens, who had replaced Alva in 1573, caused the political situation to split open. With no governor-general on hand to act for Philip II, authority was taken over by the Council of State in Brussels. The Spanish troops did not accept the council's authority; worse, left without pay, they mutinied and their rampages spread the rebellion and gave it new opportunities. The Revolt of the Low Countries, which had begun in the South and spread to the North and then had been confined there by Alva and Requesens, became a general uprising against Spanish authority. In September the States General were convened in Brussels by the Council of State despite the refusal of permission by Philip, and it began to recruit troops to protect the country against the mutineers. This was followed by negotiations with deputies of the States of Holland and Zeeland, leading in October to the conclusion of the Pacification of Ghent in November.[53]

The Pacification was a virtual treaty among the provinces, although it subordinated them to the nominal authority of the States General. It was the triumph of William's policy, which sought the freedom of the Netherlands as a whole – setting apart neither Dutch–Flemish nor Walloon–French speakers, nor religious faiths, nor social classes. It provided that the Low Countries would recognize a new governor-general named by Philip in Requesens' place, provided he accepted the Pacification, sent away the foreign troops, and governed only with "natives" (William, although German-born, was tacitly considered one) and in collaboration with the States. The States General would decide the matter of religion, but meanwhile the measures against the heretics would be withdrawn, although Holland and Zeeland, where Calvinism had become the acknowledged official religion, refused to restore freedom of religious practice to Catholics. Orange was recognized as governor (*stadhouder*) in Holland and Zeeland.

During the next two years, William's hopes soared to the highest. He dreamed of a Netherlands united and free: united under the joint rule of a benevolent prince (either a reformed Philip II or someone else of royal rank, but not himself); free from arbitrary government, the destructive fury of the Spanish soldiery, and religious intolerance and cruelty. If the Pacification of Ghent could be made to work, the dream could come true, and William therefore went to Brussels to try to achieve it there. Don John,

53 "Pacification of Ghent," 8 Nov. 1576, Kossmann and Mellink, 126–32; Rowen, *Low Countries*, 58–64.

the king's half-brother, was named by Philip as the new governor-general. He was authorized by Philip to concede much in the way of self-government to the Netherlands, but nothing to heresy, so that his acceptance of the Pacification was double-tongued. Finding that it was Orange and not himself who really led the country, Don John finally in exasperation seized the citadel of Namur in July 1577 in what he hoped would become the first act in the subjugation of the Netherlands.

The States General thereupon declared him deposed and in December invited the youthful Archduke Matthias of Habsburg, the Emperor's brother, to become the new governor-general. It was in fact a revolutionary act, since such an appointment belonged only to the king of Spain as "lord" of the Low Countries; but it was hoped that the choice of an Austrian Habsburg, his cousin, would blunt the political challenge to him, so that he could still be brought back to an agreement with his Low Countries subjects. Matthias, whose appointment had been designed by William's rivals as a means of his position, fell under his domination once he came to the Low Countries, and the real governance continued to be exercised by the Prince of Orange.

Philip II had not been swayed by the choice of another Habsburg; he wanted his own man in Brussels, not a vain and weak cousin from Vienna barely out of childhood. He continued to support Don John, but sent the duke of Parma, Alexander Farnese, whose mother Margaret had been governor-general of the Netherlands a decade earlier, to support him as his second-in-command. When Don John died in October 1578, Parma succeeded him as both governor-general and commander-in-chief. The king's cause was now in the hands of a man who was blessed with political skills as great as those of his adversary, the Prince of Orange, but was also to prove to be the outstanding military captain of his time, and the combination would be fatal to William's dream.

Orange's entry into Brussels in September 1577 had been a personal triumph, but the States of Holland and Zeeland were unhappy at his absence. They pleaded with him to return, or at least to go only to Antwerp, so much nearer than Brussels. But he had to be where the fate of the revolt was being decided, where the States General sat, and where Matthias would come before long to take Don John's place. The States General represented the murky legitimacy of the uprising against Philip II, and Matthias the hope of a reconciliation with him, or at least with his Austrian cousins. No less important was to keep under control the restless stirrings in the towns of Brabant and Flanders, where the centuries-old democratic strivings of the citizenry for a share in government overlapped with the yearning of the laboring class for an end to their hard times and with the endeavor of militant Calvinists to build a "city of God" on the model of Geneva.[54] No one but William, who had won the confidence of the people by his successes in the North as well as by his stubborn political resistance, could have any hope of keeping the turbulence from exploding the revolt into fragments, or of holding the leadership against the rivalry of other great nobles, many of them still Catholic.

Compared to the erupting disorder in the South, Holland, Zeeland and the other northern provinces had become scenes of political and social calm. Yet, as William knew full well, Holland and Zeeland were the base of his strength, and he considered it was to them that he owed his primary obligation.[55] The States General for their part treated William and the States of Holland, Zeeland and their "associates" as a unit.[56] Nonetheless the two provinces found themselves more and more assuming the full burden of self-government in the absence of the Prince, who had to give his attention to more pressing and troubling problems in the South. The States of Holland and Zeeland not only took on tasks they had never performed before, they also discovered that they had statesmen in their midst who could provide leadership and had a taste for decisive power. The very absence of William in Brussels thus contributed to the beginnings of an embryo state taking shape in the North.[57]

This development was accelerated by the two "Unions" concluded in January 1579, each of which succeeded and in so doing created a disunited Netherlands that would remain disjointed, with only one brief interval, until the present day. The first of these accords was the Union of Arras, made on 6 January by the States of the Catholic dominated provinces in the southern Netherlands. The aim of the Union of Arras was reconciliation with the king of Spain and collaboration with the Duke of Parma, his new governor-general. Government was restored upon a basis of shared authority of the king and the States, while Catholicism was restored as the religion of the country – essentially, the Pacification of Ghent without its religious provisions. Parma signed a treaty with the Arras partners in May by which the rebellion of the Walloon provinces ended upon the terms set forth in the "Union."[58]

Whether Parma could follow the conclusion of the Union of Arras and his first military success, the capture six months later of the great fortress of Maastricht, by a total reconquest of the Netherlands would depend not

54 See J. Decavele, "De mislukking van Oranjes 'democratische' politiek in Vlaanderen," *BMGN*, 99 (1984), 626–50.
55 William I, instruction for Henry de Bloeyere, envoy to the States General, 26 Jan. 1577, William I, *Correspondance*, III, 198–99.
56 William I, *Correspondance*, III, 218–25.
57 Lademacher, 149–50; P. L. Muller, *De staat der Vereenigde Nederlanden in de jaren zijner wording, 1572–1594*, 270–71.
58 Delfos, 113–15.

only on his own achievements but also on the effectiveness of the other "Union" concluded in the North. This was the "Union of Utrecht" made by the provinces of Holland, Zeeland, Utrecht and Groningen (but not by the capital city of the same name in the last of these provinces) as well as some individual members of the nobility of Gelderland, on 23 January, followed over the next year by most of the other northern provinces. A half-dozen important cities in the South in both Flanders and Brabant also joined.[59]

This day of 23 January 1579, has been the traditional birth date of the Republic of the United Provinces, but it has been observed more than once that this is a misconception, for the Republic was not conceived or born but simply grew.[60] Nonetheless the Union of Utrecht became the "constitution" of the Republic in the sense that it defined the relationship among the signatory provinces as well as the role of the stadholders in the interprovincial relationship. It did not throw off the sovereignty of Philip II, but asserted to the contrary that the defense against Spanish tyranny was being conducted in his name. It was a military alliance among rebellious provinces "for all time" (*ten ewygen daghen*), together with provisions for their political collaboration. The right of renunciation (secession, in American constitutional parlance) was explicitly denied.[61]

The Union of Utrecht was anything but specifically republican in intention or character. Indeed, later in the year the States of Holland rejected in so many words the notion that the Netherlands (*dese landen*) could be governed as a republic, "without a head and superintendent" (*zonder een hooft ende superintendent*), and the States General the next year reaffirmed that "the republican state form is not adapted to the Netherlands" (*de Republikeinse staatsvorm niet geschikt is voor de Nederlanden*). It sought to strengthen the "General Union" of the seventeen provinces, by giving it a center of force and purpose in the "closer Union and Confederation" (*naerder Unie en Confederatie*) based on Holland and Zeeland and expanding to the other provinces. A kind of partial, substitute States General of deputies to the "Closer Union" began to meet only a week after the conclusion of the Union of Utrecht, with the proclaimed intention of stiffening, not breaking, the General Union and the States General, which had moved from Brussels to Antwerp's greater safety the year before.[62]

59 "Treaty of the Union, eternal alliance and confederation made in the town of Utrecht by the countries and their towns and members," Kossmann and Mellink, 165–73, and Rowen, *Low Countries*, 68–74. Important modern studies of the formation and consequences of the Union of Utrecht in S. Groenveld and H. L. Ph. Leeuwenberg, eds., *De Unie van Utrecht: Wording en werking van een verbond en een verbondsacte*. The Hague, 1979.
60 A. Th. van Deursen, "De staatsinstellingen in de Noordelijke Nederlanden, 1579–1780," *Algemene Gechiedenis*, v, 350. His formulation is a little different but the idea is the same.
61 *Ibid.*, 351.   62 Delfos, 8–9, 88, 136–37; Kluit, I, 162–63.

Two elements of the Union of Utrecht were crucial both for the eventual development of the political structure of the Dutch Republic and for the role of the stadholderate within it. One was the assumption that the assembly of the deputies of the "Closer Union" – which after a few years merged with the States General of what remained of the "General Union" – functioned, like the larger body, upon the basis of the principle of unanimity in matters of fundamental importance. The other was the assignment to the stadholder "who is now present" (*nu ter tijt wesende*) of tasks of mediation and reconciliation among the provinces, a task he had already been given in the unions between Holland and Zeeland in 1575 and 1576. The stadholder's other powers, inherited from the time of royal rule, were taken for granted.[63] These were to be the powers that the stadholders would exercise over the whole history of the Republic; what would change would be primarily circumstances and personalities.

William, still committed to the principle of the Pacification of Ghent, reluctantly gave his approval to the Union of Utrecht and then proceeded to make it serve his own purposes. Without hope that Philip II would come to terms with his Netherlands subjects upon an acceptable basis, yet also unable to imagine that the revolt could succeed with only its own strength, Orange had been seeking the protectorate of a great power, preferably France, with Duke Francis of Anjou and Alençon[64] ruling over the Low Countries as a "constitutional prince" (in the sixteenth-century meaning of the term, of course).[65] Matthias meanwhile remained as governor-general, almost an onlooker as the great events swirled about him.

The rift between North and South – more precisely, between the rebels led by Orange and the king's adherents led by Parma – already opened by the "Unions" of 1579 was widened and deepened the next year. Parma continued his methodical reconquest, while the province of Groningen returned to Philip's obedience thanks to the so-called "betrayal" of the Catholic stadholder Rennenberg, who was on terms of intimacy with Orange.[66] For safety's sake the States General began to hold its meetings north of the great rivers, although William continued to keep his headquarters at Antwerp.

Despite Parma's military successes, Philip felt that the time had come to

---

63 Lademacher, 115–16, 138; Delfos, 145; Kluit, I, 149, 197.
64 Duke Francis (or François) is best known in English history as Alençon because that was the title he carried while courting Elizabeth I; in Dutch history he is better known as Anjou, the title borne by his brother Henry until he became King Henry III in 1574.
65 Mack P. Holt, *The Duke of Anjou and the Politique Struggle during the Wars of Religion* (Cambridge, 1986), renews the study of the relationship between Anjou and the Dutch rebels; Delfos, 113–14; Lademacher, 176; J. den Tex, *Oldenbarnevelt* (5 vols.; Haarlem, 1960–72), I, 167.
66 Geyl (*Geschiedenis*, II, 335–36) stresses both Rennenberg's Catholicism and his political sincerity in this deed.

behead the rebellion by depriving it of its leader, the Prince of Orange. On 15 March 1580, the king issued a ban of outlawry against William, authorizing anyone to kill him; the slayer would not be treated as a criminal assassin but as a servant of the public welfare, and he (or his heirs) would be rewarded with a gift of 25,000 guilders and a grant of nobility.[67] The ban was directed against William personally, but it was a threat to all who supported him. William replied with an *Apology* – a passionate defense of his own actions and a vitriolic attack upon Philip for a multitude of misdeeds, political and personal (the latter, picked up from the muck heap of malicious rumors, have been proved false). The States General declined to publish the *Apology* because of its utter intransigence, although it was addressed to them. It was then printed at Delft under the protection of the States of Holland.[68] In the covering letter which accompanied the copies of the *Apology* sent to the ruling princes of Europe, Orange defined his own status as both a servant of the States General and as "an absolute and free Prince."[69]

Deeds were necessary as well as the rhetoric and hot words of the *Apology*. First was conclusion of the long negotiations with the Duke of Anjou to take the place of Philip II as lord of the Low Countries. He had already held an ill-defined position in 1578 and 1579 as "Defender of the Liberty of the Low Countries against the Tyranny of the Spaniards," with a promise of the lordship if the rule of the Spanish king was foresworn, but he had brought only small military help to the Netherlanders. A treaty between Anjou and the States General was made at Plessis-lez-Tours in France on 19 September 1581. Its provisions paralleled the offer that had been made to the duke in 1576 by just the provinces of Holland and Zeeland: an alliance would be made between the king of France and the Low Countries; the religious peace established by the Pacification of Ghent would be kept firm; all members of the government would be Netherlanders, and they would also comprise half of the duke's court. He would govern with a council named by each province; the stadholders and other high officials would also be named from a triple list of nominees submitted by each province. The succession would be hereditary, but with the complete exclusion of any personal union with France. There would be no taxation except by authority of the States, and no foreign soldiery without their approval.[70]

On 23 January 1581, the duke proclaimed the treaty of Plessis-lez-Tours, and the deputies of the States General accepted him at Bordeaux as

---

67 The key passage of the Ban of Proscription in Rowen, *Low Countries*, 77–79.
68 There is a convenient modern reprint of a contemporary English translation of the *Apology*: *The Apologie of Prince William of Orange against the Proclamation of the King of Spain, edited after the English edition of 1581*, ed. H. Wansink (Leiden, 1969). Key passages in Kossmann and Mellink, 211–16, and Rowen, *Low Countries*, 80–91.
69 William I, *Apologie*, 3–4.   70 Blok, *Willem de Eerste*, II, 147–48.

the sovereign of the Low Countries. But he had to pay a price: a secret promise made on the same day that the provinces of Holland, Zeeland and Utrecht would be free to elect the Prince of Orange their hereditary lord (*landsheer*) or otherwise to maintain their autonomy under the nominal overlordship of Anjou.[71]

The experiment with Anjou could succeed only if he could bring French troops in adequate force to the support of the newly independent state to counter the continuing military progress of Parma, and if he could govern the country in collaboration with the States. On both counts William miscalculated. The failure of Henry III to send as large forces as were needed can be attributed to the necessities imposed upon him by the continuing wars of religion within France; but it was a defiance of experience to expect Anjou, in whom vanity triumphed over intelligence, to attempt to govern otherwise than as kings of France did. Anjou did not arrive until February 1582, and he went to Antwerp to confront the challenge from Parma. Matthias presented no problem: the archduke had put down his hollow governorship-general on 15 May 1581 and gone home to Austria to become Emperor briefly three decades later.

The most important event of these three years came at the very beginning. The nominal allegiance to Philip II that had been maintained in the first years of the Revolt had been abandoned in practice, but it was only the appointment of Anjou that made it necessary to draw the juridical consequence in a declaration of independence. This was the Act of Abjuration adopted by the States General on 26 July 1581.[72] "Abjuration" (Dutch, *afzwering*) is actually a modern term; the contemporary name was *Verlatinge* (modern Dutch, *Verlating*), which means "abandonment" or "departure." Literally, it was the Netherlands – or that part of the Low Countries represented in and controlled by the rebels – which "abandoned" Philip II, but in the deeper sense the accusation against him was that it was he who had in fact "abandoned" his subjects by his tyranny over them and so had forfeited his rule. It was a declaration of independence from *Philip*, neither an explicit assertion of the existence of a new state nor the establishment of a republican form of government. It became the founding document of the Dutch Republic because the monarchs established or sought for the new state either failed to maintain themselves or refused the honor. Republicanism was a negative, unintended product of the Abjuration.[73]

71 *Ibid.*, 162.
72 "Edict of the States General of the United Netherlands by which they declare that the king of Spain has forfeited the sovereignty and government of the afore-said Netherlands," Kossmann and Mellink, 216–28, and Rowen, *Low Countries*, 92–105.
73 Kluit, I, 198–99; Van Deursen, "Staatsinstellingen," 351–52; Van Deursen, *Het kopergeld van de Gouden Eeuw* (4 vols.; Assen and Amsterdam, 1978), III, 2. See also Lademacher, 148–49.

The Abjuration blew away the rebels' pretense that the stadholder was acting in the name of and on behalf of Philip II, but the institution of the stadholderate did not come to an end, as simple logic would have ordained. Even before Anjou had been made "lord" of the Netherlands, Holland and Zeeland returned to earlier proposals to name William their count. As such he would be a barrier between themselves and the new "lord" of the Low Countries whom they did not trust to rule them according to their lights. Constitutionally William's position as count would become more complex than ever. He would be lord of the two provinces, limiting Anjou's general lordship; yet he would not be Anjou's vassal, unlike the German princes who were vassals of the Emperor. At the same time he would exercise the political leadership of the Low Countries as a whole – or whatever part of it Parma had not yet reconquered. But there was no need to sort out the contradictions. William refused to hear of the proposal, realizing that it would be an insult to Anjou, who would consider that if anyone were to become count of Holland and Zeeland, it should be himself.[74]

William remained stadholder of the two provinces without becoming Anjou's stadholder. His position continued to be constitutionally ambiguous. The States of Holland still *recognized* and *accepted* him as their provincial stadholder, but without appointment as such; what they continued to *grant* him was the "high authority" which was not sovereignty but political leadership. This was done on 5 July 1581. They renewed William's commission as stadholder given in 1576, but no longer limited to the period of the war and with the king's name dropped. Although he was called "sovereign and supreme head," what "sovereign" meant was indicated by the description of him thereafter in official documents as "having the High Authority and Government" (*hebbende de Hooge overheid ende Regering*).[75]

While in the North William accepted the stadholdership of Friesland although he was unable to exercise it in person, but rejected the post in Gelderland following the resignation of his brother. After the enactment of the abjuration, Orange returned to Antwerp, where Anjou had established his seat of government, although the States General remained in the North. On 18 March 1582, William was badly wounded by an assassin, Jean Jauregui, and his recovery took many weeks. It had been difficult before while he had been in Brussels and Antwerp to perform the feat of governing Holland and Zeeland from a distance; now he was disabled and

---

74 Blok, *Geschiedenis*, I, 179–81; Blok, *Willem de Eerste*, II, 193.
75 N. Japikse ("Onafhankelijksdag [26 Juli 1581]," *Bijdragen voor Vaderlandsche Geschiedenis*, 5e Reeks, I [1913], 229) fails to note this limited meaning of sovereignty in equating William's "high authority" with it. The persistent ambiguity of the Prince of Orange's constitutional status is well described in Kossmann and Mellink, 38–39.

the States of the provinces had to act on their own. The key step was the decision of the States of Holland to issue on their own authority the instructions for the High Council, the newly established court of appeals for Holland and Zeeland, that had already been prepared for submission to William. He recognized that they had acted under the compulsion of necessity, and although he had previously attempted to restrict the autonomy of the Hollanders, he did not protest.[76]

Jauregui's shot was nonetheless a sign for them to intensify efforts to make William Count, and on 12 August he was persuaded to sign an act of acceptance in principle, although the offer would take effect only when conditions were worked out and all the voting towns and the Nobility had approved. William's acceptance was kept strictly secret to avoid offending Anjou, and negotiations on specific terms continued into the next year.[77]

For a while troop reinforcements from France enabled Anjou to hold off Parma's advance, but he found that the real political leader of the country remained William of Orange. Not satisfied to be a figurehead, a role that Matthias had accepted without complaint, Anjou attempted in January 1583 to seize control of Antwerp with French troops, as Don Juan had done with his Spaniards at Namur in 1577. The duke was foiled by the armed citizenry, and only the insistence of William that to depose Anjou would imperil the French assistance so necessary in the face of Parma's pressure kept the Frenchman at the head of the state. The next year he returned to France, frustrated and a failure, and he died on 10 June 1584.

Meanwhile the Prince realized that the time had come to move from Antwerp to the safer ground of Holland. He went briefly to The Hague in the summer and then settled down in Delft. On 5 April 1583 the States of Holland decided to make an offer of the countship once the conditions were worked out. They would not move, however, unless their compeers in Zeeland took the same step; the States at Middelburg had made an offer of the countship to William in 1582, but withdrew it after Anjou's attempted coup the next year. There were other obstacles. Some of the towns, Amsterdam, Gouda and Den Briel in particular, were concerned lest their privileges be imperiled by the establishment of the Prince of Orange as Count; for the first time arguments began to be heard in favor of a republican form of government. During the discussions with the Prince the States of Holland did all they could to hold on to as many as possible of the powers they had assumed during the past eleven years. A draft agreement was finally reached on 30 December, although it would not go into effect unless Zeeland also accepted him as their Count and Lord.

76 Den Tex, I, 172–73.   77 Blok, *Willem de Eerste*, II, 192–93; Kluit, I, 293.

The terms of the agreement were reminiscent of the "Joyous Entry" of Brabant, the traditional charter of the liberties of subjects and States in the Netherlands, but were more directly taken over from the treaty of Plessis-lez-Tours with Anjou. William would hold the countship as a "free" dignity and domain, meaning that it would not be held as a fief, either of the Holy Roman Empire or, presumably, of Anjou. The States alone would have the right to make laws. They would meet regularly on 1 May, but also at other times on their own authority, and they would be free in their decisions. William would name the principal officers of the province from a triple list submitted to him by the States. He could not declare war, peace or truce on his own, or negotiate with foreign powers, except with the approval of the States. If he violated the treaty and became a tyrant, he would forfeit his office. In the event of his death, the States would have the right to name one of his legitimate sons as successor (primogeniture was not possible because the eldest son, Philip William, was in the hands of the Spaniards).[78] The agreement thus gave William the name of "count," but did not make him the sovereign in the sense of absolute lord that had been introduced into political thought by Jean Bodin (who was Anjou's advisor!); indeed, the very act of conferring the countship implied the sovereignty of the provincial States.[79]

The grant of the "free" countship in Holland was equivalent to the action of Zeeland in granting their countship to William "as his property" (*in eygendom*).[80] The description of the countship as property has left modern historians at a loss for explanation, since political thought in our epoch has no place for the notion of ownership of political power.[81] Yet that principle had been involved the previous year when William purchased the marquisate of Veere and Flushing (Vlissingen) in Zeeland. It had been the property of Philip II since 1567, but had fallen into arrears in its dues to the province (that is, to Philip himself!) since the Revolt, and in 1580 the Court of Holland had ordered it to be sold publicly. Orange bought it because it gave him two more votes in the States of Zeeland (he also had a vote as First Noble for his Spanish-held son Philip William, who

---

78 Blok, *Geschiedenis*, II, 200–1; Blok, *Willem de Eerste*, II, 196–97; Kluit, I, 336–45; Den Tex, I, 199–201.
79 See Kossmann and Mellink, 41, for a discussion of this issue.
80 Blok, *Willem de Eerste*, II, 193.
81 Lademacher, in his excellent book on the stadholdership of William I, considers the formula, *in eygendom*, "somewhat unusual" (*etwas abwegige*) (p. 160). Early in the nineteenth century Kluit recognized the meaning of the term as derivative from feudalism, implying neither enslavement of the population nor direct possession of all property within the country (Kluit, I, 295 n). The problem of the ownership of the state is explored in depth for France in my book, *The King's State: Proprietary Dynasticism in Early Modern France* (New Brunswick, NJ, 1980), but the analysis given there holds, *mutatis mutandis*, for the other countries of Europe, including the Netherlands.

had inherited Maartensdijk).[82] As marquis of the two towns, William owned the government in them, both powers and revenues, although not the private property of individual residents. It was therefore a smaller version of the countship and it made William a member of the States of Zeeland.

The final approval of the town councils for the grant of the countship moved ahead slowly. William became impatient. Early in July he wrote to the States of Holland to emphasize the importance of providing for the permanent, regular government of the province. He reminded them that the offer of the countship had come from them, of their "own free will and motion," and not from him.[83] By the end of June thirteen towns had decided in favor, but others still hung back. Gouda, which had all along been a reluctant participant in the revolt,[84] balked at giving its nod despite repeated missions to the town from the States of Holland. Amsterdam still wanted to review the terms of the accord, but was very close to acceptance. The decision of 20 December was on the verge of becoming reality when, on 10 July, another assassin, Balthasar Gerard, struck down the Prince of Orange in Delft.[85]

The course of events took a very different path, the creation of a republic of the seven United Provinces. Had William lived, he would have become a count in the two maritime provinces and presumably count, duke or lord in the other provinces as well. He would have become a limited, constitutional monarch, possessed of enormous prestige but bound to govern jointly with the States. How that relationship would have worked out under William and his descendants, no one can say. What can be said with virtual certainty, however, is that their regime would not have been like that of King William I and his successors after 1815. They would have been "constitutional monarchs," to be sure, but each in the pattern of his own century.

Looking back at William's stadholdership, instead of forward to what was not to be, we can see that it had been a constant improvisation that only the countship would have brought to an end. The Prince and the States had been unlike equals, with different tasks and different powers, allies with different sources of authority. All sorts of questions in their relationship remained unsolved and even unstated, but they all came down in the end to the single one of ultimate mastery, what later would be called "sovereignty." But both sides needed each other and respected each other

---

82 Blok, *Willem de Eerste*, II, 107.
83 William I to States of Holland, early July 1584, *Archives*, 1e Sér., VIII, 428–32.
84 C. C. Hibben, *Gouda in Revolt: Particularism and Pacifism in the Revolt of the Netherlands 1572–1588* (Utrecht, 1983).
85 Blok, *Geschiedenis*, II, 199–201; Blok, *Willem de Eerste*, II, 195–96.

too much to force a determination in which one would have to suffer. For both, the cause of triumph in the war against the Spanish king was more important than the elimination of constitutional ambiguity. William had accepted as a fact – unfortunate, but one that could not be changed – that the sovereignty would remain in the hands of the provinces, that there would be no effective central authority in the republic. Political power remained widely distributed and the exclusive possession of no one. The countship as it had been designed in the resolution of Holland of 30 December 1583, might have provided a greater measure of unity. Instead of ending in fixity and clarity, however, the stadholdership of William the Silent became a time of preparation. The decision of December had come undone; a new one would have to be taken.

Maurice of Nassau: defender of the Republic

Prince William was slain during the morning of 10 July. At noon the States General met and decided that the struggle against Spain would go on without interruption. On 18 August they entrusted the government of the country "for the present time" (*bij provisie*) to a Council of State of eighteen members, consisting of deputies from the provinces, including Brabant, Flanders and Mechelen in the South, and with Maurice, the second son of the late Prince of Orange, as the only individual member. He was appointed at the urging of John van Oldenbarnevelt, the pensionary (political–legal secretary) of Rotterdam who was already a powerful voice in the States of Holland. The action recognized the special status of the House of Orange in both the Netherlands as a whole and in the provinces of Holland and Zeeland in particular.[1]

The appointment of the sixteen-year-old Maurice was more an anticipation of his future role than a grant of immediate power. The States of Holland and Zeeland did not at once name him stadholder in his father's place, although it was assumed that the governorship would be given to him when he reached adequate age.[2] There was virtually no thought of skipping over him, even though he was too young to assert a full claim to the position of his father. The feeling was strong that William's offices came to Maurice, as the older available son (the eldest son, Philip William in Spain, who became the new Prince of Orange, was beyond consideration, and Frederick Henry, born only that January, was a babe in arms), by a kind of dynastic right. In Holland and Zeeland it would be only fulfilling the expectation and the promise of the agreements with William on the countship. Yet these feelings had not yet congealed into an Orange myth, a vision of a mystical connection between the House of Orange and

---

1 Blok *Geschiedenis*, II, 224; Den Tex, I, 242; Hallema, *Prins Maurits, 1567–1625: Veertig jaren strijder voor's lands vrijheid* (Assen, 1949), 27. A systematically hostile picture of Maurice and his career is given in J. G. Kikkert, "Geen standbeeld voor Maurits," *Spiegel Historiael*, 20 (1985), 418–23.

2 Blok, *Geschiedenis*, II, 223; P. J. Blok, "Prins Maurits, Fragment," *Bijdragen voor Vaderlandsche Geschiedenis en Oudheidkunde* (hereafter abbreviated as *BVGO*), 6de Reeks, 9 (1930), 169–70.

Maurice, 1567–1625

the Dutch nation.[3] The appointment of Maurice to high office was still a matter of political convenience, not an assertion of a formal birthright in law.[4]

Without waiting for action by Holland and Zeeland, Friesland named a stadholder to replace William. Its choice was William Louis, the son of Count John of Nassau. This established a separate branch of the family in the northern province, called the House of Nassau to distinguish it from the House of Orange descended from William I; although Count John had been the eldest of the Nassau brothers, Count William Louis and his descendants were treated as the junior branch. Like Holland and Zeeland, Utrecht waited until the next year to name a stadholder to replace William, but it chose not his son but Count Adolph of Nieuwenaar, who had already been elected stadholder in Gelderland to replace Count John of Nassau when he had resigned that post there.

There was some discussion of making Maurice count of Holland. Maurice put his case before the States of Holland. He did not ask them for the countship directly, but only hinted that they should make good the promise of succession given to his father, reminding them how useful it would be to have their own count in Holland if the sovereignty of the Low Countries were given to a foreign monarch.[5] Three decades later, Oldenbarnevelt, on trial for his life, defended himself against the accusation of systematic hostility to Maurice by telling his judges that after William of Orange's death, when he was still only pensionary of Rotterdam, he had urged the city to propose the grant of the countship to Maurice. It was the other cities, primarily Amsterdam and Gouda, which had blocked it.[6] Whether or not Oldenbarnevelt actually made the proposal (there is no contemporary confirmation of his assertion),[7] no step was taken to give Maurice the crown. Nonetheless, Oldenbarnevelt continued to view Maurice as central to his plans to enable Holland to maintain its dominance in the States General, where the deputies of Brabant and Flanders lost influence as their provinces were more and more recaptured for Philip II by Parma.[8]

It was not only uncertainty over whether to renew the offer of the countship to Maurice which delayed a decision to name him stadholder, but also the efforts to persuade a foreign monarch to follow Anjou as sovereign of the Low Countries. The offer of the crown was rejected by Henry III of France in January 1585, for it was incompatible with his

---

3 For the development of the historical picture of William the Silent, see E. O. G. Haitsma Mulier and A. E. M. Jensen, eds., *Willem van Oranje in de Historie, 1584–1984: Vier eeuwen beeldvorming en geschiedschrijving* (Utrecht, 1984).
4 Van Deursen, "Staatsinstellingen," 355.   5 Hallema, 33–34.
6 Den Tex, I, 219; Hallema, 23–24.   7 Den Tex, I, 219.   8 Blok, *Geschiedenis*, II, 275.

adherence – temporary, as it turned out – to the Catholic League in the French civil wars. An embassy then went to London to repeat the offer to Elizabeth I. She too declined the sovereignty of the Low Countries; she neither wanted a troublesome personal union nor an outright defiance of Philip II. But she was not eager to see Parma, who easily took Brussels during the year and then in August at last won victory over the long-besieged city of Antwerp, complete his triumphs with total domination of the Netherlands. She therefore agreed to send an expeditionary force to help the States General, and gave its command to her darling, Robert Dudley, earl of Leicester, as lieutenant-general who would also act as governor-general. But she meant less by the term than the Dutch thought; for them the governor-general had always been the *landvoogd*, the resident representative of the sovereign, but she considered that the Dutch were accepting him as such by their own authority.[9]

She had her way, for, after his arrival in the Netherlands in December, Leicester was elected governor-general by the States General (10 January 1586). His position was equivalent to that which Mary of Hungary had held under Charles V, except that his "lord" in the Low Countries was not his royal "lady" in England, but the States. Yet the States General did not assert that they were themselves the sovereign; they still hoped that Elizabeth would relent and become their overlord. Only after she wrathfully rejected the role did they begin to rule in their own name.[10] In this sense, Leicester's appointment may be more precisely the beginning of Dutch independence than the Abjuration of 1581, for after Elizabeth's rebuff the Dutch gave up the quest for an outside lord.[11]

Even before Leicester stepped onto Dutch soil, Holland and Zeeland, at the urging of Oldenbarnevelt not to delay until it might be too late, had moved to protect their autonomy within the Union. On 13 November Maurice celebrated his eighteenth birthday and the two provinces named him stadholder and provincial captain and admiral-general, the commander of their own armed forces.[12] It was all part of the policy advocated by Oldenbarnevelt to make Maurice not only a weapon against the domination of Leicester, but also an instrument in the leadership of the Union by the province of Holland. The commission for Maurice was modeled on that which Philip II had given William the Silent in 1559, modified for the new circumstances.[13] Although an instruction was drawn up as well, it was left in draft; the powers of the stadholder remained essentially what they had been. What did change was his relationship to the States (the *provin-*

---

9 Den Tex, I, 237; J. Huges, *Het leven en bedrijf van Mr Franchois Vranck* (The Hague, 1909), 47, 61.
10 Kluit, I, 93. 11 Huges, 48–49; Den Tex, I, 251; Kossmann, *Texts*, 43–48.
12 Hallema, 35–36. 13 Japikse, *Geschiedenis*, I, 131–33.

cial assembly, for the stadholdership never became a Generality office). Maurice was elected stadholder by the States and therefore became in law their servant, not their equal partner, like his father.[14]

Two years' time was enough for Leicester to display such military ineptitude and such political folly that he returned home a total failure. He mistook from the first the character of the power that he had received. Because it was "absolute," he thought it was unlimited, but the States merely meant that it was not temporary or provisional.[15] He forgot – as his royal mistress Elizabeth never did – that the power of the purse, which remained firmly in Holland's hands, is not defied without penalty. He also failed to match the political skill of Maurice's sponsor and mentor, Oldenbarnevelt, who was named land's advocate of Holland (political and legal secretary of the States) in February 1586.

The insistence in Holland that Maurice take over the military leadership rose sharply after Deventer and the entrenchments before Zutphen, in the eastern Netherlands, were betrayed to the Spaniards in January 1587 by the English commanders, both Catholics. Maurice was given formal command of the troops in the pay of the province, and the soldiers were required to take an oath of loyalty to him as well as to Leicester.[16] The earl, having gone home to report to Elizabeth, returned to the Netherlands in July with a new army, but did not use it effectively against Parma. Instead he attempted to seize Amsterdam, Leiden and Holland north of the IJ River. He failed at this too, as he did in a desperate attempt to rescue his cause by putting Oldenbarnevelt and Maurice under arrest at The Hague. They escaped in time to Delft, and his débâcle was complete. His departure for home in December did not sever the treaty of alliance between the States General and the English queen, however, for both Dutch and English would be in equal danger when the Spanish Armada being readied for the next year, 1588, reached their coasts.

During the contest between Leicester and Holland, an English member of the Council of State, Thomas Wilkes, argued that the grant of sovereignty had been absolute and that it derived from the people, to whom power belonged in the absence of a legitimate prince, rather than from the States, who were only their delegates.[17] The States of Holland replied with a defense of their sovereignty, the famed "Brief Demonstration" (*Corte Vertoninge*) drawn up by the pensionary of Gouda, François Vrancken.[18] This short tract became the theoretical declaration of principles of the

---

14 Kluit, II, 57–59.   15 Muller, 364.
16 Blok, *Geschiedenis*, II, 255; Den Tex, II, 347.
17 Huges, 68–70; *Archives*, 2e Sér., I, 39–42; Kossmann, *Texts*, 272–73.
18 The key passages of this work are translated into English in Rowen, *The Low Countries*, 104–8, and in Kossmann, *Texts*, 274–81.

political current in the Netherlands over the next two centuries that is usually called "republican," but more precisely was "*Staatsgezind*" (literally, "in favor of the States") and denied the sovereignty either of the "people," however defined, or of the House of Orange.

Oldenbarnevelt became the dominant figure in the government of Holland after Leicester's departure. Forty years of age in 1587, he was at the height of his powers of mind and will, ready as land's advocate to prove himself the equal of any statesman anywhere in his time. Although there were no such offices or titles, he became in practice both the prime minister and the foreign minister of the Dutch Republic for more than three decades. He provided the leadership of a single person which made government possible in a country with such dispersed authority, not by attempting to pour new strength into the central organs like the Council of State but by making the province of Holland preponderant.[19] He was the true creator of the Dutch Republic, adapting the institutions inherited from the past for the work of republican government.[20]

Maurice for his part was an intense, withdrawn youth who grew into a hard, dour adult. He had experienced deep pain of spirit in his boyhood. His mother, Anna of Saxony, whose marriage to William of Orange had been utterly unhappy, had fled from Dillenburg castle soon after her son's birth. Two years later she was arrested in Cologne for living in adultery with Jan Rubens (who later became the father of the painter Peter Paul Rubens), imprisoned, and her marriage to William formally dissolved in 1574. She died in 1577 at her ancestral home in Dresden. Maurice therefore grew up without the presence of a mother. To his stepmothers, Charlotte of Bourbon-Montpensier and Louise de Coligny, he accorded respect but not love. Even his father was an emotionally distant figure, adulated but far too busy to give the time to his son that his own parents had given to him at Dillenburg. Education at the University of Leiden had not been a time of shared toils and joys with other youths growing from boyhood into manhood; he was too young, for one thing, and he learned from tutors rather than in classes, for another. He was not given to speaking his mind very much, indeed deserved the title of "silent" or "taciturn" much more than his father,[21] yet now and then broke out in exasperated impatience. He never acquired the skill of winning men over to his side by argument.

The decade that followed Leicester's departure has become known as the "Ten Years."[22] Between 1588 and 1598 the United Provinces consolidated their independence and their government received its essential last-

---

19 Den Tex, II, 31–32, 49–50.   20 *Ibid.*, 61.   21 Blok, *Geschiedenis*, II, 294.
22 This name is taken from the title of the classic study of the period, *Tien Jaren uit den Tachtigjarigen Oorlog, 1588–1598* (The Hague, 1857) by the great Dutch historian Robert Fruin.

ing shape.[23] No further effort was made to find a monarchical substitute for the foresworn Philip II, and a republican state came into existence not by deliberate decision but by the evaporation of alternatives. The Council of State ceased to be *the* national government and lost its powers as such to the States General, to which it became subordinate. The States General in turn acted thenceforth as sovereign in relations with other countries and in the conduct of the war of independence (which continued to be a revolt, of course, in the eyes of the Spaniards). But sovereignty did not really belong to the States General, and the constitutional system remained firmly federal.

The support Leicester had received from some of the lesser provinces steeled the Hollanders in their determination to keep the power of final decision in the hands of the individual provinces, which in the existing constellation of forces meant their own. Indeed, even the provincial States were in turn dependent upon the decision of their "members," the voting towns and the Nobility. (This was the situation in Holland and most of the other provinces. It was quite different in the northern provinces of Friesland and Groningen.) At all levels of the States assemblies, the rule of unanimity prevailed on matters of the first importance.

When the Count of Nieuwenaar, the stadholder in Gelderland, Utrecht and Overijssel, died in 1589, Oldenbarnevelt worked hard over the next year to obtain Maurice's election in his stead. There was no difficulty with Utrecht or Overijssel, but Gelderland resisted having a common stadholder with Holland. Nonetheless Oldenbarnevelt was able to thwart the election of anyone else.[24] Thereafter the stadholders in all the provinces were always members of the allied houses of Orange and Nassau.

The emergence of Oldenbarnevelt as political leader both of the Holland he served (by birth he was a citizen of Amersfoort and a subject of the province of Utrecht) and the Republic which it dominated meant that the stadholdership changed character. It was no longer the total combination of political and military command that it had been under the counts and William I. Instead Maurice turned away from politics to take up his tasks as commander of the army with fierce single-mindedness. He was named commander of the States forces in Brabant and Flanders. He was not commander-in-chief because his cousin William Louis, the stadholder in Friesland, retained his independent command in the northern provinces. But they worked fairly well together, and the absence of full unity of

---

23 Ivo Schöffer puts the latter date as late as 1609, but the major transformations were all complete by 1598. Schöffer, "Naar consolidatie en behoud onder Hollands leiding (1593–1717)," in: S. J. Andreae and H. Hardenberg, eds., *500 jaren Staten-Generaal in de Nederlanden: Van Statenvergardering tot volksvertegenwoordiging* (Assen, 1964), 69.
24 Blok, *Geshiedenis*, II, 276; Wagenaar, VIII, 332–33.

command did little harm.[25] The naval war did not involve Maurice directly, although his office as admiral-general was the only all-Union command he held. The supreme command of the navy had been taken from the Council of State in 1588 and given to him at Oldenbarnevelt's suggestion.[26]

The collaboration of Maurice and Oldenbarnevelt became especially important because Maurice drew the lessons of the strategic and political situation of the United Provinces: the need was to protect the heart of Dutch strength in the maritime provinces by extending the outlying glacis of the land provinces, holding off reconquest by Spain and taking back what had been lost. (That is the way it was seen at The Hague, and by Dutch historians afterwards down through the centuries; to the reconciled adherents of the Habsburgs in the Southern Netherlands, and to Belgian historians after them, Dutch successes became their own failures, and vice versa.) The best way to achieve such security was to recapture one by one the fortified cities in Spanish hands, using his studies in the military writings of antiquity and the talents of the great mathematician Simon Stevin to renew the art of siegecraft.[27] It was a way of waging war that also fitted Maurice's personality. He was slow to decide and to move, almost lethargic in the eyes of those accustomed to the drama of strategic marches and pitched battles in the open field. Siege warfare bought the decrease of risk, however, at the cost of very high expenditures. It was actually the States General that decided upon particular sieges, although of course upon his proposal and in consultation with him. Most of the time he did not resent the procedure but accepted it as strengthening his hand, and he welcomed the deputies of the States General who accompanied him in the field.[28] The detail of military administration in support of the army in the field was in the hands of the Council of State, but, as Maurice knew, it was Oldenbarnevelt who impelled it to action, acting as a kind of minister of war (as with the prime ministry and the foreign ministry, it was a title and an office that did not exist, but a function that was real).[29]

Yet their collaboration was not without eruptions of disagreement even in this period of triumphs. Maurice became restless with his subordination to the political authority and no longer accepted without question the tutelage of the land's advocate.[30] He certainly did not see Oldenbarnevelt as an enemy, however. When Count William Louis in Friesland was

25 Jan Willem Wijn, *Het Krijgswezen in den tijd van Prins Maurits* (Utrecht, 1934), 4, 29.
26 J. C. Mollema, *Geschiedenis van Nederland ter Zee* (4 vols.; Amsterdam, 1939–42), I, 167; Den Tex, I, 428.
27 Wijn, 539–41.
28 S. P. Haak, "De wording van het conflict tusschen Maurits en Oldenbarnevelt," *BVGO*, 5e Reeks, 6 (1919), 100–2, 108–10; Wijn, 29, 534–37.
29 Den Tex, II, 26; Wijn, 22–23.   30 Den Tex, II, 96–97, 144–45; Haak, 120.

caught up in a bitter conflict with the leaders of the States of Friesland, particularly the vociferous and energetic Carel Roorda, Oldenbarnevelt rallied to the side of Maurice's cousin. He was not swayed by Roorda's arguments against the stadholderate as an institution or by his warnings to Holland against Maurice. Not only was Roorda a foe of Holland's domination of the Union, he had offended the honor of the province's chosen head, and such a head, declared the States of Holland in a resolution of 26 March 1597, was necessary for the maintenance of quiet and peace in the Netherlands.[31]

Maurice's great achievement in these years was to "close the fence," as taking a series of fortified towns on the southern and eastern boundaries of the United Provinces was called. It very largely defined for all time the general area of the Republic's frontiers, although they would be pushed further forward during the half century of the war of independence that was still to come. The almost unbroken chain of victories made Maurice the most admired military leader in Europe between the death of Parma in 1592 in France and the outbreak of the Thirty Years War in 1618.

Yet by the end of the century the years of virtually ceaseless triumphs were at an end. In 1600 the States General, in which Oldenbarnevelt had become the guiding mind and impelling will, ordered Maurice to undertake a campaign of great strategic boldness into Flanders. The plan was to drive overland first to the isolated States garrison at Ostend and then all the way south to Dunkirk, the base of the sea rovers who preyed so effectively upon the Dutch shipping in the Channel and the North Sea. Archduke Albert, too, who with his bride the Infanta Isabella of Spain had become the nominally independent ruler of the Southern Netherlands, was a novice at warfare, and it was anticipated that he would falter in the face of the now famous Maurice. The decision was taken nonetheless over the reluctance of Maurice: the general was for caution, the civilian Oldenbarnevelt, as was usual for him, favored taking the chance.[32] The easy confidence of Oldenbarnevelt was proved false, as Maurice had feared. Albert, although no Parma reborn, was vigorous and ready. When he confronted Maurice on the beaches and in the dunes before Nieuwpoort, Maurice emerged the tactical victor, but Albert gained the strategic triumph and the Dutch army withdrew northward to Zeeland.

It is customary, and obviously true, to speak of the period after Leicester as the time when the Dutch Republic was born; it is less obvious but equally true that it was a republic with as yet few republicans. Among the learned, and there were many of these among the governing class, it was

31 Den Tex, II, 211, 245–46; P. Geyl, *Het stadhouderschap in de partij-literatuur onder De Witt* (Amsterdam, 1947), 18.
32 Den Tex, II, 529.

easy to identify the newly emergent United Provinces with the republics of antiquity and to preach the virtues of government without kings. Yet, although the regents (it will be remembered that in Dutch this word meant the members of the governing bodies, municipal and provincial) had grown confident of their own abilities to confront the perils and meet the challenges of rule, they were slow to see republics as fully equal to monarchies in legitimacy.[33] Nor was it forgotten that William the Silent had been an inch away from becoming count of Holland and Zeeland when he died.

Maurice's camp companions, soldiers to the core, were accustomed to the thought of obeying kings and saw no reason why their admired general should not wear the crown that would have come to him had his father lived a little longer. Kings (and sovereign counts and dukes, as they wanted Maurice to be) were in their eyes in the first place supreme commanders, and obedience to civil authority seemed denigration of their own profession. They were a loose-lipped crew, quite unlike Maurice, and what they spoke of among themselves and when in their cups was well known. The regents in the lesser provinces were another focus of advocacy for the elevation of Maurice to the countship. Some were moved by principled commitment to the doctrines of monarchical rule, others merely by the desire to cut down the preponderance of Holland within the Union by subordinating the overweening province to a count who would be its master, not its servant.

In 1594, two members of Maurice's entourage initiated activity on behalf of his elevation to the countship. One, his treasurer, Jaspar van Kinschot, was related to Oldenbarnevelt through his wife, and the advocate, when informed, indicated he would not be unfavorable provided that the title of count was given on the same terms that had been accepted by William I. Maurice's friends wanted him to be a true monarch. He himself rejected the proposal; he was politically more experienced than when, after his father's death, he had suggested that the countship be bestowed upon him, and saw no advantage in it now.[34]

Two years later, however, when a similar idea was put forward in Zeeland, Oldenbarnevelt and his adherents had already shifted their position. Maurice's support had gained the province a victory over Holland in a dispute over import duties known as *licenten*, and the councilor pensionary of Zeeland, Christoffel Roels, although near death, penned a proposal to his States urging that they take the initiative for making the country a monarchy. Maurice should be made head of the Union, but by election, not by self-proclamation or by a coup of his "creatures." Oldenbarnevelt

33 Schöffer, "De opstand," 108.   34 Den Tex, II, 219–21.

became wary as soon as he heard of the proposal. It was one thing for Holland to act for itself; it was another for Zeeland to propose action binding on all the provinces in so weighty a matter.[35]

Maurice's friends in Zeeland were not easy to discourage, however. In 1601 they raised with the Hollanders the desirability of a "better order in the government," meaning a grant of the countship to Maurice. Oldenbarnevelt was worried by rumors of a coup in preparation on Maurice's behalf, and he parried the initiative. Jacob Valcke, the provisional treasurer of Zeeland who was probably the leader in the business, did not let the proposal drop. Early the next year he made another approach to Oldenbarnevelt, who assembled a small group of the most influential Hollanders to discuss the problem of how to handle the situation. The little conclave agreed not to give in to the Zeelanders if possible, but saw that if the proposal actually came up in the States General, where the backing of Gelderland could be expected for it, it would be difficult to oppose openly. The essential problem lay in reconciling the government of a count with continued rule by the States. If Maurice were given authority less hedged than that which had been promised to William, how could he be prevented from making his power absolute? And would he not favor Zeeland, which had worked for him, against Holland, which at best had gone along reluctantly?[36]

With so many friends and would-be friends encouraging him to seek the crown, Maurice found himself in an uncomfortable position. He was no republican on principle, but he would not stoop to pick up a crown. He was little concerned with politics for its own sake, beyond what it contributed to his military activities or the prestige of his family. He did have a feeling for the difference between real power and the semblance of power, and he would not sacrifice the former for the sake of the latter. If Maurice had been offered the sovereignty without restrictions, he might have accepted it, as historians have speculated; but he did not expect it on such terms. He was not about to take unnecessary risks here, any more than upon the battlefield. This is probably what he meant when he spoke the famous words that rather than accept such a burden, he would hurl himself headlong from the tower of The Hague.[37] Whether he would have agreed with the poet who, praising him for his love of country and his self-sacrifice, emphasized that he was the servant of the States,[38] is less certain. His ambition was not quite that modest.

Oldenbarnevelt knew Maurice too well to fear that he would make a direct thrust for the sovereignty. The advocate had by the turn of the

35 *Ibid.*, 284–87.   36 Blok, *Geschiedenis*, ii, 332; Den Tex, ii, 411–16.
37 F. J. L. Krämer, in *Archives*, 3e Sér., ii, xlvii.
38 J. Bax, *Prins Maurits in de volksmening der 16e en 17e eeuw* (Amsterdam, 1940).

century grown accustomed to the almost unchallenged leadership of the state, both determining and executing policy. He was therefore a republican out of practical considerations and habit, if not on principle. Oldenbarnevelt's concern was more with the potentialities which he began to glimpse as political controversy sharpened after the failure in Flanders. But it was the very military triumphs of Maurice before that as well as his own victories in statecraft that gave rise to these changes.

A different kind of problem involving Maurice was raised by the shifting ideas of King Henry IV of France concerning the future of the United Provinces. He did not understand why they adhered to republican government when the royal form of rule was so manifestly superior. His candidate for the monarchy was sometimes Maurice and sometimes himself.

When a Dutch embassy headed by Oldenbarnevelt came to Nantes in 1598 to negotiate an alliance, the king suggested to the advocate that Maurice be made the crowned head of the United Provinces. Oldenbarnevelt, who only four years before had not been unsympathetic to the idea when it had been put forward by Van Kinschot, replied evasively. It would solve many problems, he agreed, but not all: one was the surly character of Maurice himself.[39] The king may simply have thought that with Maurice as the ruling prince, the United Provinces would hold more firmly against the enticements of the archdukes to reunite the Netherlands, North and South, under a more tolerant Habsburg rule.[40] It was not an empty concern. Only a year later Archduke Albert, asking Henry IV to mediate in peace negotiations with the Northern Netherlands, indicated his willingness to concede almost anything provided he was recognized as sovereign. He would assure Maurice a brilliant career, whereas in a democracy (by which he meant government of States) he would harvest only ingratitude.[41]

Oldenbarnevelt soon discovered that the French monarch was reluctant to abandon totally the thought of himself becoming the lord of the Netherlands, as Anjou had been. He assumed that Maurice would be his governor acting for him, a "stadholder" in the old, literal sense of the term. The king's desire was embarrassing for several reasons. How could Henry IV be refused what had once been offered to Henry III? If the French king became lord of the Netherlands, where would Maurice fit into the new government? Indeed, what would the new government be? Just what changes would result in its structure and the power of its present compo-

---

39 Den Tex, II, 313–14, 316.
40 S. Barendrecht, *François van Aerssen: Diplomaat aan het Franse Hof (1598–1613)* (Leiden, 1965), 34.
41 Barendrecht, 115; W. J. M. Eysinga, *De wording van het Twaalfjarig Bestand van 9 April 1609* (Amsterdam, 1959), 57.

nents, notably the provincial States and the stadholders? It was not until the end of 1607 that Henry finally understood that he was getting nowhere, and the matter was let drop.[42] Maurice remained concerned to protect the interests of his family. According to the French envoy, Jeannin, he asked Louise de Coligny to sound out Oldenbarnevelt about assuring the succession to the stadholderate for Frederick Henry, his half-brother, if Maurice died without a legitimate son of his own. (He rebuffed hints from the States that he ought to marry, and he would not legitimize his children by his mistress, *freule* [Miss] Margaretha of Mechelen, either.) Louise did so enthusiastically, for her passion for Frederick Henry, her only son, was, as the envoy reported, "unbounded." Oldenbarnevelt dashed cold water on her enthusiasm for immediate action, but she remained his friend and adherent in the contest of mind, will and force that would soon set her stepson and the advocate of Holland against each other.[43]

As the new government of King Philip III in Spain began to lose hope of easy reconquest of the Northern Netherlands, and in the face of its own mounting financial difficulties (themselves largely the result of the eternal drainage of the Dutch revolt), the notion of peace with the States General gained headway in Madrid and Brussels. Indeed, Archduke Albert was ready to go much further in this direction than was his brother-in-law on the throne in Spain, and he was able to initiate contacts with the States General for a cessation of hostilities. Since the war put an immense burden on the Dutch finances too, although one they were able to carry more comfortably, Oldenbarnevelt and his friends responded carefully but positively to these initiatives. It became apparent that a full peace was beyond attainment. The Spaniards would not yield to the Dutch the legal entry into the Indies, East and West, that they wanted, and the Dutch for their part would not concede the full religious and political rights the Spaniards demanded for Dutch Catholics. Discussion of a truce began.

Maurice, to make his opposition to the truce proposal heard where it mattered, used his rights as stadholder in a way that he had not followed for two decades. He wrote directly to the cities in Holland and to the States of Gelderland, Utrecht and Overijssel, in his capacity as "governor," a term he used that emphasized his political role.[44] He refused to go as far as the hotheads among his adherents desired, to rouse the people against their rulers in the towns and prevent the conclusion of the truce, using the army if need be. The advice of the moderates, who were led by Louise de

---

42 Eysinga, 57, 76–79; Den Tex, II, 313–16, 490, 555, 557, 571–72; Barendrecht, 34, 115, 152, 161–68; J. C. H. de Pater, *Maurits en Oldenbarnevelt in den Strijd om het Twaalfjarig Bestand* (Amsterdam, 1940), 32–33.

43 P. J. Blok, *Frederik Hendrik* (Amsterdam, 1924), 29; Blok, *Geschiedenis*, II, 421–22; Hallema, 156–57.

44 Eysinga, 131; Blok, *Geschiedenis*, II, 356.

Coligny and William Louis of Nassau, to hew strictly to legality was more congenial to his conservative political ideas and his customary caution.[45] Nonetheless Oldenbarnevelt began to suspect that behind Maurice's opposition to the truce lay his supposed ambition for supreme power, because it would be easier for him to seize power during war. When letters between Maurice's treasurer, Van Kinschot, who had recently died, and the late treasurer of Zeeland, Valcke, dating to 1601, were found in a street, Oldenbarnevelt read them to a secret session of the States of Holland. The correspondence, whose discovery in such a convenient way was not explained, revealed endeavors to interest Elizabeth of England in the elevation of Maurice to sovereignty.

Maurice denied to friends that he held any such ambition, and he came in person to the States of Holland to remind the assembly that under the Union of Utrecht, no peace or truce could be made except by unanimous decision of the States General; if there was disagreement, the decision would be up to him and William Louis as the stadholders.[46] An effort by the court preacher, Uyttenbogaert, to mediate the conflict between the advocate and the stadholder failed. "Let the Advocate do what he wants, and I'll do what I want," was the reply Maurice sent to the preacher, who was a friend and an admirer of both of them.[47] That was in October 1608. A month later the French envoy Jeannin also attempted a reconciliation, but with even less effect. Mutual suspicions had replaced friendship.[48]

Despite Maurice's opposition, a twelve-year truce was concluded that began in 1609 (a suspension of hostilities had gone into effect two years earlier). The truce left unsettled the issues of the Indies and Dutch Catholic rights that had prevented full peace, but fell just short of outright recognition of Dutch independence. Whether war would actually be resumed in 1621 would be decided not only by events in Madrid and Brussels, as well as on the wider European scene, where renewed war between France and the Habsburg powers seemed about to break out, but also by what would happen in the Dutch Republic.

Maurice was furious at the truce. For him the war with Spain had become a matter of self-evident principle, not the means to the achievement of one or another economic or political advantage. He wanted no truce but the total defeat of the Spaniards, the murderers of his father, and they would have to recognize the full independence of the Dutch without receiving themselves any of the concessions they sought. In this hostility to the truce he was supported by the orthodox Calvinists, especially by the exiles from the South in their midst, by his own military companions, and by those who garnered profit from the war, like Zeeland privateers. Mau-

45 De Pater, 112–13.   46 Den Tex, II, 641–42, 649; Hallema, 150–51.
47 Den Tex, II, 651–54.   48 *Ibid.*, 660–61.

rice, unwilling to grant any legitimacy to the intentions of those who made the truce, began to suspect that they had betrayed their country to Spain, or at least contemplated such treason.[49]

The estrangement between advocate and stadholder became more irreconcilable when, after the conclusion of the truce, dissension about relations with Spain fused with the religious conflict within the Reformed church. At one level, the dispute concerned a purely theological question, the range and depth of divine predestination; at another, the issue was whether the church would be restricted to only the fully orthodox or would embrace as many Protestant Christians as possible. It was this latter problem that made a theological debate a matter of the highest political concern. The orthodox Calvinists, first known as Gomarians and then as Contra-Remonstrants, demanded not only the right to define the doctrines of the Reformed church and to determine its membership, but also insisted that they alone had the right to the support of the state as the legitimate official church. They wished to expel from the nation and the body politic not only stubborn Catholics but also all errant Protestants. Such a policy was anathema to their theological opponents and their allies among the regents, first known as Arminians and then as Remonstrants, who favored toleration of a wide variety of religious groups, both out of deep conviction and from a concern for keeping the doors of the country open to traders and mariners no matter what their faith.

The stadholder and the advocate were drawn into the controversy despite their individual differences with both camps. Maurice was a sincere and strong member of the Reformed church, but he had little interest in and less understanding of strictly theological matters. The remark attributed to him that he did not know whether predestination was blue or green may be apocryphal, but it catches his opacity in such abstract ideas. He was totally convinced, however, that Calvinist orthodoxy was true and that it was an essential and ineradicable part of the Dutch war of independence: to assault the Reformed church was to put the country in peril of its very existence, and it was therefore treason. Oldenbarnevelt had a better grasp of the theological issues involved, and indeed was actually closer to the Gomarian than the Arminian position on predestination. He differed sharply with the Contra-Remonstrants, however, concerning the relation of church and state. He upheld the right of the state to determine matters of church government in the officially recognized church, and he favored keeping its doctrinal doors as wide open as possible for loyal and obedient subjects. For him, however, the "state" meant the individual provinces, Holland in particular, and not the States General.

49 *Ibid.*, 633.

We need not follow the course of this controversy in detail until its final culmination in Maurice's arrest of Oldenbarnevelt in 1618 upon the authority of the States General, his trial on charges of subversion of the state and treason, and his execution in 1619. What matters for the history of the development of the stadholderate is how it was affected by the struggle. The canker that rotted away what little remained of the good will between Maurice and Oldenbarnevelt, and hence between their adherents, was the conflict over control over the army not in foreign war but in civil strife.

Within the towns the sheriff (*schout*) and his few men were the ordinary police force. They were sufficient to arrest criminals and the like, but they could not put down full-fledged riots and insurrections. For that the burgomasters and town councils had to call upon the *schutterijen*, the civic guards recruited from the burghers but commanded by officers who were regents or their sons and nephews. The *schutterijen* were heavily enough armed and well enough trained to smash mobs; the problem lay in their readiness to disobey orders when they disagreed with authorities. The regents were helpless against them in such a case and had to call upon the provincial States to send in regular troops – an always unpalatable admission of inadequacy. There was no question of the soldiers' ability to do the job of restoring order. What did become a question for the first time during the truce years was the willingness of their commander, the captain-general, to give the necessary commands.

This novel problem arose because Oldenbarnevelt insisted upon using the army to impose unwanted decisions upon the followers of Gomarus, while Maurice refused to obey blindly orders of the States of Holland that he thought conflicted with his oath of office. In 1610, when the popular party favorable to the Gomarians seized power in the city of Utrecht, Maurice declined to head the expedition sent there by the States General at the request of the States of Utrecht. He did permit his younger brother, Frederick Henry, to accept the politically onerous commission.[50] The episode was instructive for the party opposed to Oldenbarnevelt. They could not do without Maurice at their head, for he controlled the armed force that would be needed to break the party in power. Yet he was not an ambitious *condottiere*, willing and eager to turn upon his employers and make himself master of the state. Neither was he a revolutionary, for whom armed force is the necessary and proper means for gaining control of the state. The only way for the Gomarians to win Maurice to do all they wanted was to put Oldenbarnevelt in the wrong, to trap him into using violence against the Contra-Remonstrants, violence that was illegal or at least of disputable legality. Whether or not Contra-Remonstrant leaders

---

50 *Ibid.*, 168–71.

deliberately planned such a development, that was how events worked out.[51]

Maurice after much hesitation gave his assent to efforts to obtain churches where the Contra-Remonstrants could worship, although each side in the religious conflict asserted that it alone was the true Reformed church and that the other should be barred. In The Hague the Contra-Remonstrants on 9 July 1617 took over the Kloosterkerk, which had fallen into disuse, in defiance of the municipal authorities of The Hague. Oldenbarnevelt saw it as virtual rebellion and considered having the offenders arrested that very night and punished before morning by the High Council.[52] It was not until the next day that he learned that the seizure had taken place with Maurice's approval. The pattern of events was emerging: in a showdown, Maurice would have the final say, not as stadholder but as captain-general.[53]

Two weeks later, Maurice made his choice of sides public by attending the sermon of a Contra-Remonstrant preacher in the Kloosterkerk. Yet, even at this time, he sought to avert the worst, or at least to take precautions if it happened. He permitted Louise de Coligny and Frederick Henry to attend the regular service in the Grote Kerk. Louise was outspoken in her support of the Remonstrants, but Frederick Henry kept his views in religious matters to himself, giving offense to neither party if he could and avoiding responsibility for events which he almost certainly deplored but could not prevent.[54] In sparing their predilections, Maurice assured the future of the House of Orange. If civil war did result from the controversy and the dominant party in Holland prevailed, whatever happened to Maurice himself, his brother could take over, maintaining the stadholdership and the captaincy-general in the House of Orange.[55]

The conflict over politics and religion came to a head on 4 August 1617, when the States of Holland adopted a resolution designed to avert what was seen as a Contra-Remonstrant *coup d'état* in the making. Its measures were so drastic that it was soon dubbed the "Sharp Resolution." It empowered all towns in the province to raise auxiliary troops called *waardgelders*. (The term originally described mercenary troops put on "waiting pay" [*wartgeld*] in anticipation of combat service, but it had come to mean professional soldiers hired by the towns, in contrast to those paid by the provinces and the Union.) Provincial courts were forbidden to interfere with actions of the towns. All persons who had sworn oaths of fidelity to

51 Den Tex, III, 407–8, 414; see also *Archives*, 2e Sér., II, lxxiv.
52 Maurice to William Louis, 18 Feb, 1 June, 1617, *Archives*, 2e Sér., II, 488–89; Den Tex, III, 485, 488–89.
53 Den Tex, III, 475, 489–90. 54 Poelhekke, *Frederik Hendrik*, 59.
55 Den Tex, III, 490–91.

either the province or the towns had to be ready to support their actions to maintain public order; this applied particularly to troops in the province which were required to obey the orders of the States and the towns where they were garrisoned. With these measures, Oldenbarnevelt and his party expected that the town governments would be able to enforce their authority despite the defection of many civic guard companies to the Contra-Remonstrant camp.

From Maurice's point of view, it was bad enough that the *waardgelders* would not be under his command; that they should be required to obey the municipal governments in defiance of orders from anyone else – which meant the States General and himself as captain-general – was intolerable. This is what he told Oldenbarnevelt and other members of a delegation from the majority of the States of Holland sent to seek his compliance. He insisted upon speaking to the States himself the next day. His brother, Frederick Henry, avoided conforming, lest he fall into the trap of becoming Maurice's enemy.[56]

Although Oldenbarnevelt did not realize it at once, the "Sharp Resolution" was a sword that cleaved him and Maurice apart as enemies beyond hope of reconciliation. One or the other had to go down to defeat. For Maurice it was proof that the advocate was breaking the law and was probably guilty of treason. Whatever the States of Holland might decide, he had the higher authority of the States General behind him.[57]

Events marched on, steadily but not swiftly. When the province of Utrecht began to raise *waardgelders* without informing Maurice himself, the Council of State, or the States General, he put the blame on Oldenbarnevelt and made a formal complaint to the States General.[58] On his own he prevented the swearing in of the *waardgelders* who had been hired by Den Briel. It was a direct challenge to the authority of the States of Holland which he justified as not waging civil war but preventing it.[59] It was the threat to his military command and the peril to orthodox Calvinism which stirred Maurice, however, not the desire for enhanced political power and higher title and dignity of office. He considered suspicions and outright accusations that he was preparing a *coup* to seize power and make himself sovereign count–duke a foul slander, whatever the wild ideas that ran around among some of his adherents.[60]

Ironically, it was in these months that Maurice became a "Prince" not by courtesy title but by right. His elder brother Philip William, with whom

56 *Ibid.*, 494–95.
57 H. Gerlach, "Het bestand in de Noordelijke Nederlanden, 1609–1621," in: *Algemene Geschiedenis*, VI, 307.
58 Den Tex, III, 510; Maurice to William Louis, 17 Sept. 1617, *Archives*, 2e Sér., II, 541–42.
59 Den Tex, III, 516–17.   60 *Ibid.*, 586.

he had been personally reconciled although they remained religiously and politically on opposite sides, died in Brussels on 20 February 1618, and Maurice became officially "Prince of Orange." Although the people had used the title for him for some time, he himself seldom used it even afterwards. The vanity of titles was not one of his vices.[61]

During the next year, Maurice and Oldenbarnevelt, each wishing to avert civil war, took measures which, conceived as defensive and protective of the law, made their fencing a duel to the death. The central issue continued to be the *waardgelders*, on whom the Oldenbarneveltians built their increasingly desperate hopes. It was a vain hope. Maurice used his powers as stadholder to replace friends of Oldenbarnevelt in the town governments of Gelderland and Overijssel. Then, in July, the States General resolved upon the dismissal of the *waardgelders* in the two provinces where the Oldenbarneveltians had sway, Holland and Utrecht. Maurice led a delegation to Utrecht to enforce the resolution, and a counter-delegation went out from the States of Holland to urge its rejection. After some brave talk, the Utrechters gave in, and Maurice dismissed the *waardgelders* in a massive ceremony upon the main square of the city. The Remonstrant members of the town council were removed from their seats.[62]

Finally, on 28 August Maurice exploded the mine set beneath his foe's beleaguered position. The States General ordered the dismissal of all *waardgelders* anywhere in the Republic and gave Maurice extraordinary powers to save the country. He thereupon placed Oldenbarnevelt, together with Grotius and two others, under arrest. They then faced a court of twenty-four judges, most not professional jurists, who sat as an extraordinary commission by authority of the States General. That the judges acted more as prosecuting attorneys than as impartial seekers after truth was not out of the ordinary, but merely the usual practice of the time. Never before, however, had anyone been arrested in any province by the States General without the prior approval of the States of that province, and the resolution itself was formally invalid, lacking as it did the vote of Holland. For all Maurice's concern to keep legality on his side, the arrest was an act of revolution.[63] But the conflict had come to the point where the contenders each considered the other guilty of rebellion, and its own measures as justified by the necessity which makes its own law. Maurice and his party, not considering themselves revolutionaries, nonetheless had reached that stage in a revolution when new law is created.

For Maurice the personal element was very strong. The envoys of France came to him to plead for the prisoners, but he told them to go to the States General, who alone were competent. He turned aside their request

61 *Ibid.*, 558–59.　　62 *Ibid.*, 560–61.　　63 *Ibid.*, 620–22, 626.

at least to grant clemency with bitter words: "Oldenbarnevelt gave me personal offense, boasting that he would drive me out like Leicester. The King will therefore pardon me if I do not intercede for him. He has been accused of wanting to create disorder in the country in order to put it back under the yoke of Spain. Let the court decide."[64]

The trial – more precisely, the examination of Oldenbarnevelt, Grotius and Hogerbeets, the surviving accused after the suicide in prison of Lederberg, the secretary of the States of Utrecht – proceeded methodically over the next eight months. Of the key accusations against Oldenbarnevelt, one, that he had committed treason, although it had been used to stir up the passions of the populace, was never proved. Two that involved the *waardgelders* did not require proof. The facts were plain, it was only their juridical significance that was in question, and, in the morass of Dutch constitutional law, a reply could be made only upon the basis of power, not of law. That made it certain that the accused would be found guilty, though not the sentence that would be imposed upon them. Probably the determining factor in the final judgment was a matter to which the judges gave an extraordinary amount of attention, considering that it was not in itself criminal: this was the accusation that the advocate had slandered Maurice by imputing monarchist ambitions to him. Oldenbarnevelt denied that he had suspected the Prince of Orange himself, but admitted that he had seen among Maurice's counselors some who did hold such ambitions for him.[65]

In May 1619 the court passed its sentence. Oldenbarnevelt was to die by the great sword on the scaffold, and Grotius and Hogerbeets would suffer life imprisonment in Loevestein Castle. On 13 May the advocate of Holland, aged 71 years, was beheaded in the courtyard of the Binnenhof in The Hague. "Do not believe that I am a traitor" were his last words to the onlookers. He undoubtedly thought he was the victim of judicial murder and Maurice's vengeance. He paid the price, rather, for losing in a conflict where the improvised institutions of the Republic left ultimate authority vague and indeterminate, but political passions made a decision one way or another inevitable and necessary. As for Maurice, to the end he had been not vengeful but hard. To the many pleas, not least from Louise de Coligny and the French envoys, to show clemency and give the pardon that lay in his hands as stadholder, he replied that the advocate or his family must first ask for mercy, admitting his guilt. This neither Oldenbarnevelt nor his wife or sons would do. And so the advocate's head fell, and forever after Dutch politics divided along the line between his posthumous foes and friends.

64 *Ibid.*, 670.   65 *Ibid.*, 701.

The death of Count William Louis of Nassau in 1620 was both a personal blow and a valuable political opportunity to Maurice. William Louis had been not only his cousin but a close confidant and a cherished friend, yet Maurice accepted the now vacant stadholdership of Groningen when it was offered him by the States of the province. Their reasons were significant: he permitted them henceforth to select their own town councils, and they preferred to have a stadholder who was not near by, as William Louis had been. The province of Drente, self-governing although not a member of the States General, also elected Maurice as successor to William Louis. In Friesland, however, Ernst Casimir, William Louis's brother, on hearing of his illness, rushed to Leeuwarden and gained his own election, forestalling any effort on Maurice's behalf. The States of Friesland were more concerned with avoiding the preponderance of Holland than their neighbors to the east had been.[66] The dream of having one stadholder over all the provinces, giving a new measure of uniformity to their diverse governments, would have to wait more than a century to be made real.

In the aftermath, Maurice proved by what he did (or, indeed, by what he did not do) that the crown had not been what he sought. In the town governments where the Oldenbarneveltians had dominated, they had been expelled by him in the autumn of 1618. The States of Holland, its membership purged and replaced, became obedient. The office that Oldenbarnevelt had held became an instrument in the stadholder's hand. After the advocate's arrest, his formal duties had been entrusted to Andrew de Witt, a member of an influential Dordrecht family, but only on an interim basis. In 1621 the office was given to Anthony Duyck on a regular appointment, with a five-year term, limited powers and a new title as "councilor pensionary" (*raadpensionaris*). But Duyck was as much Maurice's creature as De Witt had been. Maurice's leadership of the Dutch Republic was complete. Yet, although his supporters would have made him count and duke in their provinces at the least sign of his readiness to accept, he would not give it.[67]

His triumph left him a spiritually and physically exhausted man. He had acted against Oldenbarnevelt with great reluctance, not out of bloodthirstiness but from a sense of duty and necessity. The refusal of Oldenbarnevelt or his family to ask for pardon had deprived him of an escape from the burden of punishing the man who had guided his way to leadership of the Republic. His own direction of policy became lethargic. He soon had his

---

66 Lieuwe van Aitzema, *Saken van Staet en Oorlogh, in, ende omtrent de Vereenighde Nederlanden* (rev. edn; 6 vols. in 7 parts; The Hague, 1669–72), I, pt. 1, 7; Blok, *Geschiedenis*, II, 494.

67 To say, as does Geyl (*Geschiedenis*, II, 476), that Maurice was "all powerful" and that "so long as he lived, the Republic had become de facto a monarchy," misconstrues the constitutional meaning of his triumph. This Geyl virtually admits in his next sentence, that Maurice "was nothing more than the leader of a victorious party."

fill of the persecuting zeal of the orthodox Calvinists, but did nothing to protect its victims. He allowed his friends to govern for him in his name.[68]

Within the few years of life left to him, the popularity that had been built up over the decades began to fall away.[69] Not least among the reasons was his lack of enthusiasm for the persecution of their rivals conducted by the Contra-Remonstrant zealots. Their triumph at the Synod of Dort (Dordrecht), the national assembly of the Reformed church which they had always demanded and the Oldenbarneveltians had always refused, was sealed by their total control of the official church. Remonstrant preachers were driven from their pulpits and from the country, or else went underground ("dove under," *onderduikte*, to use the nautical phrase of twentieth-century Dutchmen during the Nazi occupation). They responded with pamphlets filled with hatred for the victors. Maurice was repeatedly called a tyrant.[70]

The venom against him found an outlet in a conspiracy against his life in 1623. The instigators were two sons of Oldenbarnevelt and several companions. Several sailors were hired to slay Maurice during a visit to his mistress, but they betrayed the plan. One son, Reinier Oldenbarnevelt van Groenevelt, was caught, tried and executed with several others. The other son, William Oldenbarnevelt van Stoutenberg, escaped to the Spanish Netherlands. Theirs had been a foolish enterprise as well as a careless one. They had had no plans for what they would do after success to revive their father's party.[71] All they achieved was to deepen the disgrace into which it had fallen, and to put off to a still later day its hopes of return.

The war with Spain was resumed in 1621. Neither side was yet ready to make the concessions which, had they been taken twelve years before, would have brought not just the suspension of the hostilities but the end of the war. Its renewal had not been a foregone conclusion in the United Provinces, where there were many, especially in Holland, who foresaw the immense costs that resumed war would bring. Indeed, had it not been for the new dominance of a war party in Madrid after the death of Philip III earlier in the year, Maurice might not have had his way.[72] The course of the fighting turned against him. He had totally lost the touch of victory.

When Ambrogio Spinola, the Italian banker turned brilliant general who commanded the Spanish army in the Southern Netherlands, put the city of Breda under siege in 1624, Maurice could do little for its defense. A treaty of alliance with France did not help. Maurice's health was shattered,

---

68 Gerlach, 313; Blok, *Geschiedenis*, II, 495; Barendrecht, 1.
69 Blok, *Geschiedenis*, II, 531–32.   70 Bax, 198–99.
71 A. Th. van Deursen, *Bavianen en Slijkgeuzen: Kerk en Kerkvolk ten tijde van Maurits en Oldenbarnevelt* (Assen, 1974), 363–64.
72 Poelhekke, *Frederik Hendrik*, 63, 216; Jonathan I. Israel, *The Dutch Republic and the Hispanic World, 1606–1661* (Oxford, 1982), 66–85.

and his capacity for effective command was reduced almost to nothing. He recognized the necessity for a deputy commander and asked the States General to authorize him to name Frederick Henry. This may have been no more than a gesture of self-affirmation as the end approached and the brother waited to take over; but it also strengthened the implicit dynastic element that characterized the place of the House of Orange in the Republic. The States General nonetheless insisted on making the appointment themselves on 12 April 1625, eleven days before Maurice died.[73]

It has become a commonplace of Dutch historical writing that Maurice wasted his chance to reform the constitution of the Republic. He took no step to make the central authority in the States General truly sovereign, although both he and Oldenbarnevelt had agreed on the desirability of a strong national government that could hold the provinces to their obligations. It was only the skewed development of the conflict in its final stages, with Oldenbarnevelt isolated from the other provinces and holding on to Holland with desperate intensity, that made it appear a conflict between central and provincial authority.[74] Maurice did not even attempt to deprive the States of Holland of their financial powers; it was sufficient that they gave what he asked of them.[75]

Some historians regret that he did not establish the hereditary leadership of the House of Orange beyond all challenge, cracking apart the self-enclosed aristocracy (in the Aristotelian, not the modern sense) of the regents in favor of a wider, more democratic participation of the burghers in government. This is, however, to impose upon him a judgment drawn from the experience of two more centuries, and one colored too by the belief that the constitutional monarchy of the modern Netherlands would have been the right form of government in the seventeenth and eighteenth centuries. It is, of course, anachronism at its purest. Maurice himself would not have understood the mission thus implicitly assigned to him which it is said he failed to perform. He had grown up with the regime and found no fault of principle with it; his dissatisfaction with policies and personalities was never given constitutional form. What concerned him was to have effective power; just where it began and ended did not matter.[76] If at the end of his life a certain sense of failure hung over him, it was not because he had not anticipated the nineteenth century, but because events had not turned out quite the way he wanted.

73 Poelhekke, *Frederik Hendrik*, 78–79.
74 Blok, *Geschiedenis*, II, 449.
75 J. H. Kluiver, "De Republiek na het bestand. 1621–1650," in: *Algemiene Geschiedenis*, VI, 352.
76 Poelhekke, *Frederik Hendrik*, 107–8; [Alexander van der Capellen van Aartsbergen], *Gedenkschriften van Jonkheer Alexander van der Capellen, Heere van Aartsbergen, Boedelhoff, en Mervelt*, ed. Robert Jaspar van der Capellen (2 vols.; Utrecht, 1772–73), I, 347.

For the history of the stadholderate, the importance of Maurice's administration lies not in the changes which he did not make, but in the definition of many of the issues that would dominate the political life of the Republic until 1795. These were the conflict between Holland and the lesser provinces, expressed in the debate over whether the individual provinces or the States General were sovereign; the political status of the Reformed church, whose preachers were the spiritual guides of an often turbulent populace; and the extent of civilian control of the military. The issue that had not yet emerged was the contest over the place of the stadholderate in the constitutional structure of the state. What was clear, however, was that the stadholder was no longer the parallel, equal collaborator of the States that William had been, but their servant, one exalted above all others in the land, but their servant still.

It had not been and would not be an easy relationship.[77] The question was whether it would be only the person and the policies of the stadholder that would be involved, or also the institution of the stadholderate itself. In hindsight, but also in anticipation of what would come, we may be surprised that no one challenged the institution during Maurice's time. It was still a supple institution that could adapt itself to changing relationships of power in the Republic; its very vagueness gave it elbow room for change.[78]

77 Eysinga, 20–21; *Archives*, 2e Sér., II, lxiv, lix.
78 Schöffer, "Naar consolidatie," 94–95.

3

Frederick Henry: firm in moderation

The significance of Maurice's refusal to become count and duke in the United Provinces became clear with his death. Had he taken the crown when it was within his grasp, his brother Frederick Henry would have succeeded him as stadholder by established right. Now, however, Frederick Henry did not step at once into his brother's boots, but had to wait for the States to act.

There was no question about his succession in command of the army. He had been named deputy commander on 12 April, when Maurice's incapacity and approaching death had become evident, and then, when his brother was no more, he was appointed captain-general of the Union by the States General, as they had promised Maurice they would do. His command was therefore more extensive than Maurice's had been, for it included all troops in the service of the States General, including those in the northern provinces, where, however, all significant military operations had ceased. There was discontent in some of the provinces that the States General had not waited for their customary prior approval, but Holland pressed for Frederick Henry's universal command over the troops of the Union.[1]

The haste with which Frederick Henry was given command came from two concerns. One was that no opportunity be given to the Spaniards to exploit a period of uncertainty. It was bad enough that they took Breda on 5 June; but Spinola was a bold general whose enterprising spirit there was every reason to fear. The other was that the loyalty of the army itself could not be taken for granted; most of the soldiery and many of the officers were not Dutchmen but foreigners serving for pay, with little or no commitment, religious or political, to the cause for which they fought. *Condottiere* captains like Count Ernst von Mansfeld and Duke Christian of Brunswick might well proclaim themselves the leaders of the army and treat with the States General not as servants but as equals. Any such untoward happening was forestalled by the swift appointment of Fred-

1 Blok, *Geschiedenis*, II, 533; Blok, *Frederik Hendrik*, 67; Van der Capellen, *Gedenkschriften*, I, 349.

Frederick Henry, 1584–1647

erick Henry, and the troops easily transferred their fidelity to the new Prince of Orange.[2]

Politically the election of Frederick Henry as stadholder did not go as smoothly. Holland was ready to act quite quickly, although Contra-Remonstrant towns gave hints of second thoughts because of his inclination toward the Remonstrants.[3] Zeeland, which from the beginning of the Republic had made its stadholdership joint with that of Holland, moved hesitantly. The question there was not whether Frederick Henry would become the new stadholder, but whether as Prince of Orange he could name his deputy as First Noble of Zeeland even before his own election as stadholder. At the request of the Hollanders, their sister province sent deputies to The Hague to work out common terms of appointment. Frederick Henry was named stadholder of Holland and Zeeland on 1 May, but it was not possible to come to agreement upon the terms, and the commission that was adopted some three weeks later was largely a verbatim copy of that which had been given to Maurice in 1585. In any event, the sovereignty of the States as the stadholder's master was reaffirmed. Frederick Henry took his oath of office as stadholder of both provinces in his camp at Waalwijk on 1 June.[4]

Holland urged the other provinces to follow suit by naming Frederick Henry as their stadholder too, "for the sake of better relation with this province." In Utrecht province, although the eventual election of Frederick Henry as stadholder was never in question, a sharp debate raged before it was done. Holland's initiative in calling upon the other provinces to follow its lead was resented, and the States decided instead to name him on their own. The city of Utrecht opposed putting back into the stadholder's instruction clauses taken over from Maurice's instruction of 1590 which provided that the stadholder would name members of the city's government. Although he had to act with the advice and consent of the States, the clause had been employed on behalf of the "elected members" (*geëligeerden*, those chosen to replace the former ecclesiastical members of the States), who were now usually noble. It had been dropped in 1618 at the insistence of the so-called "democratic" party supporting Maurice. An appeal to the States General and the States of Holland did not break the impasse, and finally Frederick Henry was simply given a commission as stadholder without any instruction, but with the powers that Maurice had had at the time of his death.[5]

2 F. J. ten Raa and F. de Bas, *Het Staatsche Leger, 1568–1795* (8 vols. to date; Breda, 1911–), IV, 4.
3 Poelhekke, *Frederik Hendrik*, 84.
4 Blok, *Geschiedenis*, II, 532–33; Blok, *Frederik Hendrik*, 71–73; Aitzema, I, 186–87; Poelhekke, *Frederik Hendrik*, 85–86, 88–90.
5 Poelhekke, *Frederik Hendrik*, 91, 93–96.

The election in Overijssel went without difficulty, although Frederick Henry did not take his oath as stadholder there until 6 July.[6] Gelderland was the last to act. There had long been discussion of naming a nobleman from the province itself as its stadholder, but the military situation overrode such considerations, since there was no thought of separating the stadholdership and the captaincy-general. Frederick Henry was not named until 5 July, and took his oath on 25 July.[7]

While a young man Frederick Henry had been a gay blade, roistering with the wildest of his army camp companions. The thought of binding himself to a wife was distasteful, and he had insisted upon retaining the privileges of bachelorhood. Maurice, whose relationship to *freule* Margaretha of Mechelen had been emotionally a kind of marriage, but without the public and ceremonial aspects of formal wedded status, had not interfered with his brother's preference until he realized his own death was nearing; then he had put down his foot. Frederick Henry, already forty-one years of age, must marry at once and assure the continuation of the family; else Maurice would legitimize his own children by his mistress. Since this would deprive him of the heritage that would otherwise come to him, Frederick Henry knuckled under. He took as his bride his current mistress, the German-born Countess Amalia of Solms-Braunfels, a lady-in-waiting in the miniature court-in-exile of Queen Elizabeth of Bohemia.[8]

Life changed dramatically for both Frederick Henry and his twenty-two-year-old wife (who is henceforth known in Dutch history by the Dutch form of her name, Amalia van Solms). He turned from a rake into a model husband and father, and she from a minor noblewoman with few prospects to the first lady of the land, proud and ambitious. Initially, Frederick Henry's preference for simplicity and avoidance of ceremony triumphed over Amalia's pride. He continued to have people call him "Excellency," not "Your Grace," as the Germans did to persons of his rank. He spurned a proposal that Amalia be called "Your Excellency's consort," replying, "I am a Hollander, born in Delft, and there they say wife, housewife or lady (*vrou, huysvrou off wijff*)."[9]

He began to give up this stark simplicity when a son was born to him and Amalia on 27 May 1626. The States General and the States of Holland joined in becoming the babe's godfathers, and it was the latter assembly that chose for him the name of his grandfather, William, who by this time had become a mythic figure, a noble and selfless "father of the fatherland." It was a political choice of name, indicative of the unique role of the House of Orange in the Republic. When the baptism took place on 1 July, the expectation was repeatedly voiced that "in his time" William would

---

6 *Ibid.*, 97–98.   7 Blok, *Frederik Hendrik*, 67; Poelhekke, *Frederik Hendrik*, 98–99.
8 Blok, *Frederik Hendrik*, 61–62.   9 *Ibid.*, 73–74.

become "a good instrument for the protection of the freedom of this country," and Frederick Henry replied that "a servant of Their High Mightinesses [the States General] had been born" who would follow the example of his forefathers in worthy fashion.[10]

Now Amalia was able to win her husband over to a more ostentatious pattern of life. By turning the soldier with the habits of camp life into a nobleman of refined taste and conduct, she performed for him a subtle but important service. The air of the *condottiere*, the soldier who sold his services, had still hung over his brother, because that was what so many of his companions really were. Now Frederick Henry not only devoted much of his time and thought to political questions, he acted the part of the statesman. By siring a son and daughters, he found himself thinking ahead to their fortunes, and he became a dynast, one who mingled his destiny with that of the state he ruled or served.[11]

Frederick Henry and Amalia established a court that was modest by the standards of foreign royalty but outshone by far the public display of any family, noble or regent, in the country. They were not satisfied to reside in the cramped stadholder's quarters in the Binnenhof, in buildings shared with the States of Holland (their proprietor) and the States General, but over the years built a number of sumptuous homes near The Hague and out in the countryside. These stately residences were decorated with furnishings and art works in the fashionable international style.

The transformation of Frederick Henry was swift but not really surprising. His childhood had not been scarred by the tragedies and near-neglect that had marked the growing up of Maurice. He had not known his father, slain when his youngest child was only five months old, but he had a warmhearted, devoted mother. Louise de Coligny respected the position of her stepson Maurice but nonetheless kept her highest hopes for her own adored child, especially when Maurice backed away from marriage. Maurice had retained in his character much of the rough-and-ready quality of the German Nassau counts, but Frederick Henry, thanks to his mother, became both Dutch and French in culture and connections. In his youth he spent time in France with his relatives there, great French noble families like the La Trémoïlles and the Bouillons. His oldest brother, Philip William, was little more than a name in his life, but Maurice, who was William's second son but the true head of the family in the Dutch Republic, was a far more important influence in his life.

Maurice and Frederick Henry were separated by seventeen years of age,

---

10 *Ibid.*, 90–91; Poelhekke, *Frederik Hendrik*, 151–53.
11 Poelhekke, *Frederik Hendrik*, 149; J. J. Poelhekke, "Een gefrustreerd Antwerpenaar: Frederik Hendrik, Prins van Oranje, 1584–1647," in: J. J. Poelhekke, *Met Pen, Tongriem en Rapier: Figuren uit een ver en nabij verleden* (Amsterdam, 1976), 48–49.

but this would not have impeded intimacy had they lived under the same roof. Maurice was a tough-skinned soldier who became interested in his brother when he became of age to learn the trade of war. Frederick Henry responded with respect, and when he grew into maturity something like friendship developed between the brothers. Maurice watched over the career of his brother who already represented the future of the House of Orange. He permitted him to acquire the experience in warfare that prepared him for the career of military leadership that was foremost in the life pattern of Orange princes, but kept him from taking needless risks. He was cautious too to keep Frederick Henry from falling into political traps. The youth and young man had been brought up as a pious Calvinist, for his mother was a Huguenot whose Protestantism was in her blood; her father had been the leader of the Huguenot party until his murder in the Saint Bartholomew's Day massacre of 1572. In the Remonstrant versus Contra-Remonstrant struggle, she had been strongly inclined to the Remonstrant side, and that sympathy became her son's as well; but both obeyed Maurice even when they did not follow his religious journey to the other side.

From the mutual protectiveness that Louise and Maurice displayed in those difficult years, Frederick Henry probably learned much of the breadth of his own religious toleration as well as the ability to subordinate considerations of faith to political necessities. In character he was even in temperament, disliking violence; he was adept at persuasion, sure of himself but flexible. When he took over the political and military leadership of the United Provinces from his brother, therefore, Frederick Henry was ready to employ the skills he had learned under his brother's guidance, but with his own policies and predilections.[12]

In politics he could let matters ride until he had got the regents accustomed to taking their lead from him. In the war, however, he had to take on the supreme command at once and act with vigor, lest the fall of Breda, which came so soon after his own elevation, presage a series of victories from Spinola's master hand. Frederick Henry continued the style and the method of waging war that had been his brother's, with skill and success at least as great. He was a master of siegecraft who engaged in open field battle as seldom as he could manage, and for the same reason that impelled Maurice: to minimize the risk to a country whose territory was so small. He displayed the same ingenuity, the same patience and persistence.

The discouragement caused by the fall of Breda was dissipated when the tide of war turned back in favor of the Dutch within a year.[13] Deputies from the States General accompanied him in the field, as had been customary with the captain-general since the days of William I. Their presence

12 Poelhekke, *Frederik Hendrik*, 105–6; Aitzema, II, 602.   13 Aitzema, I, 418.

may have been annoying on occasion, as during the siege of 's-Hertogen-bosch (Den Bosch in ordinary speech, Bois-le-Duc to the French) in 1629, when they set up their headquarters as close to his as possible, and in 1631, when they required him to retreat in the face of the Spanish army at the canal from Ghent to Bruges, leading to abandonment of an effort to reach Dunkirk. But for the most part he preferred to have them on hand, not only because they were usually confidants, but also because their presence facilitated approval of his plans and activities by the States General.[14]

The first Dutch victory came in 1626, with the taking of Oldenzaal, in Overijssel, by Ernst Casimir, Frederick Henry's cousin who was stadholder of Friesland. It was followed the next year by Frederick Henry's capture of Groenlo, in Gelderland. After Spinola was sent off to Italy in 1628 to become governor of Milan, almost every year passed with some fortress falling to siege by Frederick Henry. In 1629 he took Den Bosch, a well-fortified and strongly-defended fortress in the midst of marshlands. In 1631 he drove across Flanders toward Dunkirk, but, before he could reach and reduce the pirates' nest that continued to cost the Dutch merchant fleet dearly in ships and lives every year, he was met by a Spanish army and withdrew without accepting the challenge of battle. The next year he was able to take the great fortress of Maastricht, which dominated the Maas River where it flowed down from the hills in the southeastern corner of the Low Countries. Despite the promise of two Belgian commanders of the Spanish army who came in secret to The Hague to organize a common campaign to drive out the Spaniards, no uprising of the population followed, and Frederick Henry decided against attempting a bold thrust to Brussels. In 1635, after a treaty of alliance was signed with France, Frederick Henry attempted another campaign in the open field, but again the local population failed to rise in support of the invading foes of Spain and a siege of Leuven (Louvain) had to be abandoned. Returning to his preferred mode of warfare, he retook Breda from the Spaniards in 1637. It was the culmination of his career, not only for the strategic importance of the town, but also because it was the ancestral home of the Nassaus in the Netherlands. In recognition of these achievements, he was given the name of *stedendwinger*, the forcer of cities,[15] even though he lost Venlo and Roermond to the Spaniards not long afterwards and the next year was defeated with heavy losses in an attempt to capture Antwerp. The last major achievement of the Dutch army on land was taking Sas van Gent, strengthening the Dutch hold on the southern side of the Schelde estuary, in 1644.

---

14 Poelhekke, *Frederik Hendrik*, 267, 277–78, 349–50.
15 See Caspar van Baerle, "Eerdicht op de Beschryving van de Wyt-Beroemde Belegering van 's Hertogen Bosch," in P. S. Schull, ed., *Poezy van Caspar van Baerle* (n.p., 1835), 46.

Perhaps even more important than the military accomplishments of Frederick Henry were the triumphs of the Dutch navy. In 1628 Piet Hein, commanding a fleet of West India Company ships, captured the Spanish "Silver Fleet" near Havana, and Frederick Henry received 20 per cent of the prize money. In 1639 a "Second Armada" was destroyed in the Battle of the Downs. All in all, the military events of these decades merely consolidated the great glacis of the outer provinces protecting the inner fortress of the Dutch Republic in Holland and its neighboring provinces of Zeeland and Utrecht; their only direct political consequence was the negative one of failure to reunite the Low Countries, North and South. The naval victories, by contrast, kept the seas open for Dutch shipping and trade, which provided the resources on which the preservation of the independence of the Republic depended. Yet, although he was admiral-general of the Union, Frederick Henry was little involved in the conduct of the war at sea. It remained the affair of the admiralties and, behind them, the port cities and the maritime provinces.

Frederick Henry's military campaigns were closely allied with his political work as a stadholder. He had two fundamental political aims. The first was to bring the war of independence to a triumphant conclusion, if possible with the reunification of the Netherlands. In the quest for victory, however, the Hollanders favored a basically defensive policy, which would not run up extraordinary costs, while Frederick Henry maintained that only a policy of offensive action would yield results.[16] He told the deputies from the States to the army that the country had either to make peace or wage war. The only way to wage war, he added, was to take the offensive; a defensive posture would ruin the country.[17]

The last chance for reunification of the Netherlands, a repetition of the Pacification of Ghent with better prospects, was the campaign of 1632. Its failure was an event of long-lasting historical importance. Archduchess Isabella (Albert had died in 1621) had been skillful in keeping the southern provinces in obedience to her nephew, the king of Spain, Philip IV, despite the readiness of some of her army leaders to lead them into a union with the North. The popular rising on which they counted did not occur, partly because of the respect she had won for her government and partly because it was evident that Frederick Henry could not carry along the States General to grant the guarantees regarding the maintenance of Catholicism that he was personally willing to give.[18]

Frederick Henry was the last of the Princes of Orange to take the reunification of the Low Countries as a serious political objective. He viewed not Holland but Brabant as the keystone of the Netherlands. Had the country

---

16 Poelhekke, *Frederik Hendrik*, 127–28; Aitzema, I, 513.
17 Aitzema, I, 900.   18 Kluiver, 358.

been reunited, he would probably have sought sovereignty for himself and his family in one form or another, not the absolute monarchy of France or Spain but the restrained government of prince with Parliament that had characterized the rule of Elizabeth I of England whom he so admired. Whether he would have converted to Catholicism, after the example of Henry IV of France, in order to win and hold the South, as his biographer suggests, is speculation. It would have been an *arrière-pensée* so dangerous that he would never have spoken it or put it on paper. All that can be said with certainty is that, as the Venetian ambassador observed, he did not hate Catholics and the idea would not have appalled him, as it would have his grandson William III.[19]

In any case, it was not Frederick Henry who determined ultimate policy but the States General, where he accepted the primacy of Holland. Accompanied by the Council of State, he would come to the States of Holland to urge the assembly to support the war budget, known as the "state of war," in the States General. He would warn them of the great problems that would come upon the country if they refused, almost like a modern cabinet minister who threatens to quit his portfolio if his policies are rejected.[20] Even in the matter of appointment of officers, he could not act on his own but had to obtain the approval of the States. This he almost always gained, but not without a good deal of politicking. Nor could he increase the number of troops in any place by his own authority.[21]

The second of Frederick Henry's political aims was to prevent a recurrence of religious turmoil. He himself inclined toward the Remonstrant side, but he sought to avoid arousing the fury of the orthodox to the point where his political leadership was endangered. His policy was to soften the enforcement of the edicts against the Remonstrants rather than to seek their outright repeal; he declined to use troops against the Remonstrants and urged moderation. Yet he tried not to offend the Contra-Remonstrants publicly. Not until his prestige rose did he begin to work more openly for a "moderate freedom" for all religious dissenters.[22] His policy was pithily stated to a burgomaster of Haarlem in 1629: "Vooght, I have always said we must champion the government in the church, but we must also accommodate the others. I have said this many times and no one wants to believe me."[23] When orthodox dominees demanded troops to put down their foes, he replied angrily, "Soldiers, soldiers? No, I have no soldiers to torment burghers with."[24]

19 Poelhekke, "Een gefrustreerd Antwerpenaar," 52–54; Poelhekke, *Geen Blijder Maer in Tachtig Jaer* (Zutphen, 1973), 21, 27–28.
20 Poelhekke, *Frederik Hendrik*, 129–30, 259–60.
21 *Ibid.*, 132; Blok, *Frederik Hendrik*, 106.
22 Blok, *Frederik Hendrik*, 83; Poelhekke, *Frederik Hendrik*, 182.
23 Kluiver, 355; Poelhekke, *Frederik Hendrik*, 166, 182–83. 24 Blok, *Frederik Hendrik*, 81.

His policy of moderation was put to a hard test in Amsterdam. Control of the city government had gradually passed from Contra-Remonstrant to Remonstrant hands between 1622 and 1627, but the orthodox Calvinists refused to submit to the new authorities. Rioting ensued in 1627 and 1628, and the municipal government asked Frederick Henry to come in person to restore order by his "high authority." He did so, but only with the approval of the Delegated Councilors (the permanent executive committee of the States of Holland) and accompanied by two of their number. His appearance in the city brought brief calm, but after his departure rioting resumed and Contra-Remonstrant civic guards declined to serve under Remonstrant officers. Finally troops were sent in.[25] Where the Contra-Remonstrants remained at the helm of a city's government, however, Frederick Henry did not attempt to remove or displace them or override their decisions. Each town, he said, should be its own master.[26]

Over the years this policy in domestic affairs more and more won the acceptance and approval of the province of Holland. At the very same time, however, the province found itself more and more reluctant to give its support to the active and expensive policy of Frederick Henry in foreign affairs.[27] The desire to reduce the burden of war costs, present and past, was a powerful impulse of Holland's policy. This led to an estrangement between Frederick Henry and the leaders of Holland with regard to foreign policy, especially when, in the 1630s, Amsterdam came under the domination of the Bicker brothers, John, Cornelius and Andrew. They were immensely wealthy merchants and busy regents, sitting in the town council and frequently as burgomasters. Their leadership of the great city was marked by strong self-confidence and a readiness to go to the very end for their policies.[28] But the city and the stadholder maintained a posture of courtesy toward each other, so that their relations continued on the plane of friendship.[29] All the same, it was Holland, and such Amsterdammers as the Bickers, whose policy of religious toleration would have brought within the realm of possibility the winning over of the population of the Southern Netherlands, while, paradoxically, the orthodox Calvinists who most vigorously supported Frederick Henry's military enterprises thwarted his policy of conciliating the Catholic population there.[30]

Frederick Henry exercised his political leadership of the Dutch Republic with the same persistence and skill that he employed as an army commander. The key to his influence was his right to appoint magistrates in the

25 Poelhekke, *Frederik Hendrik*, 206–11; H. Brugmans, *Geschiedenis van Amsterdam van den oorsprong af tot heden* (8 vols.; Amsterdam, 1930–34), III, 209–11; Aitzema, I, 657, 702–3.
26 Aitzema, I, 1022.   27 Poelhekke, *Frederik Hendrik*, 180–81.
28 Brugmans, III, 231–35.   29 *Ibid.*, 228–31; Poelhekke, *Frederik Hendrik*, 512.
30 Poelhekke, "Een gefrustreerd Antwerpenaar," 54–55.

municipal governments, so that he chose those who were ultimately his masters.[31] He tried to select persons most favorable to his policies, yet avoided direct clashes with politically powerful groups. Although the deputies from the provincial States to the States General were not in his appointment, he used all his means of influence to gain the choice of men favorable to him. The deputies from the outlying provinces were usually named for life, and most decisions in foreign affairs were left to their judgment; these were matters in which the provincial States, apart from those of Holland and to a lesser extent Zeeland, had little close interest or knowledge. Furthermore, the provincial States were not in constant session, as were the States General, so that most decisions were not subject to prior approval by the provincial States before they were put into effect; only matters of the highest importance, like war, peace or treaties of alliance, required such confirmation.[32]

Frederick Henry also strengthened his control over the daily determination of policy by obtaining from the States General the formation of a secret committee for foreign affairs, the famed *Secreet Besogne*, which met with him and had the power to take binding decisions. It had begun as an informal meeting of deputies to the States General who were in his confidence, and in 1634 had been given formal powers to draw up resolutions in the name of States General, a power never before given to a committee of the assembly.[33] In this respect, it more closely corresponded to the Delegated Councilors of the States of Holland than the "usurpation" and "semi-monarchical government" that it has been called.[34] But the Delegated Councilors were primarily an administrative body with limited decision-making powers while the States of Holland were not in session. The *Secreet Besogne*, to the contrary, was important because it was a political body and overcame the dilatory decision-making and leaking secrecy that so hampered Dutch foreign relations and the conduct of the war.[35]

Ever since Frederick Henry had been old enough to comprehend politics, he had been familiar with the debate over whether the Prince of Orange should be raised from the stadholdership to sovereignty over the provinces as duke, count and lord. He himself never sought to become a monarch, although the ambition was often imputed to him, and the imputations received confirmation of a kind from the obvious attitude of Amalia and many members of the Prince's court.[36] Foreigners in particular, when

---

31 Geyl (*Geschiedenis*, II, 518) puts the contradiction in the relationship more strongly.
32 Poelhekke, *Frederik Hendrik*, 484–85.   33 I. Schöffer, "Naar consolidatie," 89.
34 By A. Waddington, in *La République des Provinces-Unies, la France et les Pays-Bas espagnols de 1630 à 1650* (2 vols.; Paris, 1895–97) I, 29.
35 Kluiver, 356–57.   36 Japikse, *Geschiedenis*, II, 602.

they saw that he was the effective head of the Dutch government, asserted that Frederick Henry was really sovereign in all but name.[37]

The House of Orange, by its international connections and the beliefs and ambitions of its courtiers, was thus representative of what a modern historian has called a "continental-monarchical" element in Dutch political life.[38] That principle was fed, too, by the political theory taught in Dutch universities, where so many of the regents' sons received a legal education as a preliminary to political careers. Roman law doctrines were reinforced by the Calvinist political teaching, which was not republican in character, as is so often asserted,[39] but rather favored a moderate, limited, constitutional monarchy governing in combination with the States, a dualistic *Ständestaat* in the modern terminology.[40] The general principle of "mixed government," embodying elements of monarchy, aristocracy and democracy, was applied to the Dutch constitution. It did not actually fit properly, but it was the best that could be done to describe a situation in which the States were sovereign but the leadership was in the hands of a servant of the States.[41]

The difference between France and the Netherlands was succinctly explained by Frans Aerssen van Sommelsdijk, one of the stadholder's closest advisors, to the French soldier Count Godefroi d'Estrades, who had been serving in the States army under Frederick Henry since 1632. The Prince of Orange, Aerssen told Estrades,

is in a different position from the King [of France], who has only to express his wishes. Here he [the Prince] needs money to put his ideas into effect, and this goes slowly; it can be obtained only from the provinces, which are tired and most of them exhausted, by a persuasive demonstration of some major advantage, which some of them do not see in the conquest of cities by which their burdens are increased. They can be led only by persuasion... our provinces find it difficult to agree on how the army should be used, one demanding it be used here and the other there. One considers it should not change its position, another that it should remain at the size the state can afford. In the midst of such a diversity of interests and opinions, His Highness [the Prince] must come to a decision and then, gradually clearing the way, bring matters to where they should be. This cannot be done without much controversy and loss of time.[42]

37 Van Deursen, *Bavianen en Slijkgeuzen*, 356.
38 J. C. Boogman, "The Union of Utrecht: Its Genesis and Consequences," *BMGN*, 94 (1979), 401.
39 For instance, among Dutch historians, Japikse, *Geschiedenis*, I, 196.
40 E. H. Kossmann, "The Low Countries," in: *The New Cambridge Modern History* (14 vols.; Cambridge, 1957–70), IV, 360–61.
41 Kossmann, "The Low Countries," 365. Kossmann expresses this idea rather more abstractly.
42 Aerssen van Sommelsdijk to Frederick Henry, 10 April 1638, *Archives*, 2e Sér., III, 114–15.

Aerssen knew the reality of Frederick Henry's conduct of politics in a country where the States assemblies held the ultimate power, and how much it differed from a king's (or prime minister's) mode of leadership in an authentic monarchy, with which Aerssen was familiar from his days as the Dutch envoy in France. It is surprising how little attention historians who emphasize the monarchical element in the government of the Princes of Orange have paid to this passage, which points not to aspirations but to actuality.

The very leadership in Amsterdam that Frederick Henry had helped to bring into power, the religious moderates led by the Bicker brothers, nonetheless began to look with anxiety at the increasing power of the Prince of Orange, all the more because of the all too visible monarchist aspirations of so many in his camp. Pamphlets advocating a crown for him caused a stir, and the loose talk of his supporters at court and in the army, and the obvious ambitions of Amalia van Solms, all heightened these concerns. The populace, for all its Orangist fervor, seems to have wanted his power strenghtened *within* the framework of the Republic, and Frederick Henry himself seems to have been satisfied with the real power and influence he possessed, which he preferred not to risk for the sake of a higher title.[43]

Another sign that Frederick Henry's political power, however impressive, was not total, came when the councilor pensionary of Holland, Duyck, died in September 1629. After much delay, a slate of three was presented to the Prince by the States of Holland for his consideration. The candidates were Adrian Pauw of Amsterdam, Jacob Cats, a Zeelander who was the town pensionary of Dordrecht, and Rochus van den Honart, a native Dordrechter. The stadholder replied to the delegates who brought the slate to him that all were competent and acceptable to him. Still he was probably surprised and annoyed when at last Pauw, who represented the vigorous independence of Amsterdam, was elected on 9 April 1631. Yet, for a time, the stadholder and the new councilor pensionary, the two most important figures in the political life of the country, got on well together.[44] That easy collaboration did not last, however, for Pauw soon made it obvious that he saw his office as one of strong initiative and leadership. He was not a passive servant of the stadholder's will, as Duyck had been.[45]

Pauw also represented the hesitancy in Amsterdam about the limited alliance with France renewed in 1634, a year before Louis XIII openly entered the war against Spain. Aerssen realized that Frederick Henry's power, great as it was, had limits and that a peace party led by Amsterdam

---

43 Brugmans, III, 224; Poelhekke, *Frederik Hendrik*, 130–32, 136.
44 Poelhekke, *Frederik Hendrik*, 360–61.   45 *Ibid.*, 362–63.

was a formidable force.[46] But the contest over the alliance was waged primarily between Holland, for which peace and a chance at fiscal recovery were becoming paramount, and Frederick Henry, who had the forthright backing only of Zeeland among the provinces. The new element that entered the situation was an awareness beginning to take shape that France, the friend whose alliance would alone make possible final victory over Spain, might itself become a threat to the Netherlands once shorn of the burden of its own contest with Spain.[47] Indeed, the defensive–offensive alliance made in 1635 included an arrangement for partition of the Southern Netherlands that would have brought about this very danger.

Pauw finally paid the price for his, and his city's, opposition to Frederick Henry's policy. In 1636 he was forced to resign as councilor pensionary of Holland. His replacement was one of the other candidates of 1630, Jacob Cats, who represented a policy of tame obedience to the stadholder. Cats looked upon the Republic as a state whose head was the Prince of Orange, although he governed in collaboration with the regents. He became Frederick Henry's willing instrument in the States of Holland, and although he may have had no policy of his own, he was anything but weak when it came to doing the Prince's bidding and preventing his opponents from achieving their aims.[48] Pauw's dismissal did not change the fact that the balance of political forces in the country was fundamentally shifting. The States of Holland, especially from 1638, balked more and more at providing the funds for an active military policy. They kept the obligations flowing from the alliance with France to a minimum. The other provinces could be prodded, but they too became more reluctant to support the Prince in a bold policy.[49]

The care that Frederick Henry had to use in sparing their sensibilities was shown during 1636 when the Emperor offered to elevate his territorial possession of Meurs, in Germany near the Dutch frontier, from a country to an Imperial principality. Frederick Henry asked the States General for their approval and was perhaps a bit put out when they let him know they did not like the idea. Among the common people, too, there was surprise, as if they had not realized that "prince" in political parlance elsewhere meant a sovereign ruler in a monarchical state. In any event, Frederick Henry, with his customary preference for real power over rank, let the matter drop.[50] The ironical aspect of the whole affair was that, as a pam-

46 Sommelsdijk to Johan Hoeufft, 5 June 1634, *Archives*, 2e Sér., III, 61.
47 Aitzema, II, 93.
48 A. Th. van Deursen, "De raadpensionaris Jacob Cats," *Tijdschrift voor Geschiedenis* (hereafter abbreviated as *TvG*), 92 (1979), 153, 158.
49 Poelhekke, *Frederik Hendrik*, 496.
50 *Ibid.*, 472; W. G. Brill, ed. and trans., "Verslag van den Ambassadeur in Den Haag, Francesco Michiel, aan Doge en Senaat, 27 Mei, 1638," *Bijdragen en Mededeelingen van het Historisch Genootschap* (hereafter abbreviated as *BMHG*), 7 (1884), 75–76.

phleteer remarked a decade later, when it came to real power, the stadholder of Holland had more of it than a dozen of the likes of the electors of Mainz and Trier,[51] and electors held the highest rank in the Empire after the Emperor himself.

To counter the temptation offered by the Emperor, King Louis XIII of France decided to bestow upon Frederick Henry a new title of address, "Highness" (*Altesse*), instead of the "Excellency" he had been accorded until then. This put him on an equal footing with the princes of the blood in France and Spain and with small sovereigns elsewhere, as in Italy. The French ambassador brought the letters informing the States General, Frederick Henry and Amalia of the decision and presented them to the States early in January 1637. They received coolly the news of the Prince's honor, but it was soon realized that the title could not be refused without an open insult to him. Frederick Henry and Amalia were much taken with his new title, Amalia more than her sober husband, as was to be expected.[52] The States General responded to his honorific elevation by taking the next year as their own title of address "High Mighty Lords" (*Hoog Mogenden*), which had been in occasional informal use before, and henceforth they were known as "Their High Mightinesses."[53]

Frederick Henry suffered an important political defeat with long-reaching consequences in 1632. Ernst Casimir, the stadholder of the northern provinces, died in battle, giving the Prince of Orange an opportunity to become general stadholder of all seven provinces. But, before Frederick Henry could bring his interest in these stadholderships to bear, Friesland confirmed as Ernst Casimir's successor his eldest son, Henry Casimir, who had received the survivance (automatic succession) for the province that Spring. Under the insistent pressure of Friesland, the province of Groningen also named Henry Casimir as stadholder, but imposed upon him a requirement that he not seek to influence the choice of his successor. The province of Drente followed Groningen's example.[54]

The contest between the two branches of the House of Nassau was renewed in 1640 when Henry Casimir, still unmarried at twenty-nine, died in action in States Flanders. Frederick Henry, with the support of both the States General and the States of Holland, again attempted to gain the northern stadholderships for himself. But Henry Casimir on his deathbed had recommended that his younger brother William Frederick be named to follow him, and the young man rushed to Leeuwarden to obtain his

51 *Fransch Praetie. Sic vos non vobis* (Munster, 1646). (W. P. C. Knuttel, *Catalogus van de pamflettenverzameling berustende in de Koninklijke Bibliotheek* [9 vols.; The Hague, 1888–1920; hereafter abbreviated as Kn.], no. 5,297.)
52 Blok, *Frederik Hendrik*, 174; Poelhekke, *Frederik Hendrik*, 478–79.
53 Blok, *Geschiedenis*, II, 569.
54 Blok, *Frederik Hendrik*, 152–53; Blok, *Geschiedenis*, II, 156; Aitzema, II, 9.

election. To a suggestion that he permit Frederick Henry to become stadholder over all the provinces, with himself as stadholder-lieutenant, he replied, "It's better to be a captain than a lieutenant."[55] A mission of the States General supporting Frederick Henry's candidacy arrived too late in Friesland, but Groningen and Drente named him as their stadholder. Although the significance of these stadholderships in the North was more symbolic than substantial, the prestige of the senior branch of the house would have been enhanced if the Prince of Orange had become stadholder in all seven provinces, putting him in practice if not in law in the position of governor-general of the Republic.[56]

The ensuing bitterness between the two branches of the house lasted for several years. Finally Frederick Henry realized the peril it posed for his own dynastic ambitions, while William Frederick found that he needed his cousin's support against political turmoil in Friesland. A sweet-sour reconciliation was arranged, with Frederick Henry's son William receiving a survivance of the Frisian stadholdership should William Frederick die without an heir.[57]

Whether or not Frederick Henry himself in the secret recesses of his mind dreamt of putting the crown on his own head as count and duke, he acted upon dynastic principle in arranging the advancement of his son William.[58] Yet he was careful to stay within the bounds of the existing political structure of the Republic. The first, purely symbolic step was taken when William was only three years of age. In 1630 the States General gave the little boy the post of general of cavalry; it had been his father's command for many years before he became stadholder and captain-general. The next action was more than symbolic. The States of Holland and Zeeland, following the example of Utrecht and Overijssel the year before, gave William the survivance of the stadholdership, to succeed upon his father's demise. Survivance was an election procedure that corresponded to the election of a king of the Romans as successor to the Imperial throne in the Holy Roman Empire. Holland and Zeeland did not make their gift blindly, however; if William was not of age when his father died, the States would have the right to reconsider his election.

The possibility of a minor stadholder was a novel notion, implying as it did the possibility of possessing an office while still unable to exercise its powers; it would be one step along the path to monarchy, where the reign

55 Aitzema, II, 706; Van der Capellen, *Gedenkschriften*, II, 49–50.
56 Blok, *Geschiedenis*, II, 569–70; Blok, *Frederik Hendrik*, 205–7; Poelhekke, *Frederik Hendrik*, 512–14.
57 Poelhekke, *Frederik Hendrik*, 516–17.
58 Breaking with the dominant Orangism among Dutch historians, Geyl treated this dynasticism as contrary to the interests of the Republic (see *Oranje en Stuart*, Utrecht, 1939, and *Geschiedenis*, II, 522–23).

of a minor was a familiar situation. There was therefore some hesitation about granting the survivance for the captaincy-general of the Union, but this too was done six years later, in 1637.[59] The arguments in favor of the survivance did not mention any implicit dynasticism, but stressed the gratitude of the country for the services of the House of Orange and especially of Frederick Henry. Nonetheless there was anxiety among more thoughtful politicians about the introduction of hereditary elements into the state, and republican ideas were strengthened, although as yet without clearly distinguishing between the stadholderate and monarchy as such.[60]

The great event of the new decade was the marriage between William and Mary Stuart, the eldest daughter of the king of England. The original initiative was taken by the exiled queen mother of France, Marie de Médicis, who stopped off at The Hague in 1638 on her way from Brussels to London. It was eagerly picked up by William's mother and father. For Amalia van Solms the wedding would be the culmination of her dream and ambition, linking her family with one of the preeminent royal houses of Europe. Frederick Henry was certainly more realistic about politics, far less of a dreamer, but he was carried along by her enthusiasm. He was aware that such a marriage would be seen by the English royal family, most of all by Queen Henrietta Maria, the sister of King Louis XIII of France, as a *mésalliance* consented to only because Charles I, facing imminent civil war with the Scots, counted upon Dutch assistance and exaggerated the power of the Prince of Orange over Dutch policy.[61]

Yet Frederick Henry did not really deceive the English monarch. He informed him that he could not give assurances that Princess Mary would be allowed to use Anglican services, for "it is not I but the States who are sovereign in these provinces," and they alone could innovate in matters of religion. He would not promise "what everyone knows is not in my power."[62] But his asseverations that the alliance was a purely private matter, "which has no relation to public business," were not at all accurate. When Frederick Henry officially informed the States General of his plan in December 1640, they named a ceremonial mission to negotiate the final details with the English. The marriage of his son, with his survivances of the stadholderships and the captaincy-general, was obviously a matter of state.[63] The Dutch negotiators avoided the linkage, at least in formal documents, but Charles continued to expect repayment for consenting to the

59 Poelhekke, *Frederik Hendrik*, 349.
60 G. W. Kernkamp, *Prins Willem II, 1626–1650* (2nd edn; Rotterdam, 1977), 14–15.
61 Geyl, *Oranje en Stuart*, 12.
62 Frederick Henry to Heenvliet, 1, 6 Sept. 1640, *Archives*, 2e Sér., III, 302–4.
63 Frederick Henry to ambassadors in England, 5 Feb. 1641, *Archives*, 2e Sér., III, 336; Geyl, *Oranje en Stuart*, 10–11.

mésalliance by support against his domestic foes.[64] The marriage between William and Mary was solemnized in 1641, although she was still a child.

Frederick Henry was in fact anything but enamored with Charles's policy toward Parliament. Early in 1642, with conflict between king and Parliament about to flame up in open civil war, the Prince of Orange sent repeated pleas to London deploring the situation. He told the Dutch ambassador he fully supported the efforts of the States General to bring the contending parties to terms. He sent a warning for the king that if matters ever came to the extreme, it would be very difficult to find a way out. When one takes up arms, everything then depends on victory, which is very uncertain. Reconciliation was best, as Queen Elizabeth had shown.[65] This was, of course, advice that Charles I would not take, at a cost that even Frederick Henry did not anticipate. Yet the Prince of Orange was also defining his own political aims and strategy – civil peace not by force of arms but by reconciliation, government with the States, not against them or without them. Whatever the desirability of these aims, neither side in Britain was willing to consider the proposals from over the North Sea.[66]

A half year later Frederick Henry was compelled to give active support to the king's cause because Charles I would neither follow his advice nor forego the assistance for which he had made the sacrifice of accepting a *mésalliance*. Queen Henrietta Maria came to Holland and sought ready funds upon the security of the English crown jewels. Parliament protested that these belonged to the English nation, not to the king personally. To carry the Amsterdam lenders over their reluctance, Frederick Henry allowed the jewels to be treated as if lent by him, pledging his own credit.[67] But he could not thwart an official policy of neutrality in the English civil war.

Henrietta Maria, before her return from the Netherlands, made a last effort to pull Frederick Henry away from the official Dutch policy of neutrality. The marriage between William and Mary might be followed by another, even loftier, between the Prince of Wales (the future Charles II!) and Frederick Henry's oldest daughter, Louise Henriette. How seriously this hint was meant we do not know, but the bait was taken. Frederick Henry arranged for arms and munitions to be shipped to the royalist forces, and English and Scots officers in his army, including Prince Rupert of the Palatinate, were given leave to serve the king. And the loan in Amsterdam upon the security of the crown jewels was consummated.[68]

64 Kernkamp, 25.
65 Frederick Henry to Joachimi, 1 Feb., to Heenvliet, 1, 19 Feb. 1642, *Archives*, 2e Sér., IV, 9, 11–12, 24.
66 Joachimi to Frederick Henry, 22 Feb. 1642, *Archives*, 2e Sér., IV, 25.
67 Frederick Henry to Heenvliet, 28 July 1642, *Archives*, 2e Sér., IV, 56.
68 Poelhekke, *Frederik Hendrik*, 532–33; Kernkamp, 30.

The royal alliance aroused wide suspicion that Frederick Henry was seeking sovereignty for himself and his descendants, and the result was a heightened republican feeling, joining for once regents and Calvinist clergy and the populace they led in supporting the endeavors of Holland to keep the country's neutrality intact. In November 1642 the States General issued a general ban on the export of war materials to either side in Britain, so that Frederick Henry's continued shipments had to be made surreptitiously, indeed illegally. The squadron that carried Henrietta Maria back to England in January 1643 did carry both troops and supplies for Charles I, however.[69] As it became clear that Frederick Henry's dominance was lessening, whatever chance there might have been of a marriage between the Prince of Wales and Mademoiselle d'Orange, as Louise Henriette was called, now vanished. The negotiations with Charles I were abandoned in April 1646, just a month before the king's surrender to the Scots marked the beginning of the last act of his reign.[70] The matrimonial negotiations of the House of Orange, successful or not, were no longer viewed passively by the Dutch, as they had been since the death of William the Silent. Two elements were involved. The first, which was republican in character, was directed against the notion that rulership was inherited, so that the choice of bride or bridegroom could become a matter of the highest political importance. The other, which we may call, with a word not yet used, "nationalist," emphasized that foreigners were being called into the body of the state. It spoke for the resentment against the Frenchmen and Englishmen who peopled the Prince of Orange's court at The Hague and who gave their style of life even to the native Dutchmen among their fellow courtiers.[71]

The strain in the relations between the House of Orange and the States, especially the States of Holland, came at a time when the war of independence was obviously in its very final stages, depending on how the negotiations with Spain for peace, which shifted to Münster in 1643, worked out. The complicating element was that France had finally begun to turn the tide of its war with Spain in its own favor. The defeat of the Spanish army at Rocroi by the duke of Enghien, later to be famed as the prince of Condé, marked the beginning of France's wave of triumphs, but it would take a decade and a half of continued fighting before Spain would admit defeat. For the French it was crucial to keep the Dutch in the war; for the Dutch, to stay in the war meant the continuation of enormous expenditures without significant gains beyond what Spain was already visibly ready to offer. Frederick Henry contemplated this prospect with more equanimity than

69 Geyl, *Oranje en Stuart*, 21–22, 28–29; Kernkamp, 29.
70 Geyl, *Oranje en Stuart*, 42–43, 47.
71 *Ibid.*, 48; Poelhekke, *Frederik Hendrik*, 541–43.

the civil rulers, particularly in Holland, who had to find the funds by high taxation and continued borrowing.

The Spaniards for their part tried to bait Frederick Henry into accepting their peace overtures by offering him the ducal title of the Upper Quarter of Gelderland, which they had been able to hold in their possession. The other three quarters, which formed the Dutch province, at once demanded that the Upper Quarter be rejoined to them as part of the peace terms. Avoiding the Spanish trap, Frederick Henry merely referred the matter to the Dutch negotiators at Münster.[72]

In 1646 Frederick Henry's health broke. In April, although his memory was failing, he was still strong enough to handle the Hollanders with skill. All eyes were upon his son, as with crown princes everywhere when the king is dying.[73] The French looked to the young man to keep the United Provinces in the war, but observed that the States were more suspicious than ever of monarchical tendencies in the House of Orange.[74] The French also kept a close eye on Amalia, for, although she saw the advantage of war to the House of Orange, she also saw that peace could not be prevented and that the country could not be expected to wage war forever.[75]

As the year neared its close, William became blatantly impatient. He told the French envoy Brasset that once he was free to decide matters for himself, he would show who he was. His wiser friends urged him to abandon the wild debauchery which harmed his reputation.[76] The French hopes for advantage through the maintenance of the authority of the Prince of Orange now focused on William. Unity of military command and political leadership in the States was essential, in the view of the French court.[77]

The end came for Frederick Henry on 17 March 1647, slowly and evenly, so that all the ceremonies of leave-taking could be carried out to the full. He received delegations from the States General and the States of Holland as they paid their final respects on 11 March, and his last words to them, "I have been the servant of the States" (*Ick ben der Heeren Staten Dienaer*),[78] were literally true but also may have held a note of irony.

As their servant, he had been in most things their leader, almost their

72 Poelhekke, *Frederik Hendrik*, 553; Israel, 358.
73 Brasset to Mazarin, 2, 9 April, La Thuillerie to Mazarin, 11 June 1646, *Archives*, 2e Sér., IV, 151–52, 155.
74 Estrades to Mazarin, 29 Aug., 5, 24 Sept., Brasset to Mazarin, 10 Sept. 1646, *Archives*, 2e Sér., IV, 164–67.
75 Brasset to Mazarin, 23 July, La Thuillerie to Mazarin, 31 July 1646, *Archives*, 2e Sér., IV, 159; Poelhekke, *Geen Blijder Maer*, 10.
76 Brasset to Mazarin, 17 Dec. 1646, Servien to Mazarin, 5 Feb. 1647, *Archives*, 2e Sér., IV, 176–77, 181–82.
77 Brienne to Servien, 25 Jan. 1647, *Archives*, 2e Sér., IV, 180.
78 Poelhekke, *Frederik Hendrik*, 563–64.

master, but the ultimate authority had always been theirs. He had not been a king without a title, as some outsiders thought at the time and later historians were to repeat. If a comparison must be made, his political status had been much like that of his contemporaries, the first ministers of France and Spain, Richelieu and Olivares. He too made the policy for the state he served and carried out the decisions that his sovereign accepted. His advantage over them was that his posts were given to him for life while they remained always utterly dependent upon the good will of a single man, the king whose minister they were. But the instrument of power in their hand was a true monarchy with a highly developed (for the time) bureaucratic apparatus, while he had to work with the diffused Dutch political system, with no single person at its peak except himself.[79]

79 *Ibid.*, 314–15.

4

William II: the challenger

William II was stadholder for a shorter time than any other Prince of Orange, but none had a more powerful impact upon the institution of the stadholderate. He challenged to the quick the ambiguity upon which the government of the Dutch Republic had always rested – the sovereignty of the States overlapping the leadership, always military and sometimes political, of the House of Orange. On the one hand, in law the ultimate power rested beyond question in the States assemblies, although just how it was shared between the provincial States and the States General was not settled with absolute clarity and precision; on the other hand, the Princes of Orange were not mere subjects but a quasi-hereditary if not quasi-monarchical power whose judgment and will could not be neglected by the sovereigns. William II drew together some of the most significant threads of the political life of the country until his time, and in the dramatic events of the summer of 1650 almost created a new constitutional fabric. That he did not do so may have been only a question of his early death a few months later, hacking off intentions of revolutionary transformation which he kept concealed, as some historians have contended; or he may have had in mind much less than they thought, seeking only new policies rather than a crown. In either case, he brought about a deep change in the character of political debate and struggle in the United Provinces.

The self-image of the House of Orange may be most clearly seen in the sermon preached at the inauguration of William II on 8 May 1647 (*inhuldiging*, "inauguration," is what the ceremony of royal installation of the kings and queens of the Netherlands is still called, not the usual "coronation"). The preacher was a Delft dominee, Hermannus Tegularius. The sermon swings throughout between two different conceptions of the stadholderate. One compares it to kingship, the other to any government whether in kingdoms or republics.[1] In conformity with this ambiguity,

---

1 Hermannvs Tegvlarivs, *Inhvldings-Predicatie, Op de Vermaerde Intrede van Syn Hoogheyt, Den Doorluchtigsten ende Hoogh-gebooren Vorst ende Heere Wilhelm, By der gratie Godts Prince van Orangien, &c., Gedaen op den Bede-dagh, den 8. Mey, Anno 1647* (Delft, 1647) (Kn. 5579), *2–*3.

William II, 1626–1650

Tegularius uses the celebrated warning of Asaph in Psalm 82 that earthly rulers are gods but die like men, and applies it to all "mighty" men, "Kings, Princes, Magistrates and high States," not just to kings, as was customary.[2] That Tegularius supported the call of the States General for success of the peace negotiations, anticipating that William's leadership and deeds would contribute to the defeat of the foe's designs, indicates that he was not close to William himself, but spoke rather the mind of Amalia van Solms.[3]

William II was the first Prince of Orange to succeed to his high posts by a right he had known since he was a child, the survivance as stadholder in the provinces where his father had governed and as captain-general of the Union by decision of the States General. He also had the survivance of the stadholdership of Friesland in the event that William Frederick died before him without heir. Since his cousin was unmarried and at the age of thirty-three was thirteen years older than William, this was not at all improbable.[4] William grasped power with the eagerness that he had already displayed when Frederick Henry was still alive, arousing a resentment that soured the dying man's last months and persisted in bad feelings between Amalia van Solms and her son. Yet that unseemly ardency of anticipation was the result of the character they had shaped in him and the role they had taught him to expect.

William's pride of rank and place was immense. Frederick Henry had given his son the customary initiation into the craft of war such as he himself had received from his own brother, for command of the army was the task par excellence of the Princes of Orange in the Dutch Republic. Since William never exercised command in a military campaign against a foreign enemy, it is not possible to weigh his talents as a commander, although the glory of military victory was his highest desire. It may be assumed that young William was at least taught the elementary facts of Dutch political life, the structure of the state and the forces at work, but he seems not to have absorbed its intangibles, both its spirit and the informal understandings that made it possible to achieve results in a political system of extraordinary cumbersomeness.[5] Like his father in his youth, but even wilder, William entered manhood – one can scarcely speak of adolescence in his case – as a rakehell, sampling the diversions and vices available to a young and rich man in Holland. Was this the man who would, indeed who could, lead the country? It was not an idle question, for the character of the stadholder was immensely important to the exercise of his office.

The personality that had emerged by the time William II took on the tasks of manhood was quite unlike his father's, or indeed that of any of his

2 *Ibid.*, 1–2.   3 *Ibid.*, 2–3.   4 Kernkamp, 17.
5 *Ibid.*, 51–55; Kossmann, "Low Countries," 382.

immediate ancestors. He had a quickness of mind that impressed those who met him, but it was a mind that was not disciplined by systematic education in either the classroom or the school of life. As a child, he had been unsure of himself, at least if hesitation in speech is a sign of such uncertainty. But by the time he was twenty years of age, he displayed no such self-doubt, whether by overcompensation we can only speculate. He had not learned to seek or take advice, although he was open to suggestions that confirmed what he already wanted to do. He did take counsel with himself, arranging his ideas on paper in orderly fashion before coming to a decision. He disliked contradiction and disagreement. He was extremely strong-willed, but he had learned to hide his feelings and his thoughts in order to get his way. These feelings and thoughts were centered upon himself; he showed little warmth of affection for others, including his parents and his wife. His self-image was quite different, however, from what others saw. He thought of himself as indulgent, even gentle, disliking cruelty even when it was necessary.

It was, all in all, the character of one who, given or taking the opportunity, could ruthlessly smash opposition and shatter the complicated compromises and ambiguities upon which the Dutch political system rested – or, failing, suffer losses as great as the gains he sought.[6] He won, however, the first battle he had to wage – with himself. Within a few months after succeeding his father, he put aside his disorderly life and applied himself seriously to the tasks of statesmanship.

He exerted his rights to the full whenever he could and tolerated no reduction of them on any pretext, however justified in law. No sooner had he heard of his father's death than he renamed John de Knuyt as his deputy as First Noble of Zeeland, although he knew quite well that the province found De Knuyt a hard-fisted and unpalatable figure.[7] In Nijmegen in January 1649 he used both political influence and the threat of military force to compel the city to continue to accord him the right of appointment of the magistrates even after the end of the war, although it had been ceded to Maurice in 1590 as an exception only for the duration of the conflict.[8] He did the same a little later in Dordrecht, replacing some members of the town council against the desire of the town and against the advice of the Court of Holland. This act, which was illegal, embittered the city fathers greatly.[9] He did not hesitate to enter into a direct conflict with the province of Holland and the city of Amsterdam over the arrest of Admiral Witte de With, who had returned with his fleet from Brazil in violation of orders. He insisted that the admiral be tried by the States General, but the province

6 Poelhekke, "Frederik Hendrik en Willem II," in: Tamse, 143–44.
7 J. Eysten, *Het leven van Prins Willem II (1626–1650)* (Amsterdam, 1916), 94.
8 Eysten, 114–16; Poelhekke, "Frederik Hendrik en Willem II," 146.   9 Eysten, 116.

and the city rejected it as a violation of their jurisdiction. The test of strength between them and the Prince continued without resolution until William's death, when Witte de With was released.[10] It was an anticipation, however, of what would be the major conflict during William's administration, the dispute between Holland and the stadholder over the province's demand for reduction of the army.

On the mid-March day in 1647 when he became Prince of Orange, William's dominant passion, however, was to prove himself on the battlefield against the Spanish enemy; he therefore bitterly resented Holland's action in preventing him from undertaking a campaign that summer. His hatred of the Spaniards was intense and personal. The grandson of William I loathed his murderers with blinding fury. It was as if the idea of vendetta had suddenly come alive in him, shorn of its political aspects. More precisely, it shaped the politics of William II in very large degree.

England was equal to Spain in his political concerns. Just what the consequences of his marriage to Mary Stuart would have been if England's internal history had developed differently is hard to say: the civil war and Commonwealth-Protectorship are events too massive to be simply thought out of existence for the sake of speculation. Yet such speculation can be more safely ventured on the Dutch side. There we can surely say that the developments already begun under Frederick Henry, notably the concentration of political leadership in the hands of the Prince of Orange, would probably have continued, enhanced by the prestige of a royal connection. The friendship between the Houses of Stuart and Orange would have complicated the expression of the commercial and maritime rivalry between the two countries; it might even have prevented such competition from spilling over into open war.

William II began his administration as the Stuarts were passing off the stage of history, whether for all time or for a more or less long period of defeat and exile no one could then know. But the Oranges cast their lot with the Stuarts, and for a dozen years the burden of support passed to them. It was a burden that William II was not only willing but zealous to take up, especially after the trial and beheading of his father-in-law, Charles I. Even some of his own devoted servants worried about his getting involved more deeply in the English labyrinth, but they did not influence his decisions.[11] An appeal by the Prince of Wales to the States General for intercession on behalf of his father in January 1649, as Charles I was about to go on trial, won half-hearted action, despite William's efforts. A delegation from which Orangists were pointedly excluded was sent to London, but its audience a day before the king's execution was useless.[12]

10 Kernkamp, 87–88; Poelhekke, "Frederik Hendrik en Willem II," 145.
11 Geyl, *Oranje en Stuart*, 52–53.   12 *Ibid.*, 55–57.

The beheading of Charles I turned the bulk of Dutch opinion away from the Commonwealth, although the States of Holland maintained their policy of neutrality and living at peace with the Parliamentary party.

France was the third great power in William II's constellation of foes and friends (the adjacent Holy Roman Empire and its Habsburg Emperor played virtually no role in his concerns). His attitude toward France was strictly businesslike, a consideration of what Mazarin had to offer him and what he could give in return. He did believe that the obligation not to make a separate peace which was part of the alliance of 1635 continued to hold good, and hence he vigorously opposed the conclusion of the peace with Spain in 1648. What troubled him, however, was not that the Dutch broke their given word, but that Spain would not be finally and totally defeated until France was victorious as well as the Dutch Republic, and that France could not achieve this on her own. Before an alliance with France could be restored, however, it would be necessary to undo the peace with Spain, and that could not be accomplished without establishing his own domination within the Republic.

Winning over William was so important that Mazarin instructed his envoy at The Hague to tempt him to seek "a grandeur far beyond that of his predecessors" with French support, although suspecting that he would not be a wholly reliable friend.[13] William entered into secret negotiations with Mazarin regarding a new partition of the Spanish Netherlands. Whether William could have carried the Dutch Republic into a new war cannot be known, for the French part of the plan, an invasion along the Meuse (Maas) River valley, had to be abandoned when the intended commander, Turenne, went over to the Fronde.[14]

In any case, the French bet on William's ability to command Dutch policy was a very big gamble, given the Prince's failure to prevent conclusion of the Peace of Münster in January 1648.[15] All he had been able to do was delay it, but finally all the provinces except Zeeland swung to Holland's side, and even that obdurately Orangist province could not prevent either conclusion or final ratification in May. It had not mattered that the members of the municipal governments everywhere but in Amsterdam had been named by William's father (in the northern provinces, by his Nassau cousins). The regents had come to feel the urgency of peace and, serving for life on the town councils, they could not be unseated except by a massive countrywide *wetsverzetting* (changing of the governments) that would have amounted to a revolution for which at the moment William had neither the will nor the means.

13 Mazarin to Servien, 5 Apr., Louis XIV to Servien, 5 Apr. 1647, *Archives*, 2e Sér., IV, 203.
14 Kernkamp, 61–62.
15 The principal clauses of the treaty in Rowen, *Low Countries*, 178–87.

To make sure that he did not block the conclusion of the peace at the very last moment, the States of Holland did not confirm him in his office as stadholder until the treaty was an accomplished fact. It was a warning that the implicit dynasticism of the survivance must not be strained too hard,[16] that he could not make policy on his own and impose it upon the States if they balked. William was able, however, to defeat a proposal in the States of Holland that an instruction be drawn up for him to which he would have to take an oath. It was set aside upon the argument that the country could not afford a delay in having a stadholder and captain-general. His commission as stadholder still provided for an eventual instruction, but none was ever adopted.[17] The terms of the peace were essentially those of the Twelve Years' Truce of 1609, made permanent and unconditional, but the significance of the treaty was much wider. The United Provinces were fully accepted by the rulers of Europe as an independent power, indeed a great power.[18]

The insistence of Holland upon the conclusion of peace had been based upon more than Spain's willingness to grant at last terms that were satisfactory. At least equally important was the fiscal pressure upon the Dutch treasuries. The war of independence had been financed by a combination of taxation and borrowing, made possible by the immense earnings of Dutch trade and industry but nonetheless a very heavy burden upon a small country. With peace taxes could be cut and the debt and the interest upon the debt could be reduced as well. Since the expenditures of both the national and the provincial governments consisted overwhelmingly in outlays for the armed forces, the Hollanders turned to the army as the principal object for trimming. The navy was financed principally by the import and export duties called "licenses and convoys"; furthermore, the need for a fleet to protect Dutch merchantmen continued, with English royalist privateers based in the Scilly Islands as the principal marauders. The border with the Spanish Netherlands was assured by the peace, while the Emperor had endorsed the treaty made at Münster. No threat from the East was therefore visible, and only the roving troops in the pay of the duke of Lorraine continued to annoy the countryside of westernmost Germany, with a few incursions into Dutch territory. The States of Holland therefore called for a reduction of the army to the much smaller size needed for precautionary purposes in peacetime.

Another motive for the Hollanders was not openly spoken but was

---

16 J. J. Poelhekke, *De Vrede van Munster* (The Hague, 1948) 468–69; Poelhekke, *Geen Blijder Maer*, 8–9; Poelhekke, "Frederik Hendrik en Willem II," 145; Brugmans, III, 240; P. A. Samson, *Histoire de Guillaume III. Roi d'Angleterre, d'Ecosse, et d'Irlande, &c.* (3 vols.; The Hague, 1703), I, 102.
17 Eysten, 94–95.   18 Poelhekke, *Geen Blijder Maer*, 9–10, 24.

clearly visible. This was a desire to limit the influence of William II.[19] For him, to the contrary, reduction of the army would mean defeat of all his great plans even before they were worked out in detail, not to say before he had begun to put them into operation. Furthermore, the Hollanders' insistence that the troops and officers to be dismissed be drawn principally from the foreigners in Dutch service, mostly Frenchmen, Englishmen and Scots, was particularly discomfiting, for these gave their fidelity more to him personally than to the civilian authorities who paid them. If it came to a conflict between William and the States, there was no question as to whom they would obey, as there was with the Dutch troops who remained under the jurisdiction of the towns and provinces of which they were subjects.

The problem was further complicated by the system of "apportionment" (*repartitie*) by which the troops were paid. The soldiers were volunteers raised by and in the name of the States General and technically paid by them; indeed, it was their pay as well as the other costs of the army that were the largest expenditure of the national government. The Generality (as the central government was often called) had no significant revenues of its own. Its funds all came from the provinces, each paying according to a ratio that had been fixed early in the history of the Republic. Holland's portion was a fraction less than 58 per cent, of which Amsterdam paid about half. For many decades, it had been the practice for each province to make payments directly to companies assigned to it, whether stationed on its territory or elsewhere; this was the specific meaning of "apportionment." These companies had come to be considered as in that province's service rather than that of the States General. So long as there was a strong stadholder and captain-general, this was more a theoretical than a real difference, but there was always the possibility of genuine conflict between the provincial States on the one hand and the captain-general on the other.

This is what happened between 1648 and 1650. Holland asserted that the troops which it paid were subject to its instructions and orders, and that it therefore had the right if it so decided to dismiss those it did not wish to continue to pay. Contrariwise, William, arguing from the precise juridical status of the army as well as from the practical necessity to maintain its unity, affirmed that only the States General had the right to dismiss troops, as they alone had the right to raise them, and that their agents in such operations were only the Council of State (which, it will be recalled, now functioned chiefly as a kind of war ministry) and himself as captain-general. Both sides knew full well, of course, that it was not only the constitutional place of the army within the state that was being debated.

19 Blok, *Geschiedenis*, III, 128.

Also at stake was the choice between alternative policies for the Republic – maintenance of the peace or resumption of war.[20]

In form this was a controversy between the States General and the States of Holland, but, with the Prince of Orange having a firm hand over the deputies from most of the other provinces, the contest was really between him and the Hollanders. Their initial positions were far apart, but, as the talks continued month after month all through 1648 and 1649, the two sides gradually moved toward agreement. At last, during the Spring of 1650, it seemed as if a final accord were at hand, for the difference between what the Hollanders still demanded and what William was willing to accept had been reduced to only a few hundred men. Yet the tiny difference became an uncrossable chasm, for neither the captain-general nor the Hollanders were willing to make the final concession, which had become symbolic of effective political triumph. The abyss was therefore still one of principle, and behind principle lay a fundamental conflict of policy.[21]

The Prince built his plans with support from the French in case of need. His preferred means of communication with Mazarin was the French ambassador, the soldier–diplomat D'Estrades, to whom he wrote in his own hand, in code and without signing his letters. By early 1650 the Frenchman realized that William was planning something so confidential that he would trust only Mazarin himself. Mazarin, despite a warning from D'Estrades that William might be overestimating what he could achieve, had the envoy inform the Prince that France would support him in maintaining his authority. Encouraged, William drew up no later than May but probably as early as February an instruction for an unnamed "gentleman" who would go to Mazarin to get assurance of French backing if it came to a break between Holland and the other six provinces and himself. This would mean recognition of the six provinces as a separate state and the grant of a large subsidy and the promise of troops to be used against Spain if, as anticipated, she intervened on Holland's side. The new state would join France in war against Spain and, if and when victorious, would partition the Spanish Netherlands. Mazarin would also be asked to send French ecclesiastics to assure Dutch Catholics so that they would not declare for

20 Geyl (*Geschiedenis*, III, 644) treats the debate over the distribution of sovereignty between the provinces (specifically the province of Holland) and the States General as a theoretical matter that did not touch the reality of the conflict. His reason was that the States General had become a corrupt body in which the deputies were obedient to the commands of the Prince of Orange rather than those of their own constituents. This is confusing sovereignty and policy. On the other hand, he considers that the position of Holland with regard to the army was "unconstitutional."

21 Kernkamp, 95–96; Poelhekke, "Frederik Hendrik en Willem II," 148. This whole episode from its beginning until its denouement is described and analyzed in Herbert H. Rowen, "The Revolution that Wasn't: The *Coup d'Etat* of 1650 in Holland," *European Studies Review*, 4 (1974), 99–117.

Spain. The "gentleman" apparently did not actually make the journey, for there is no record of either his departure from the Netherlands or his arrival in Paris. But the document reveals the drastic character of William's intentions.[22]

The States of Holland decided to send their own representative, Gerard Schaep of Amsterdam, to London to watch over the province's interest. The opponents of the province accused Holland of giving him instructions to obtain a separate treaty between the province and England, in violation of the Union of Utrecht, but Holland denied that this was what he had been sent to do. It affirmed, however, the right of each province to discuss its private interests with a foreign state, as had been done before without contradiction. Schaep denied that he had any such instructions. He sought only to protect the interests of Dutch merchants and not to harm those of William II, "whose glory provides the basis of our prosperity."[23] Yet Schaep's mission was indeed a threat to the unity of the Dutch state. William treated it as virtual treason and some observers thought it was the real reason behind the great conflict of 1650 between William and Holland.[24] But it was no more than wind upon the tinder of an already smoldering antagonism.

The concessions made by the Prince during the first half of 1650 in the discussions with the Hollanders were in any case largely hypocritical, for he had decided by the onset of the new year to settle the conflict in his own way, by force or the threat of force.[25] He was encouraged in this decision for a hard solution both by his cousin, Count William Frederick, the stadholder of Friesland, and by the envoy of France. William Frederick in fact suggested a specific strategy, aimed at military occupation of Amsterdam and replacement of the recalcitrant magistrates, and offered to take personal command of the troops that would be given the task.[26]

William's plan was bold, almost reckless, for it meant civil war, actual or potential. It would pit the poorest, weakest and least populous provinces and foreign soldiery against the wealthiest, most densely populated province and its great city. This was the kind of challenge to fate that is usually taken either by a devil-may-care adventurer or by a man of absolute principle who cannot settle for less than everything. Yet, although there was a bit of the former in both William and William Frederick, and a tiny touch of the latter as well, both were confident of easy success. William and William Frederick were alike in their restlessness to affirm themselves (to "gain

22 Kernkamp, 65–67; Geyl, *Oranje en Stuart*, 78–79; S. Groenveld, *De Prins voor Amsterdam* (Bussum, 1967), 23–25.
23 Kernkamp, 77–78.   24 *Ibid.*, 76–77; Geyl, *Oranje en Stuart*, 74–76.
25 Kernkamp, 95.
26 William Frederick to William II, 19/29 Dec. 1649, 27 Jan./6 Feb. 1650, *Archives*, 2e Sér., IV, 336–37, 344–45.

glory," in the contemporary phrase) and their impatience to achieve their purposes.

The political tactics they employed to prepare an appeal to arms were subtle and effective. The conflict over the size of the army was presented as a controversy over ultimate sovereignty in the Republic, setting the province of Holland against all the other provinces as represented in the States General. The underlying ambiguity of the Dutch political system was therefore reflected in the relative strengths and weaknesses of both sides. William II as captain-general upheld the unity of the army, and as the defender of the rights of the States General over the army the ultimate unity of the Republic, which had been formed for mutual defense but now faced the unprecedented situation of complete peace.

In asserting the authority of the States General, or, more precisely, of a majority of its member provinces, to compel an unwilling province to pay its share of expenditures to which it did not and would not consent, William was introducing what the Hollanders considered to be a new constitutional principle. It was, of course, not completely new, for it had been the grounds for the arrest and trial of Oldenbarnevelt and his associates and the convocation of the Synod of Dort in 1618–19; but it had been imposed then by military force at the risk of civil war. Now William II reasserted the supremacy of the States General over the individual provinces. William and Holland each sought to clarify this ambiguity to its own advantage by a symbolic victory over the other in extracting the final concession in the negotiations over the army reduction.

The Hollanders miscalculated in carrying over the principle of provincial autonomy into the sphere of military pay and command. It was one thing to assert that the States General could take no decision by majority vote over Holland's opposition; it was quite another to treat the troops which it paid as its own, subject to its orders. The difference was a subtle one, but of extreme importance. If the soldiers owed their ultimate fidelity to the province that paid them, then the power of command of the captain-general was conditional, and he was at the beck and call not just of the States General but of each provincial assembly as well. This was an impossible situation which in a crisis might lead to dissolution of both the army and the state. The situation was further complicated because there was no good way of settling differences between States and stadholder; the system which worked well when they collaborated creaked to a halt when they fell out.

The situation was at a standoff, with William working secretively to gain the initiative and the Hollanders without strong leadership.[27] Never one to

---

27 Geyl, *Oranje en Stuart*, 81.

enjoy practicing the art of persuasion, William decided that the time for talk had passed. Then, late in the Spring of 1650, Holland played into his hands, as he had hoped they would. Exasperated at the delay now running past two years in reducing the army, the States of Holland finally decided to dismiss a number of the companies it had been paying and sent orders to the affected captains informing them of their decision. This was a direct violation of the powers of the captain-general, to which he responded by calling upon the States General to reaffirm his rights. On 4 June he obtained a resolution by majority vote, with Holland protesting, which instructed him to make proposals for remedying the situation. He took this limited decision as the basis for vigorous action. He informed the States General that he was forming a delegation to visit the towns of Holland whose municipal governments had opposed his army reduction program, in an effort to persuade them to go along with the majority in the States General. He would lead the delegation himself, but he insisted that Van der Capellen tot Aertsbergen, a Gelderland nobleman who had long served Frederick Henry as an advisor and was known for his facile tongue, join the delegation and act as its spokesman, despite his reluctance to take on the thorny task.[28]

The delegation to the towns was a violation of established law and practice. It was a confirmed constitutional principle that the States General treated the provinces as unitary entities; the "members" of the provincial States, which varied from province to province but in Holland comprised the Nobility and the eighteen voting towns, were beyond the legal ken of the States General. This was an essential part of the "sovereignty" of the provinces.[29] William II as *stadholder* possessed an unquestioned right to visit the towns to discuss problems of policy with their magistrates, but now he deliberately avoided presenting himself to the towns of Holland in that capacity. In the letters of credential drawn up for presentation, he was identified only as "His Highness" and the term "the stadholder" was used only for Count William Frederick, without specifying that he was stadholder of Friesland. Such vagueness carried with it implications that William II was more than a stadholder and even hinted at a constitutional reorganization of the Republic.

The delegation left The Hague on 28 June and returned on 25 July. It numbered not only the delegates themselves but also an impressive military escort which William insisted be admitted along with him. Although some of the towns allowed William to present his case in person and through the mouth of Aertsbergen, others vigorously asserted the impropriety and irregularity of the procedure. Particularly vehement was the

---

28 Van der Capellen, *Gedenkschriften*, II, 267.   29 Poelhekke, *Geen Blijder Maer*, 73–77.

burgomaster of Dordrecht, Jacob de Witt, who was well known for his sharp tongue, although usually it was the burghers of the town who felt its sting rather than the stadholder of the province. After the meeting in Dordrecht, Aertsbergen appears to have warned William that he was running great risks, but the Prince was not deterred.[30] Several towns, notably Amsterdam, refused even to admit the delegation, although they were willing to open their gates to William provided he came in as stadholder only and without his companions and his threatening military escort.[31]

As an exercise in political persuasion, the delegation was a total failure. No votes in the States of Holland were changed. William was angry and bitter at the offenses to his dignity.[32] Yet although, his wrath was genuine, he had gained an end he clearly wanted. He had not expected his opponents to capitulate, but he had put them in the wrong and he had the justification he needed for the far more drastic action he was planning. On his return to The Hague, he informed the States General of what had happened and received from them authority to consider and propose measures to restore good order in the Republic. He went beyond the letter of that authority, however, to undertake a *coup d'état* at the end of July and the beginning of August.

William Frederick came down from Leeuwarden to take command of the military part of the operation, while William remained in The Hague for what was to be done there. The first stroke of the *coup* was made in The Hague on the morning of 30 July, when six deputies to the States of Holland from cities which had most offended William were arrested in the Binnenhof and sent off during the night to imprisonment at Loevestein Castle.

The arrests came as a surprise and a shock. The councilor pensionary of Holland, Jacob Cats, had been an easy-going official, anything but a foe of William's, yet when the Prince informed him of what he had done, Cats was thunderstruck.[33] At the Prince's request, Cats went at once to give the news to the States of Holland. The assembly responded with great caution, although without the fright that William had hoped to put into them. They did not at once demand the release of the six deputies but took a quite different step, which could mean far more if the conflict widened. Each voting town was asked to keep one or more of its deputies at The Hague to speak for it, while the other deputies returned to their respective cities to consult their principals about what should be done, and to come back in two days.[34]

---

30 Kernkamp, 94.   31 Poelhekke, *Geen Blijder Maer*, 97–100.
32 Poelhekke, "Frederik Hendrik en Willem II," 148.
33 Jacob Cats, "Twee en Tachtigjarig leven," in: Jacob Cats, *Alle de Werken* (Amsterdam, 1712), 54.   34 Kernkamp, 119.

The second part of the *coup* came the same morning when troops appeared before the gates of Amsterdam under the command of William Frederick, demanding entry to present a message from the Prince of Orange. The troops had been sent from the eastern Netherlands, but they had missed their route during night fog in the Gooi, the desolate region east of the city, and word of their presence had been carried to burgomaster Cornelius Bicker by a post courier from Hamburg who had not been detained by the troops when he rode into their midst at Hilversum because they did not know the purpose of their mission. Although it was thought at first that the threatening soldiery were marauding Swedes or Lorrainers, Bicker acted vigorously through the remainder of the night to put the city at the ready. When William Frederick's forces arrived outside Amsterdam around dawn, they found the gates closed. There was mutual surprise, William Frederick that the Amsterdammers were forewarned, the Amsterdammers that it was Dutch troops who stood outside the gates.

William Frederick had instructions only to present a message from the Prince and did not dare to undertake an assault upon the city on his own, even though he had at least 10,000 troops at his disposal. He therefore awaited the arrival of William, who came quickly after the dismaying news of the failure of his planned surprise had been brought to him at The Hague. Over the next few days, he negotiated with a delegation from Amsterdam outside the city walls, and a compromise settlement was reached on 3 August. William's sole significant gain was the agreement of Andrew and Cornelius Bicker (their brother John had died some time earlier) to resign their posts in the city government. They abandoned their intransigence when they found themselves deserted by some of the most influential regents. The crisis generated by William's threat to the city enabled those who resented the Bickers' domination to ease them out of power.

It was only after the agreement was made and signed that two delegations, one from the States General and the other from the States of Holland, arrived with a request that he terminate the siege and return to The Hague. The action of the States General, although submerged in the general relief that combat had been averted, undercut William's assertion that he was acting on their behalf. Nonetheless he made preservation of the Union and of religion – orthodox Calvinism, of course – the reasons he gave for his decisions in a letter to the magistrates and in a declaration of "reasons and motives" which he presented to the two assemblies, which they left unopened.[35]

The Prince did not gain dominance within the city of Amsterdam, how-

35 *Ibid.*, 110–12.

ever, for the new magistrates who replaced the Bickers and their friends, although more flexible, were equally committed to the interests of the metropolis. Unexpectedly, the entire population of the city remained vehemently loyal to the government of the city.[36] As for the deputies held at Loevestein, they were released later in the month. They had not faced trial by special judges and the fate of the defendants in 1618–19, as they feared and William probably planned; but they were freed not by action of their "natural judges," the courts of Holland, as would have been normal, but by William's personal decision.[37] William required each of them individually to agree to withdraw from political life, as the Bickers had done, and their town councils had to cast their votes for acceptance by the States of Holland of the resolution of the States General setting the size of the army. There was no general replacement of the municipal governments in the province, as there had been in 1618–19 in the towns that had supported Oldenbarnevelt.

The grandiose plan worked out by William II and William Frederick had gone awry, and the Prince of Orange had to be satisfied more with the appearance of victory than with its substance, except for the ouster of the Bickers and the six deputies. He still did not have the States of Holland subjugated, although they had to be more cautious than before in opposing him.[38] He had to be satisfied with a compromise on the army reduction issue as well. The States General on 18 August adopted a resolution, with Holland consenting, that set the figure for the military forces at what William wanted, but weakened his triumph by providing that all those dismissed would be from foreign units. Holland's effort at individual action was rejected, and the dismissal was done by the Council of State. But the principle remained intact that the decisions of the States General had to be taken by unanimous vote of all the provinces.[39]

Nonetheless, although William had not gained the total victory he had counted upon, the advantage went to him. He had gained the initiative. Yet, how far he could go in the policy of renewal of war with Spain and hostilities against the English Commonwealth, which remained his firm goals, would depend upon the extent of the fear that he had instilled in the Hollanders. It soon proved much less than he needed to have his way with certainty.[40]

On 26 August the Delegated Councilors of Holland decided to oppose William's endeavor to force Dutch mediation upon Spain as well as France. They correctly read his intention as to put Spain in the wrong if it

36 Kernkamp, 104; N. Japikse, *Prins Willem III: De Stadhouder-Koning* (2 vols.; Amsterdam, 1930–33), I, 19.
37 Kernkamp, 126–27.   38 *Ibid.*, 113–15.   39 *Ibid.*, 127–28.
40 Geyl, *Oranje en Stuart*, 83–85.

refused, so that resumption of the war would be justified. They warned that they would instruct the deputies of Holland in the States General to enter a protest if such a resolution were adopted over their opposition, and furthermore would call the States of Holland back into emergency session. This did not have to be done, because William backed down; the resolution adopted on 30 August was mild and removed the immediate threat of war, although William continued to harbor hopes of reviving the mediation trap for Spain.[41]

Clearly, if William was to take the country back into war with Spain as well as into another with the Commonwealth regime in England, he would have to build up his party within Holland. This meant the slow and laborious process of putting different people in the municipal governments, although he was hampered in such an operation because the town councils retained the right of nomination. It was a period of anxious uncertainty in the country, an anticipation of something about to happen again, with each side suspecting some action by the other.[42]

In any case, William continued his negotiations with the French government. In late October Mazarin and D'Estrades drew up the draft of a treaty to be presented to William. Although its text has never been found, it probably provided for the partition of the Spanish Netherlands, with William established as Marquis of Antwerp and the provinces within the zone assigned to the Dutch incorporated into the United Provinces in some unspecified way. William himself never saw the proposal, so that it represents not his own ideas but rather what the French thought he would agree to.[43] Exactly how the southern provinces would have fitted into the republic's constitution can only be guessed at, although it is obvious that it would have required not only significant revision of the existing system but also would have shifted the balance of political forces, severely cutting down the preeminence of Holland and Amsterdam. The secrecy about these negotiations was not complete, however. Suspicions arose about what was afoot, and some were quite accurate.[44]

While these talks with the French were continuing, William made no effort to impose his will upon the States General or the States of Holland beyond what he had already achieved. He spent most of his time relaxing,

41 R. Fruin, "De bemiddeling tusschen de kronen van Frankrijk en Spanje door de Staten der Vereenigde Nederlanden in 1650 aangeboden," *BVGO*, 3e Reeks, X (1897), 221–25; Kernkamp, 133–35; Poelhekke, *Geen Blijder Maer*, 163–79; Poelhekke, "Frederik Hendrik en Willem II," 152.

42 Poelhekke, *Geen Blijder Maer*, 165; Poelhekke, "Frederik Hendrik en Willem II," 151.

43 Kernkamp, 137–39; R. Fruin, "Over de oorlogsplannen van Prins Willem II na zijn aanslag op Amsterdam in 1650," *BVGO*, 3e Reeks, IX (1896), 15; Fruin, "De bemiddeling," 197–234.

44 *Hollantse Mercurius* (41 vols.; Haarlem, 1651–91), I, 46; J. N. de Parival., *Abrégé de l'histoire de ce siècle d'or* (Leiden, 1653), 430.

in particular hunting from his lodge at Dieren, in Gelderland. He may only have been trying to lull his rivals for power in the country while he prepared another stroke against them, or he may have come to terms with the limits of the effective power that he could wield. The sources do not permit us to decide between the two alternatives, although they represent quite antithetical patterns of development. It is probable that he was waiting for the Spring to resume the initiative, for there is no reason to believe that he had abandoned his plans for action in combination with France. His hope for immediate action against England was dashed by Cromwell's victory at Dunbar against the Scots.[45]

Meanwhile political debate resumed with more turbulence and vehemence than ever.[46] One pamphleteer hostile to the Prince reaffirmed that he was "nothing more than a governor and stadholder, and a servant of the States," but admitted that if he had succeeded with his *coup*, he would have become the sovereign, more absolute in his power than any king, who would never seize and carry off the States of their provinces for taking decisions of which he did not approve.[47] Such confidence in monarchs elsewhere may or may not have been sincere, but it pointed up the denial that stadholders were chosen to rule absolutely.[48] Another writer charged William with seeking supreme power over all the States and towns. If he had gained it, he would have been sovereign, and those who contradicted him would face arrest and imprisonment. "For what difference can there be between him and a sovereign, and can a monarch have more power than that?"[49] It was in the nature of things that the army should want to make William a sovereign, commented another pamphleteer. He added that "it is the character of princes and governors of countries that they always try to climb higher and higher, first for a time and then for all time, rising from elective to successive and hereditary, from limited to absolute and sovereign."[50] Whether he was truly, as these authors imply and the modern historian Geyl asserts in so many words, the representative of the "monarchical principle," can neither be proved nor disproved, however, in view of his untimely death. It is probably safer to say that he lacked any commitment, intellectual or emotional, to the republican principle. As for his

45 Geyl, *Oranje en Stuart*, 85–86.
46 See Groenveld, *De Prins*, for a good sketch of these pamphlets.
47 Wel-hem Recht-hert van Vry-land. *Brief Rakende het vangen der Ses Leden van de Groot-Mogende Heeren Staten van Hollandt en West-Vrieslandt, en 't belegeren van Amsterdam* (In 't Vrije Hollandt, Meenrecht Vredericxsz. Stavast, 1650) (Kn. 6,771), 4.
48 Wel-hem Recht-hert van Vry-land, 6.
49 *Hollants praatjen, Tusschen vier personen, Een Geldersman, een Hollander, een Vries, en een Brabander, Aangaande de Souveraintiteyt van Syn Hoogheyt. Het eerste deel* (Antwerp, 1650) (Kn. 6,824), 3–4.
50 *Amsterdams Buer-praetje. Dat is, Discours tusschen twee Amsterdammers, Claes Torenssen, en Kees Vries, over de doot van Syn Hoogheydt* (Amsterdam, 1650) (Kn. 6,868).

opponents, what may well have been the most witty comment on the *coup* was much more down to earth. Constantine Huygens, the Prince of Orange's secretary, in a rhyming quatrain built around the dual meanings of the word *voor* in Dutch, "for" and "before," punningly summed up the event: Amsterdam was no longer *for* the Prince because he had been *before* Amsterdam.[51] This was sarcasm at Amsterdam's expense, for immediately after the settlement Huygens observed that "their manners are becoming better" (*le monde devient plus sage*).[52]

Accident now intervened in the course of events, leading to an outcome that no one had expected. William had not been deterred from hunting by the harsh October weather, and late in the month he came down with a fever. When he did not recover quickly, he was carried by river boat to The Hague, where his ailment turned out to be smallpox. He seemed to be recovering when, on 4 November, he suddenly took a turn for the worse and died in the stadholder's quarters in the Binnenhof.

It was a most impolitic death. He had challenged the most powerful province in the country, and if his triumph had been incomplete, it was still his. Now he was gone, and the institution of the stadholderate, which had not been in dispute as such since the beginning of the Republic, was in question.

---

51 Eysten, 172. The quatrain: Hoe quam 't, dat Amsterdam soo gramm was, / En waarom was 'tniet voor den Prins? / In seven woorden gaet veel sins; / Om dat de Prins voor Amsterdam was.

52 Constantijn Huygens to Count Henry of Nassau, 6 Aug. 1650, *De Briefwisseling van Constantijn Huygens (1608–1687)*, ed. J. A. Worp (6 vols.; The Hague, 1911–17), v, 47.

5

The first stadholderless period: 1 exclusion

Never did unanticipated circumstance bring a more profound transformation of the political scene in the United Provinces than occurred with the death of William II. At a time when Dutchmen had to think very hard about the necessity and desirability of the stadholderate, the Prince of Orange was a posthumous child for whose succession no provision had been made.

Proof that leadership in the Republic resided in the province of Holland no less than in the House of Orange was instantly provided. The States of Holland moved with a swiftness that would ordinarily have been astonishing in a constitutional system notorious for its dilatoriness. William II died on the night of 6 November; before midnight the Delegated Councilors of Holland had already sent word to the voting towns that the new situation would be the subject of a meeting of the States of Holland already convoked for 9 November. When they met, Their Noble Great Mightinesses the States of Holland acted with speed and vigor to consolidate their own leadership within the Republic and to reassure the other provinces, their "allies" in the accepted nomenclature, that they did not consider the Union of Utrecht to be dissolved but rather sought to maintain its permanency.

For this reason they called upon all the provinces to participate in a "Great Assembly" of the States General. According to the original plan proposed by Holland, this would be a meeting of all the provincial States together and simultaneously, so that there would be in principle no "deputies" from the provincial States to the States General; differences could then be worked out in person and without delays caused by the requirement that deputies consult their principals before voting. Not all the provinces consented to the procedure, but the "Great Assembly" that met in the Binnenhof in January 1651 was sufficiently empowered so that it could engage in the large work of reconciliation and pacification.

One fundamental change had already taken place before the assembly met. On William's death, the provincial States and the town governments took over the prerogatives that had belonged to him as stadholder, notably the election of municipal councilors and burgomasters. In the Great

Assembly, Holland persuaded all the provinces except Friesland and Groningen to refrain from appointing a new stadholder or captain and admiral-general, but this was actually not part of the assembly's activity, although elaborating its consequences was. It was decided that there would be no supreme commander unless and until the necessity arose, and then a field marshal could be named just for the time he would be needed; it would not be an appointment for life. Furthermore, he would be subject not only to the States General and the Council of State, as had been true from the formative years of the Republic, but also to the provinces and towns. The assumption of command and movement orders ("patents," as they were called) for troops by the provinces which paid them was given official status. Furthermore, no military force could henceforth be moved into any town without the approval of its military government. Colonels and captains, the effective commanders of troop units, essentially became responsible to Generality, provincial and local authorities. As a precaution against misuse of the armed forces for a political *coup*, this decision would no doubt be effective, but little thought was given to what might happen if they had to be called upon for quick and decisive military operations.

No formal change was made in the Union of Utrecht, although the absence of a stadholder (except in Friesland and Groningen) meant that the dominant force within the national government became the individual provinces, and most of all the preponderant province, Holland. No new right of taxation was given to the States General; the national treasury continued to receive its funds from the provinces according to the unchanged quota that was now decades old and did not reflect the shifts in relative wealth among the provinces.

All in all, the most important decision of the Great Assembly was the implicit one of an action or actions *not* taken that would have been customary and unquestioned before. No measure was taken to acknowledge or grant a specific political or military role to the Prince of Orange, the infant William III, but neither was any positive action taken against the House of Orange. Holland's essential achievement had been to persuade the other provinces to accept the absence of the stadholder–captain-general. Holland was successful with the other provinces primarily because, in the absence of a counterbalance in the Prince of Orange, its own preponderance became enormous. Not to be neglected, however, is the resentment that had built up in other provinces against the appointment of their governments and the determination of their policies by Frederick Henry and William II.[1]

Once the Great Assembly had concluded its work, the councilor pen-

---

[1] Japikse, *Prins Willem III*, I, 21.

sionary of Holland, Cats, insisted upon putting down his office and retiring into a sinecure for the remainder of his life (nine years, as it happened). If only domestic policy had been involved, it would have been possible for the States of Holland to search carefully and systematically for a new councilor pensionary. The worsening relations with England did not permit a leisurely exploration of talents, however, and there was an immediate need for someone experienced in diplomacy. The States of Holland therefore turned to Pauw, who had been councilor pensionary before Cats and then ambassador to Paris, although he was only a few years younger than Cats. He was not allowed to remain in the retirement he had already entered, but was pressed to become councilor pensionary again for at least a short time.

His attention was almost entirely focused upon the problem of relations with England, and for a time he even went to London for direct negotiations with the new republican government. During his absence, his tasks in the management of the States of Holland (and, less officially, of the States General) fell according to custom to the permanent deputy of Dordrecht, the senior city of the province. This was John de Witt, who was one of the two town pensionaries; he had already been singled out as a leader in the Great Assembly.[2] He helped Pauw with his tasks so effectively after his return and then while he was mortally ill during 1653, that the States of Holland turned to him to become councilor pensionary in July, after Pauw's demise.[3]

The election of De Witt was another accident with great historical consequences, no less than the death of William II. The new councilor pensionary proved himself over the next years to be a statesman of immense ability, in more than one sense the "Oldenbarnevelt Resurrected" that his enemies called him. He was not a state-builder like Oldenbarnevelt but a consolidator. What made him crucially important not just for the history of the Dutch nation in general, but for the stadholderate in particular, was his ability to provide the stadholderless regime with stability and guidance. He took the incipient principles of stadholderless government, to which the name of "True Freedom" was given, and gave them consistency and persuasiveness. His gifts of statesmanship enabled the stadholderless regime to endure for more than two decades. He defined therefore the great historical alternative to government by a stadholder, government by the States under the leadership of the councilor pensionary of Holland. The party of

---

2 *De rechte ondeckinge Vande Hollantsche Regeerende Loevesteynsche Heeren* (Dordrecht, 1652) (Kn. 7,302).

3 This and the subsequent chapter, which encompass the whole "first stadholderless period," draw throughout on my biographies of De Witt, *John de Witt, Grand Pensionary of Holland (1625–1672)* (Princeton, 1978), a full-scale work, and *John de Witt: Statesman of the "True Freedom"* (Cambridge, 1986), a short version.

the Princes in turn had to define itself against this new rival. He was therefore even more important for the development of the stadholderate as an institution than Oldenbarnevelt had been, for the land's advocate had never been a foe of the stadholdership as such, but on the contrary had been one if its foremost sponsors.

The government led by De Witt should not be seen, however, as an emanation of his personality. It was able to function as well as it did for two decades because there were in addition to the councilor pensionary many able regents in the towns, experienced in domestic affairs if less so by far in foreign policy.[4] In a political structure such as that of the Dutch Republic, where there were so few paid officials and these were usually administrators rather than leaders, and where political power was distributed all up and down the scale and across the country, governance was more a matter of persuasion than of command. Yet De Witt as councilor pensionary exercised his leadership not only by the undoubted power of his words and his skill in manipulation of the system, but also by the existence of what, for want of a better term, historians call the "States party." It was not a modern organized party, of course, no more than its competitor, the "Orange party," but a clique or a congeries of cliques, as they have been called.[5] It was at one level the body of those regents in Holland and other provinces who more or less regularly upheld the doctrine and the practice of stadholderless government. At another level, it also comprised those in the wider nation who accepted and favored such government; but it did not succeed in extending that support deeply or widely, and it always remained a narrow party of the elite.

Like the States party, the Orange party was not a party in the modern sense, but only a loose assemblage of disparate elements brought together by their common affection and fidelity to the Prince of Orange, a "side" in the political struggle. What it did possess above all was a candidate and a historic myth. From the beginning of the Revolt, the Princes of Orange had had both a personal entourage and a wide band of supporters. Ordinarily no effort was made to assemble the followers into an active force, but in critical times guidance was given to key individuals, especially among the regents and the clergy. The informality of this structure of leadership meant that it could not function well with passive, pallid persons at the helm; but, for all their differences, from William the Silent to William II, the Princes had all been strongly defined persons, although each in his own way. Now, however, the Orange party had to function with a child at its head. The key person thus became his guardian. This would ordinarily be the mother, and the strain upon her capacities would be all the greater

4 Geyl, *Oranje en Stuart*, 97.   5 *Ibid.*, 338–39.

because Dutch society remained almost totally patriarchal and women who exercised influence usually did so through their men, husbands or sons, and not directly.

The struggle between the two parties was waged about intertwining constitutional and political issues. It was a contest between various groups of the population, although there was much overlapping, and within each group there were subgroups which had interests which often clashed. The constitutional form in which these controversies were expressed was in the first instance a weapon with which the contenders fought,[6] but it was more. A constitution, by distributing power and defining its range and character, also creates interests and favors particular groups. In addition, the constitutional debate contributed to the formation of explicit ideologies, to which men committed themselves often without much consideration of personal advantage, out of family or local traditions or friendships.

How well either Mary, who became the "Princess Royal" in recognition of her birth, or Amalia van Solms, who remained "Princess Dowager," as she had been called since Frederick Henry's death, would have done had she held the guardianship individually, cannot be known. The fact was that daughter-in-law and mother-in-law were caught in the grip of an intense political and personal rivalry, and they thwarted each other of any chance of successful leadership of the Orange party. Her *mésalliance* still rankled with Mary. Her pride verged on brusqueness.[7] Her residence in Holland was a kind of exile, necessary for the sake of the family, like most dynastic marriages, but unleavened by love of its people. She made little effort to learn Dutch well but continued to feel as well as to speak English. More significant was that her affection for her royal brother was stronger than that for her son. As for her mother-in-law, Mary had haughty disdain for Amalia.[8]

The Princess Dowager was different in almost every respect. Her background as a German countess of modest importance paled in her memory compared to the rank her husband had achieved and that she aspired to see her grandson attain. She deeply resented the scorn her daughter-in-law showed for her, perhaps all the more because she knew that in the rank and precedence-conscious world in which they both lived, Mary's attitude was wholly legitimate, if hardly flattering. She had become quite Dutch in feeling, seeing the interests of her family as bound to the United Provinces in a way that Mary did not. She had learned much about the craft of

6 *Ibid.*, 97–98.

7 *Les Mémoires du Burgrave et Comte Frédéric de Dohna, 1621–1688*, H. Borkowski, ed. (Königsberg i. Pr., 1898), 142.

8 Dutch historians are generally not admirers of Princess Mary. The best biographer of her son, the American Stephen Baxter, reviewing her whole life, does not agree with them. For him she was doing her best, a lonely foreigner in a hostile land. Stephen B. Baxter, *William III and the Defense of European Liberty, 1659–1702* (New York, 1966), 27.

politics from her husband, and even more about the realities of political power in the Dutch Republic. She was not at all eager to see the cause of Orange restoration sacrificed to the needs of the House of Stuart. She did not lightly offend such powerful persons as the burgomasters of Amsterdam. Her perpetual aim remained to see her grandson become stadholder and captain-general like the Princes of Orange before him. He should be brought up to see this as the central purpose of his life.[9]

The first clash between Mary and Amalia concerned the name to be given to him at his baptism on 15 January, which would be symbolic of the direction of his upbringing. Mary wanted him to be named Charles, after her father, with its implied English commitment; Amalia insisted upon his receiving the name of William, after his own father and great-grandfather. Amalia won out, a victory that was all the more important because she understood the significance of achieving for him acceptance from the various States assemblies in recognition of his place at the head of the "eminent House."[10]

Immediately afterward, control over William's education and management of his estates and properties came into dispute between Mary and Amalia. William II had left only an unsigned and undated testament which gave guardianship to Mary and several still unnamed deputies to the States General. Amalia contested its validity and appealed to the States of Holland to decide between her and Mary. Her grounds were that Mary was herself a minor and that the guardian should come from the father's side, all the more because all of the young Prince's property came from him. She claimed therefore a special status for the House of Orange in law as "illustrious," making its members subject to the decisions of the States rather than of the ordinary courts finding according to ordinary law.

Amalia's appeal to the States of Holland rather than the States General catered to the principle of provincial sovereignty; but acceptance of the House of Orange as "illustrious" would imply that its head, the Prince, would at some time receive the high office of stadholder (and captain-general from the States General) as his due. Furthermore, it could do nothing but harm in the already difficult relations with the English republican government. It was these considerations rather than Mary's counter-appeal for her rights to which the States of Holland responded in rejecting Amalia's request. They decided instead to leave the matter of the Prince's guardianship to the Court of Holland as a matter "concerning ordinary Justice."[11] Finally a compromise was arranged. Unlike the

---

9 Japikse, *Prins Willem III*, I, 22–24; Geyl, *Oranje en Stuart*, 88–95; Baxter, 27–28.
10 Japikse, *Prins Willem III*, I, 30; Geyl, *Oranje en Stuart*, 93.
11 J. A. Worp, "Inleiding," Huygens, *Briefwisseling*, V, x–xi; Japikse, *Prins Willem III*, I, 31–36; Baxter, 17–18.

babe in Solomon's judgment, the guardianship could be split down the middle, and this was done, half going to Mary and half to Amalia and Elector Frederick William of Brandenburg, her son-in-law, jointly.[12] The guardians were helpless to change the legal status of their ward. Even Zeeland, the most zealously Orangist of the provinces, followed up its action in leaving the stadholdership unoccupied by declining to accept the Prince as First Noble of the province on the grounds that the dignity adhered to the stadholdership and not to proprietorship of Veere and Flushing.[13]

The Orangist party was also weakened by the renewal of the rivalry between the House of Orange and its cousin of Nassau-Dietz in Friesland, which William II had overcome. The stadholder of Friesland, Count William Frederick, hoped to become lieutenant-general, but he found he was opposed both by Amalia, who worried that he would try to usurp her tiny grandson's position, and by the province of Holland, which remembered all too clearly his role in the events of 1650.[14] Amalia's suspicions, which were shared by Mary, were heightened when William Frederick accepted the stadholdership of Groningen province on 1 December 1650, less than a month after William's death.[15] In 1652 he married Amalia's daughter Albertina Agnes, but the relations of the two allied houses improved little.[16] He continued, however, to be no more than a thorn to both the Orange princesses and the now dominant States party, for he was a man whose ambition and readiness for reckless action was matched only by his lack of political talent.[17]

William's death dashed any hope that Charles II may have had of restoration by foreign troops, but it did not remove the fear of the English republicans that the Orange party would drag the United Provinces into armed conflict with their newly-established Commonwealth. Their anxiety was heightened by the impunity with which Stuart adherents in exile in the Netherlands were able to molest and even murder representatives of the republican regime in England.[18]

The relationship was ideological on the English side, not on the Dutch, for whom the English were primarily rivals in trade and shipping. They saw at once the significance of the Navigation Act passed by Parliament in 1651 in an effort to deprive the Dutch of their advantages in trade. Adopted on 9 October, the statute was translated into Dutch and published

12 Japikse, *Prins Willem III*. I, 34–36; Baxter, 17–18.
13 Japikse, *Prins Willem III*, I, 37.
14 Sommelsdijk to William Frederick, 16, 21 Dec. 1650, *Archives*, 2e Sér., V, 12–13, 15.
15 Geyl, *Oranje en Stuart*, 87–88.
16 Japikse, *Prins Willem III*, I, 41; Geyl, *Oranje en Stuart*, 131.
17 Japikse, *Prins Willem III*, I, 29–30.
18 Geyl, *Oranje en Stuart*, 105–6.

before the year was out.[19] Oliver Cromwell, already the most powerful force in the new regime in England, was much more concerned, however, about the political threat from Dutch Orangism than he was about the greedy yearnings of English merchants and shippers, but he had to take their interests into account. Furthermore, if the Dutch would not give him the political assurances he wanted, he had no reason to restrain the bellicosity of the inveterate foes of the Dutch. The war that broke out in 1652 was therefore not "Cromwell's war," as one historian has dubbed it.[20]

So important, in fact, was Cromwell's desire to thwart any effort by Charles II to use Dutch power for restoration of the monarchy that he proposed to the Dutch a merger of the two Republics. In effect he offered them free entry into the English market and an end to the Navigation Act in exchange for an absolute guarantee of Dutch rejection of the Stuart cause. Rebels and refugees from each county would have to be expelled from the territory of the other. This would apply even to Princess Mary and her son. The Dutch were flabbergasted by the proposal, which was utterly without precedent. They realized that in the proposed union the United Provinces would be the junior partner, and they had no desire to give up the independence they had won in an eighty-years war. They therefore rejected the offer out of hand. But they nonetheless very much wanted peace and even an alliance with England, which they recognized held the strategic upper hand.[21]

The profound political suspicions of the English rulers contributed to their readiness for war, which came when the English and Dutch fleets clashed. In the First Anglo-Dutch War (1652–4), which the Dutch call the "First English War," the advantage of battle soon went decisively to the English. Their navy was a battle fleet whose ships had been built specifically for combat, while the Dutch force was constituted mainly by converted merchantmen. The English Republic also benefited by the vigor and enthusiasm of its leadership, while the Dutch nation found itself under the flabby guidance of old, worn-out men. Furthermore, the English leadership was far more united than the Dutch. In the United Provinces the

---

19 *Een Placcaet tot Aenwas der Schepen, ende Moet-ghevinge aen de Zeevaert van dese Natie. Donderdag den 9. Octob. 1651. Gheordonneert by het Parliament dat dese Acte terstont ghedruckt ende ghepublicert sy.* (The Hague, 1651) (Kn. 6,955)
20 The historian was myself, and it was Charles Wilson who pointed out the error in the chapter title of my De Witt biography. See Charles Wilson, "Arbiter of the Republic" (Review of Herbert H. Rowen, *John de Witt, Grand Pensionary of Holland*), *TLS: The Times Literary Supplement*, 29 Sept. 1978, p. 1070.
21 See *Redenen Waerom het oorbaerder is Dat de Vereenichde Nederlanden Haer met de Republyq van Engelandt verbinden...* (Kn. 6978) for an expression of this attitude. The author of *Christelijcke en Politique Redenen Waer om dat Nederlandt en Engelandt tegens malcanderen niet moghen Oorloghen* (Rotterdam, 1652) (Kn. 7,204) is unusual in citing (p. 3) as another reason for friendship the fact that they were both free republics.

States party was trapped by the inconsistency between the need on the one hand to wage hard war against the English to save the country, which fell into deep economic depression because of the enemy blockade of the coasts, and the importance, on the other side, of not playing into the hands of the oppositional forces of the Orangists within the country.

The Orangists faced no such split of mind. For them everything was clear. The way to fight the English republicans was to support the restoration of Charles Stuart.[22] The provinces where the Orangists carried weight did not, however, make any move to increase support for the navy, which they saw as the responsibility primarily of Holland (and to a lesser degree of Zeeland and Friesland) and the admiralties; after all, the benefits of success at sea visibly went to Dutch trade, in whose profits they did not directly share. The Orangists were not cool analysts, weighing resources and strategic possibilities in order to produce effective policies, but worried, fearful men knowing not much beyond their immediate surroundings and responding to their desires and their hopes. Yet, understanding of the reasons for the Orangists' political myopia cannot blind us to the fact that they undercut the war effort of the country.

The Orangist regents were a problem and a threat to the regime because their strength came not only from their own numbers, but also from the support of the broad population, especially in the towns. The role of the populace was significant not because they possessed any vote, with a few minor exceptions and certainly not in Holland where it had been formally forbidden by law since the 1590s. Furthermore, the very term "vote" is misleading when applied to the populace, for it gives the impression of modern elections, with parties and candidates contending at the ballot box. The method of popular influence was riot, which could put unpopular regents at peril of their property and lives unless the burgher guards or the army was available and ready to put down the disturbances. The popular riots, which were concentrated in Holland but also broke out in Zeeland, had distinct causes – religious acrimony, economic hardship, love of "Our Prince"[23] – but they ran together now in a threat to the stability of the local governments, especially in the smaller towns. But they never became more than a problem that could be handled. When regular troops were sent in, order was always restored.[24]

22 *Eenvoudigh advis* (Kn. 7,257); *Hoe veel den Vereenighde Provintien Gehoort gelegen te zyn, de her-stellinge van den Coninck van Groot-Britangie. Uytgegeven op de tegenwoordige gelegenheyt van Oorlog tusschen Hen, en de Engelsche Rebellen* (The Hague, 1653) (Kn. 7,426); *Ontdeckinghe, Van den tegenwoordigen standt onses Vader-landts, waer het hapert, en hoe de In-ghesetenen, uyt haer groot verstel, spoedelijck wouden connen verlost worden, en uyt de Engelsche Oorlog ghereddet.* (Middelburg, 1653) (Kn. 7,462).
23 R. M. Dekker, *Oproeren in Holland gezien door de tijdgenoten: Ooggetuigeverslagen van oproeren in de provincie Holland ten tijde van de Republiek (1650–1750)* (Assen, 1979), 8–9.   24 Geyl, *Oranje en Stuart*, 139–41.

Nonetheless there was a deeper importance to the rioting. As the Orangist party discovered that it could not effectively bring together enough forces within Holland and in the other provinces to endanger the stadholderless regime, the realization arose that a mob could bring down a government which had ceased to command the loyalty of the burgher guards in the towns, or when the regular army had been defeated in war. This was a new element in the Dutch political system, one that would play a role of the highest importance in the years and decades to come. Yet Princess Mary refused to make systematic use of the instrument of popular riot in an attempt to overthrow the government. What she wanted was to persuade the States of Holland that they had no need to fear her, and she deterred those supporters of Charles II – the Presbyterians, not the Anglicans – who wanted a direct appeal to the Dutch people.

The economic resources of the country, from which Dutch naval power was drawn, were being sapped by the highly effective blockade of the Dutch coasts that the English were maintaining. They had the whip hand, but, except one or two naval commanders who faced the problem at first hand, few in the Dutch Republic were willing to admit it. With no foreign friends to give help, the Dutch were caught in an impasse of policy, unable to move forward to victory or backward to acceptance of defeat. The Republic needed a leader of strong will and clear mind to persuade it to accept the latter if the former was not feasible.

It found that leader in John de Witt, the young Dordrechter who was doing Pauw's work after the councilor pensionary's death. In July 1653 De Witt was unanimously elected councilor pensionary of Holland for a five-year term. He soon discovered that rebuilding the navy sufficiently to give a chance of victory over England would be the work not of months but of years, and he decided that coming to terms with England to end the war was necessary, even though the terms would be largely imposed by the victor. Most of the terms, although painful, were politically acceptable in the Netherlands. There was, however, one basic demand by Cromwell, who had meanwhile become Lord Protector and as such a quasi-king in Britain, that was much harder to swallow. This was that the States General exclude the House of Orange from the high offices it had traditionally held in the Republic. De Witt and his principal collaborator among the Dutch ambassadors in London, the Gouda deputy Van Beverningk, were put in a strange position. They did not at all favor the restoration of the House of Orange, but they had no liking either for the notion of a foreign power interfering in the internal affairs of the Dutch Republic. Worse, they recognized that such a proposal would arouse a storm of anger in the country.

Cromwell, after some balking, agreed to a substitute proposed by De Witt, a promise by the States of Holland that they would never name a stadholder or permit the stadholder of any other province to become captain-general. Cromwell insisted, however, that the Prince of Orange be excluded from both offices. This became known as the "Seclusion," after contemporary Dutch usage; the meaning is very rare in English. De Witt tried every argument to persuade Cromwell to accept something less offensive, but it was precisely the commitment of so many Dutchmen to the cause of the House of Orange and through it to support of the House of Stuart that caused the Lord Protector concern, and although he gave way with regard to exacting such a promise from the States General, especially after it was explained to him that the stadholdership was a purely provincial office, he insisted all the more implacably that it had to be given by the States of Holland. "Seclusion" would do what he had not been able to obtain by the proposed combination of the two countries into one.[25]

De Witt soon discovered that his powers of persuasion, already admired, did not extend so far as to gain the adherence of all Their Noble Great Mightinesses of Holland to the terms of the "Seclusion." It was only when he promised every effort to win a concession from Cromwell that he extracted a secret decision that if worst came to worst, they would swallow this bitter pill. Word of what was afoot got to opponents in the States General, and there a resolution was adopted directly instructing the ambassadors not to give any such promise. Before this decision, which would have doomed the Republic to continued war and defeats, reached London, De Witt got a message through to the two Hollanders among the ambassadors informing them that it was coming and hinting to them in the plainest words that they should present the copy of Holland's "Act of Seclusion" to Cromwell at once if they had not already done so (the hint was so plain that it was really a command).

This subverting of the decision of the States General he kept from the knowledge not only of Their High Mightinesses but also of the States of Holland, where there was much reluctance to defy the higher body. If peace were to be obtained, it had to be done by deceit that verged on outright disobedience by De Witt to his own masters, the States of Holland.[26] He was risking not only a political defeat but his head. He won through safely, however. The ambassadors of Holland delivered the Act of Seclusion in time, Cromwell and his Council of State signed the Peace of Westminster in April 1654, and all that remained was to get it ratified.

That became another battle, almost as hard as the one for the "Seclusion" itself. News of what Holland had done, despite a promise of secrecy

25 *Ibid.*, 152.   26 *Ibid.*, 156–57.

given by all who took part, quickly reached the deputies of the other provinces as well as the streets. A storm of fury broke over the Hollanders, with De Witt and Van Beverningk at the center of the accusation that the province had violated the Union of Utrecht. De Witt was depicted as having prompted Cromwell to make his demand for the "Seclusion," thereby obtaining from the country's enemy a measure he could not extort on his own. De Witt was able to hold the States of Holland behind him, and he doggedly defended the Act of Seclusion as a purely provincial matter. He drew up a formal defense of their conduct and their rights in a "deduction," or detailed exposition of their case, that was adopted by the States of Holland for presentation to the States General and the other provinces. Whatever the cogency of its arguments, the States General settled back and ratified the Treaty of Westminster simply because peace had already come. It was one thing to hang on in a losing war, it was another deliberately to go back into combat with awareness of the near certainty of defeat.

De Witt's *Deduction* – although his name did not appear on the title page, his authorship was no secret – became a central document in the debate over the stadholdership.[27] For the first time it brought together the themes of the opponents of the stadholderate in a coherent treatise, written in a clear, vigorous prose that carried a message of strong convictions. Its central argument was that the province of Holland, represented by its States assembly, was sovereign. It held all political powers except those explicitly transferred to the States General in the Union of Utrecht, and the Act of Seclusion concerned a purely provincial office. This was a narrowly constitutional argument, and De Witt had it pretty much won from the beginning because of the terms of the Union. He went beyond the constitutional issue, however, to a broad political one, the place of the House of Orange in the Dutch Republic. Admitting the services of earlier Princes of Orange as stadholders and captains-general, he held that they had been more than adequately recompensed by the salaries and grants to them over the decades. There existed no unpaid debt of gratitude.

Even if there had been, he held that it would not obligate the province of Holland to elect the Prince of Orange as its stadholder. The office, indeed,

---

27 *Deductie, ofte Declaratie van de Staten van Hollandt Ende West-Vrieslandt; Behelsende Een waerachtich, ende grondich bericht van de Fondamenten der Regieringe vande vrye Vereenichde Nederlanden; ... Ingestelt ende dienende tot Justificatie Van 't verlenen van seeckere Acte van Seclusie, Raeckende 't employ vanden Heere Prince van Oraigne, By d'hoogh-gemelte Heeren Staten van Hollandt ende West-Vrieslandt op den vierden Mey 1654 gepassert; mitsgaders vande procedure van de selve daer ontrent gehouden: met grondige REFUTATIE van 't gene daer jegens by, often van wegen eenige Provincien is voortgebracht* (The Hague, 1654). The key passages are translated in Rowen, *Low Countries*, 191–200.

was not an inherent part of the structure of power in the province, as were the order of Nobility, the town governments, and the States of Holland; it was only a post which the States of Holland, exercising the sovereignty of the province, could create or abolish at its pleasure. In any case, it was not a hereditary post. There was no hereditary office in a republic, certainly not in the Dutch Republic, and no family, however eminent, could claim any office by birthright. Such a right belonged only to monarchies, and monarchy formed no necessary or proper part of the Dutch regime. The Dutch Republic and its constituent provinces were aristocracies, a term which De Witt used in its precise Greek meaning as the rule of the "best" and therefore the few, not as a synonym for nobility.

De Witt rebutted the claim of the Orangists that the proper functioning of the Dutch state required the presence of a single head at its leadership, thus introducing the element of *"eenhoofdig"* (literally, "one-headed") or monarchical government into the republican system of the Netherlands. De Witt resolutely rejected such an argument; he favored a pure republicanism. Yet he totally agreed with his opponents in treating the stadholderate as equivalent to monarchy. Thus, like them, he did not examine the stadholderate in the specific, largely informal role that it had developed beginning with William the Silent. There is no reason to believe that he was avoiding the question as too ticklish: he found the simple constitutional argument quite sufficient.[28]

For all its elaborate argumentation, the immediate political purpose of the *Deduction* was to give the impression, subtly and without outright prevarication, that the ambassadors had turned over the Act of Seclusion to Cromwell before they knew of the decision of the States General.[29] In the long term it became one of the classic texts of a more assertively republican theory. It was no longer a doctrine defending rebellion against a tyrant but an affirmation of an existing regime.[30]

The most cogent of the replies was another *Deduction*, this one by the States of Zeeland. The essence of its argumentation was that the stadholderate had been an inherent part and parcel of the constitutional practice of the Dutch Republic from the very beginning, and that this was the meaning of the various references to the stadholderate in the Union of Utrecht. It affirmed the importance of "one head" in the governance of a federal state with many diverging interests, drawing up the arguments for monarchy that had been elaborated over the years by the adherents of the Orange house, but sidestepping the equation of stadholdership with kingship that De Witt (and pamphleteers of *Staatsgezind*

---

28 Geyl, *Oranje en Stuart*, 165–67.   29 *Ibid.*, 155–56.
30 I. Schöffer, "De Republiek der Verenigde Nederlanden," in: *Winkler Prins Geschiedenis*, II, 181–82.

convictions)[31] had made. Most of the *Prinsgezind* pamphlets[32] did not attain such a level of abstraction. At their best they were affirmations of the principles better stated in Zeeland's deduction, at their worst vituperations against De Witt, Van Beverningk and their friends, accusing them of the most incredible crimes and vices. Yet, for all the fierceness of these interchanges, they came to little in the short run.

The two Princesses might complain together to the States of Holland that the Seclusion had struck them "with astonishment and great pain,"[33] and William Frederick might speak bold words to the French ambassador about carrying things to extremes with the help of the other provinces,[34] but their protests and his boasts were empty of consequences. The fact of the matter was that the country needed the peace badly and benefited quickly when it came. Trade picked up, and the population of the country began to breathe more easily as life improved. The war of words in the pamphlets fell off to almost total peace.

De Witt used his immense talents as a statesman for almost all the major tasks of government: returning the finances to health, rebuilding the navy, guiding the internal policies away from conflict by deft political management, and directing the foreign policy of the country in the same way and essentially with the same tools that Oldenbarnevelt had used half a century before. The army was allowed to slumber on, lacking a supreme commander and adequate only for keeping a Dutch military presence on the frontiers and policing the towns when needed.

All the while the Prince of Orange was growing up. Until 1658 he resided principally in the "stadholder's quarters" in the Binnenhof which were not taken from him and his guardians by the States of Holland, to whom the buildings belonged. His household, at first small, expanded somewhat over the years. His education, which began in 1656, was regular, concerned with the customary skills of a noble gentleman as well as with religion. In these years, he spoke mainly English; Dutch and French had to be taught.[35]

31 For instance, *Zeeuwze Ratel, geroert Tusschen dry Persoonen, Een Hollander, Zeeuvv en Hagenaar, over Het Uitsluiten en deporteren van een Stadhouder Generaal* (Middelburg, 1654) (Kn. 7,564); *Korte Vragen en Antwoorden, Over de Deductie ofte Declaratie van de Staten van Holland ende West-Vrieslandt* (Amsterdam, 1654) (Kn. 7,552); *Leeven en Bedrijf Van sijn Hoogheyt Willem Hendrick de Derde, Prince van Orangien, En Nassau, &c. ... Door een Liefhebber der Historien* (Amsterdam, 1675).

32 For instance, *De oog-geopende Zeeuw, Gestelt in maniere van een t'samenspreking Tusschen een Hollander Ende een Zeeuw, Aengaende de seclusie van sijn Hoogheydt den Prince van Oranjen* (N.p., 1654) (Kn. 7,565); *Bedenckinge Op de Deductie van de Ed. Gr. Mog. Staten van Hollant, Noopende den Artickel van Seclusie Van den Heere Prince van Oraenjen; Ingestelt door een Patriot van 't Vaderlant* (N.p., 1654) (Kn. 7,550).

33 Memorial of Princesses Mary and Amalia to the States of Holland, 9 May 1654, Algemeen Rijksarchief, The Hague, Staten van Holland, #1698.

34 Chanut to Mazarin, 14 May 1654, *Archives*, 2e Sér., v, 145.

35 Japikse, *Prins Willem III*, I, 61.

Amalia resisted Mary's efforts to put a strong British coloration upon his ideas and associations, and a Dutch dominee, Dr Cornelius Trigland, who preached in The Hague, was named to instruct him in religion. In these early years William acquired a firm Calvinist faith, amplified as he matured into a fairly good understanding of its doctrines.[36] The military education directed toward his anticipated eventual role as army commander was small in these years, consisting more of physical hardening and athletic exercises than in real training, which in any case would not have been appropriate to a boy not yet in his teens. He needed to be made physically stronger because he suffered from asthma, which would dog him for the rest of his life, and his body was pulled out of shape by a small hump on his back. He was not a lovely child to look upon and would not grow into a handsome man to whom women were quickly drawn, but his face already indicated intensity of character and personality. He seems not to have developed strong affection for either his mother or his grandmother, whose concern for him was more generalized political aspirations than simple love of a young human being.[37]

Most of the persons in his entourage were women. This made the role of two men in it all the more important. One was his governor, Frederick of Nassau-Zuilestein, a bastard son of Frederick Henry and therefore actually William's uncle. He was named to his post by Mary in 1659, when William went to Leiden to continue his education, although without enrolling at the university, as was usual even for such young persons. Amalia assented to Zuilestein's appointment, although she thought him too pro-English, because there was no one else upon whom the guardians could agree. It was Zuilestein who filled in as best he could the empty place of a father upon whom the child could shape his personality and his developing identity, and William was deeply devoted to him.[38] The other male among William's elders who was a force molding his character was a Frenchman serving in the Dutch army, Henry de Fleury de Coulan, chevalier de Buat. He was a dashing soldier, not very bright but recklessly brave.

From neither of them could the young Prince learn much about the political world in which he would eventually act. Zuilestein was always a soldier rather than a statesman. Buat was just a soldier too, but one of utter simplicity of mind, without any real comprehension of the world of statecraft. Thus William had Zuilestein as his model of mature wisdom and Buat as that of virile strength. Neither, as events would show, was the best of examples, but William's essential character had probably already been formed. What they did give their young charge was a sense of himself, and

36 Baxter, 21–22; Geyl, *Oranje en Stuart*, 176–77.
37 Japikse, *Prins Willem III*, I, 11, 100–1; Baxter, 24, 37.
38 Geyl, *Oranje en Stuart*, 177; Baxter, 22–23; Japikse, *Prins Willem III*, I, 69–71.

of course they reinforced the feeling inculcated by his little court that he was born to a high mission and to high offices. Observers were struck in particular by his ability to hold his tongue.[39]

We can only speculate what would have come of the aspirations he was taught if events in Britain, taking a course upon which the Dutch had no influence whatever, had not reversed the fortunes of the House of Orange. Oliver Cromwell died in 1658 and was succeeded as Lord Protector by his son Richard, who proved inept in office and let power slip from his hands. Finally the English army, in the person of General George Monck, brought back the exiled Charles II in the Restoration of May–June 1660.

Had Cromwell lived on and consolidated the new regime in Britain so that it could survive the test of succession – and there seems to be no good reason why inherently it could not have lasted in this way – then the fate of the House of Orange within the Dutch Republic would have certainly been very different. To the extent that the Cromwellian regime would have continued with its unbending opposition to any restoration of the Prince of Orange in the Dutch Republic as a threat to its own security, we can say with confidence that it would have required the most monumental of internal political overturns to unseat the established government. The solidity of the government led by De Witt was not really endangered by occasional riots, and by 1658, when he was reelected as councilor pensionary of Holland, he had already gained such respect for his abilities and leadership that the task of his opponents seemed hopeless.

Save for some miracle, the House of Orange could have been expected to hang on in its torpor, believing in government by "one head" but itself without a real head until William reached manhood in another dozen years, according to the normal requirement for majority in Holland. What he could have done to regain the position of his house, short of the intervention of some external force, is hard to say. It is likely that the Princes of Orange would have remained in a kind of internal exile, excluded from power, their once impressive record of achievement thwarted of repetition. It would have passed from the stage of great events, declining into a vestigial curiosity. The various forces within the Dutch Republic that joined to form the movement we call the "Orange party" would have continued to exist and would have found outlets in one or another way that we can try to imagine, but with a result that is irrelevant to our concern in these pages.

The customary way the history of the Dutch Republic is told, which makes the government of States-with-stadholder the normal pattern and the two stadholderless periods (the second would last from 1702 to 1747)

---

39 Japikse, *Prins Willem III*, I, 75, 112–14; Baxter, 37.

interruptions that distort the pattern, may be as false as the opposite vision of the followers of De Witt in his own time and in subsequent generations who saw the Republic in its purity as government without a stadholder. Neither John de Witt nor William III can be easily thought out of Dutch history. Both conceptions suffer from the imposition of a historical necessity that does not really arise out of the events themselves. But events which do not happen have no consequences in other events.

6

The first stadholderless period: 2 return

The event of 1660 that shaped Dutch history no less than that of England was the call to Charles II to come home from his travels. The Orangist party passed in an instant from apparent moribundity to vigorous vitality. The governing States party, in accordance with its principle of always staying on good terms if possible with whatever government happened to hold power in London, in the same brief moment went over from a disdainful wariness toward the Stuarts to an effusive welcome.

On his way home, King Charles was entertained in The Hague in the most ostentatious fashion, with gala banquets, receptions and entertainments. His sister, Princess Mary, was in constant attendance in this triumph of her aspirations after a bitter decade of defeat and (for a royal person) poverty. Her son, William III, watched too, although his future rather than his person was at the center of discussion. We know little about how he felt or what he thought then, but he was old enough to realize that much was at stake in these talks between his mother, his uncle and the councilor pensionary who had been the bane of the House of Orange ever since he could remember.[1] Amalia van Solms was almost a stranger at the festivities, present but neglected by the jubilant and triumphant Stuart partisans.[2]

Charles wanted, of course, the abolition of the Act of Seclusion, and it was repealed without fuss; but he also sought the parallel restoration of his nephew, or at least a firm agreement to give him the stadholdership and captaincy-general when he came of age. De Witt fended off this embarrassing request with the notion that William III would become a "great hope," to be educated for high offices but to receive them only as the unforced gift of the States when he should prove himself worthy of them.[3] The difference between a promise, which was binding, and a "hope,"

---

1 Baxter, 25; Japikse, *Prins Willem III*, I, 80.
2 Japikse, *Prins Willem III*, I, 86.
3 Charles II, statement to States of Holland, holograph, De Witt, drafts of reply to Charles II, 1 June 1660, Minute Resolutions, States of Holland, Algemeen Rijksarchief, The Hague, States of Holland, #436.

which could be piously empty, was crucial.[4] The king, still deeply uncertain of the solidity of his rule once he returned to Britain, put high value at
the moment on the friendly support of the government in The Hague and
did not attempt to force the issue.[5]

There was a peril to the House of Orange to which it was blinded by its
joy at the resuscitation of its prospects. This was that, by seeking the
advancement of the Prince from the pressure of his royal uncle, the Orangists were enabling Charles II to use his nephew for his own advantages
and those of his own country. The Orangists were putting themselves in
the position of possibly condoning treason if there were a repetition of the
war of 1652–4, and thereby risking the mystical marriage of Dutch nationhood and the House of Orange that was the central element of the Orange
myth.[6]

One immediate consequence of the Stuart restoration was the triumph of
Mary over Amalia in the guardianship of William III and the leadership of
the Orangist movement. She was readier than Amalia to put her confidence
in De Witt, not out of failure to recognize his deep-lying antipathy to what
he had agreed to do, but rather in her cynical certainty that the councilor
pensionary would pay the inescapable price for her brother's friendship.
Amalia was more dependent upon inner-Dutch forces, although she found
constant support from her son-in-law, Frederick William of Brandenburg,
and his envoy at The Hague was her closest advisor. She was willing to
play the game of inter-provincial and intra-provincial rivalries in a way
that Mary felt was beneath her dignity.[7]

In September, three months after her brother's departure, the Princess
Royal left for England for her first visit to her homeland in almost two
decades. Amalia did not go to the little port of Hellevoetsluis in time to see
her off, so tense was the relationship between them. William stayed behind
because his education as "Child of State" was about to begin.[8] The States
of Holland had agreed to take on her son's education, and the committee
Mary named consisted of De Witt and friends of his; the exclusion of
Amalia and her friends, and most of all of any representative of Zeeland,
infuriated the Princess Dowager, but to no effect.[9]

Accident – the event that no one expected – intervened at the end of the
year, as it had a decade before. On 3 January 1661 (it was 24 December
1660, by the English "Old Style" calendar), Mary fell victim to smallpox,
the same disease that had killed her husband. The delicate compromise
that had been devised with De Witt was put under great strain, but it did
not shatter at once. Mary's testament, fully elaborated and properly signed

---

4 Geyl, *Oranje en Stuart*, 195–96.   5 *Ibid.*, 187.
6 Baxter, 28; Geyl, *Oranje en Stuart*, 185–86.   7 Geyl, *Oranje en Stuart*, 189.
8 Japikse, *Prins Willem III*, I, 87.   9 Geyl, *Oranje en Stuart*, 198–99.

and authenticated, named Charles II to be her son's sole guardian, with all power over his person and estates until he came of age. This was a total denial of Amalia's claim of a share in the guardianship, which had set her and Mary battling in 1651 without a victory for either; it was Mary's last, posthumous victory over her mother-in-law. But it was also a blow to the conception of William III's position held by the powers that be in Holland, and this was probably not in her mind. For the councilor pensionary, William remained a subject of the States of Holland, even if the most illustrious in the province and now destined for service at the highest level. As such, he continued to be under the laws of Holland, including its binding regulation of inheritances and guardianship. Mary therefore violated the rights of the States of Holland as "superior guardians."[10]

The inconsistency of Mary's status – British royal princess and at the same time, in her widowhood and motherhood, a Hollander – had been tolerable while she lived, although it created problems. But Charles II was a foreigner and a foreign ruler, purely and simply, and it could be taken for granted that in his guardianship of the young Prince of Orange he would be looking out for himself and his subjects and not for Dutch concerns. How the Prince of Orange would fit into such a situation was a worrying puzzle for De Witt, but unlike some of the blunter-minded *Staatsgezinden* he did not want to abandon at once the hope of maintaining the "Child of State" plan and the educational committee for the Prince. But his upbringing would have to be wholly in the hands of the States of Holland, without the king's involvement or interference.[11]

When it became clear in 1662 that Charles had abandoned the tacit agreement made in The Hague regarding his nephew, the States of Holland at De Witt's initiative abolished the education committee outright and set aside the plan to make William a "Child of State." He's yours, they in effect told Charles, do with him what you will. If you want to educate him yourself, bring him to England.[12] But don't forget that while he is in Holland he is under our laws and has no special privileges. William's guidance continued to remain in the hands of Zuilestein despite Amalia's efforts to reduce his influence.

Although the "Child of State" scheme was put aside, the lion of Orangism had been uncaged, and it would not quietly retreat behind the bars of neglect and disregard as it had had to do after 1654. But for the moment it was a lion that might roar but could not bite. Amalia, supported by the Elector of Brandenburg, successfully negotiated a settlement of the guardianship dispute, by which she and Frederick William shared one-half of the

10 *Ibid.*, 204–6.   11 Japikse, *Prins Willem III*, I, 89–94.
12 This is what Van Beverningk told Buat, the Orangist family confidant, a year before. See Wicquefort to [Brienne], 14 Apr. 1661, *Archives*, 2e Sér., v, 208–9.

custody of William III and the other half was retained by Charles II. In practice, this meant that the king turned over to her the leadership of the Orangist movement in the Netherlands, subject to his veto over her measures and his readiness to put the Orange forces to use in his own advantage.[13]

The debate over the necessity to have a Prince of Orange in power continued to rage in print. The best statement of the Orangist position had been made in a "deduction" presented by the States of Zeeland to the States of Holland in September 1660, urging election of William III as captain-general, and no new arguments were adduced thereafter. The States party case was stated most vigorously in a book that has remained a central document in the history of Dutch political and economic thought.

The *Interest of Holland* by Peter de la Court, a Leiden cloth manufacturer, was a passionate affirmation of the superiority of republican government and a denunciation of monarchy, both in the world at large and in the Netherlands in particular; it was also a close analysis of the economic situation and needs of the country, with arguments anticipating some of the key free trade ideas of Adam Smith. No more than any other important writer on either side of the debate over the stadholdership did De la Court distinguish the stadholders from authentic monarchs. If De la Court had confined himself to these issues, however, the book would not have stirred up the furious refutations in both serious tracts and in a horde of pamphlets that continued to come off the presses for years. The particularly offensive passages did not involve the stadholderate, or indeed his economic notions, but concerned such matters as a denial of the necessity or utility of the Union of Utrecht for Holland and a statement of rank Machiavellian "reason of state."[14]

The attacks upon the stadholderate in pamphlets and formal treatises as essentially identical with monarchy were having an effect upon the Orangists themselves. Many, perhaps most, still accepted the equation, which both flattered the Prince and placed upon his shoulders the mantle of representing what in that age was generally considered the best form of government. Others recognized, however, that the republican form of government was established and accepted in the country, and they defended the stadholderate as inherent in the Dutch constitution, not contradictory to it. There was no thought of abolishing the rule of the regents as such.[15] The office of stadholder was not inherited, they granted, but they argued that it should be given to the Princes of Orange out of gratitude for the

---

13 Baxter, 31; Geyl, *Oranje en Stuart*, 210–12; Japikse, *Prins Willem III*, I, 94–98.
14 [Pieter de la Court] V. D. H., *Interest van Holland, ofte Gront van Hollands Wel-varen* (Amsterdam, 1662). Key passages in Rowen, *Low Countries*, 200–13.
15 Geyl, *Het stadhouderschap*, 63–64.

services of their fathers. "What enriches Nassau does not make the state poorer." The family inherits a right to be preferred in the election, like the Habsburgs in the Empire.[16]

Meanwhile relations with England were turning sourer in general, notably with the reenactment of the Navigation Act of 1651 and the persistence of claims for lost shipping that supposedly had been settled in the Peace of Westminster of 1654. Charles began to feel more sure of his position once his first year on the throne had passed safely, and he felt less concern about catering to Dutch concerns. Indeed, he went almost gaily into war with the United Provinces in 1665. A formal declaration of war followed quickly upon a clash off the west coast of Africa late in 1664.

Although this Second Anglo-Dutch War was a repetition of the first in that it originated in maritime and commercial rivalry, it differed crucially from the First Anglo-Dutch War in the part played by the connection of Orange and Stuart. Now, although a Stuart sat upon the throne of England, he did not enter war with the Dutch Republic in order to restore his nephew to his forefathers' offices. Although many of the Orangists believed as a self-evident truth that this had been the king's paramount concern in his relations with the United Provinces, it had largely slipped from his mind after 1661. Once war broke out, however, it returned swiftly, not as the primary English objective, but as a means of defeating the established government in The Hague. It became all the more important to English policy because it soon became evident that the English were not going to win easily; the Dutch navy had been rebuilt and maintained at a high level of effectiveness under the guidance of De Witt and proved more than a match for the English fleet.

The Orangists played into the king's hands by proclaiming that peace could be had simply by putting William III into office as stadholder and captain-general, and that De Witt and his friends were therefore guilty of needlessly extending the conflict for the sake of their own usurped power. The populace bought this notion, with its appealing assurance that peace could be had by an action that they favored anyway.[17] The king fed their naive belief with repeated declarations that he fought for that reason, although he always included capitulation of the Dutch in the matter of trade and colonies in his terms for peace. He went beyond mere words, however, and sought to arouse rioting and outright rebellion in the United Provinces

---

16 *Den Herstelden Prins Tot Stadt-houder en Capiteyn Generael vande Vereenighde Nederlanden, ... tegens de boekjens onlangs uytgegeven met den naem van Interest van Hollandt, ende Stadt-houderlycke Regeeringe in Hollandt, &c.* (Amsterdam, 1663) (Kn. 8806a), 108–13; A. van den Berg, *Verdediging, of Antwoort op het schandaleuze en monstrueuse Boek, Genaamt Hollandts Intrest* (Dordrecht, 1663), 1–3.

17 Geyl, *Oranje en Stuart*, 250; Japikse, *Prins Willem III*, I, 119.

through members of the Prince of Orange's entourage and some of their friends in the towns.[18]

Their first opportunity came when the councilor pensionary went aboard the fleet with several other deputies of the States General in the Autumn of 1665 to spur decisive naval action in an effort to win the war quickly. Storms thwarted the ambitious plans and De Witt had to return without victory and with a storm-battered fleet. While away, he had been ceaselessly pelted with urgent calls to come home from his stand-in as councilor pensionary, his cousin Nicholas Vivien, the pensionary of Dordrecht, because rioting and plotting were beginning to shake the stability of the government. In October two deputies from Overijssel proposed that William be given the supreme command of the army and navy, with a competent lieutenant-general to assist him, and that he be sent to England at the head of an extraordinary embassy to discuss peace. The plan, a masterpiece of political inanity, fell through.[19] De Witt had rebuffed the entreaties, putting the defeat of England ahead even of domestic stability within the Republic, but he returned in time to reestablish his effective leadership and to restore calm and self-assurance in the government. His friends and opponents alike recognized how crucial he had become to the government, especially in a time of crisis.

For the moment, the Orangists lost their bid for power, but they had discovered the key to success. Defeat in wartime could set in motion forces beyond the ability of the government to hold down, and determined opponents could unseat it, with riotous and rebellious crowds in the cities their instrument of victory. This had not been possible during the first war because then the victorious English had not wished to displace the Dutch republican regime but rather to strengthen its grip. Now the contrary was true, so that all depended upon who won the contest at sea.

As the course of the naval war had turned against him, Charles II had turned more and more to the diplomatic tactic of offering peace if the promotion of the Prince of Orange was accorded to him. He sent agents to Buat, who was so close to William III, to open an apparent discussion of possible peace terms with De Witt, to which the councilor pensionary responded with the knowledge of the States. What Buat did not tell De Witt was that he was also instructed to organize a conspiracy to overthrow the government and to put a pro-English regime in its place. Working with Buat in the background were Zuilestein and Orangist magistrates in Rotterdam. The plot went awry when Buat by error handed over to the

18 [Antoine de Gramont, Comte de Guiche], *Mémoires du comte de Guiche, concernant les Provinces-Unies des Pais-Bas* (London, 1744), 45, 57; *Politique Aenmerckinge over den Oorlogh, Tussschen Engelandt en de Vereenigde Nederlanden* (n.p., 1665) (Kn. 9,128), 4.
19 Japikse, *Prins Willem III*, I, 119–20.

councilor pensionary not only letters from England written to be seen by De Witt, but also another "for yourself" about the insurrectionary conspiracy. He was arrested and tried on charges of high treason. He did not admit that his actions had been treasonous, but the court found him guilty and he was beheaded. The Orangists saw him as a martyr, not as the clumsy if brave conspirator that he had actually been, and the hatred for De Witt acquired a bloodthirstiness such as had marked the hostility toward Oldenbarnevelt in the Truce period.

William himself felt the loss of Buat deeply, although disapproving his conduct and denying any knowledge or participation in the plot. Fortunately for the future of the House of Orange, the plotters had not confided their dealings to Amalia, who saw her grandson's advancement as a work to be sought from the Dutch themselves and not from the enemy. In any event, she and William had been away in Germany visiting the Elector of Brandenburg when the plot had come to its climax.[20]

Well before Buat made his mortal misstep, Amalia had broken decisively with the pro-English faction around the Prince. On 2 April 1666, she repeated a request to the States of Holland that she had made without success in 1663 that they assume the responsibility for William III's education, an endeavor that had been abandoned in 1661. Now it was accepted within two weeks. A committee was named of which De Witt was the foremost member. At the same time, Zuilestein was replaced as the Prince's governor by a Gelderlander, Baron Joseph van Ghent, and Buat was also barred from his accustomed place in his entourage.[21] It was a victory for De Witt, but only a partial and possibly a pyrrhic one. The States of Holland had conceded at last the principle that the House of Orange was an "illustrious" family and the Prince of Orange more than just an ordinary subject of the province. William became a "Child of State," although this was never a formal title.[22] The way now lay open for the other provinces to seek the Prince's promotion, that is, to put into practice the implicit promise of Holland's decision.[23]

William had sought desperately but vainly to avert the dismissal of Zuilestein, the uncle who had become almost a father to him. He did not protest so bitterly the sending away of other members of his little court whose loyalty was more to England than to the Netherlands. He vented his anger at the loss of Zuilestein at Amalia, and he never again gave his confidence to his grandmother.[24] He informed the States of Holland, not without at least a hint of sarcasm, that he would thereafter consider them as

20 *Ibid.*, 128–29; Baxter, 423–24; Geyl, *Oranje en Stuart*, 329–42.
21 Japikse, *Prins Willem III*, I, 121–22; Geyl, *Oranje en Stuart*, 318–20.
22 Geyl, *Oranje en Stuart*, 320–1.   23 *Ibid.*, 323.
24 Japikse, *Prins Willem III*, I, 127; Baxter, 41; Geyl, *Oranje en Stuart*, 322–23.

his "fathers." He put up no resistance to De Witt, who became his principal educator, but worked diligently and carefully with him, soaking up
knowledge from a man of peerless understanding.

For the next two years the Prince and the councilor pensionary met
regularly, usually once a week, for lessons in the craft and art of politics.
The instruction seems to have been in the form of case studies, with
explanation of background, fundamental interests of state involved, why
decisions were taken, and what consequences had followed. De Witt knew
full well that his pupil might eventually put him out of office, or at least
deprive him of his dominance in the Republic, yet this did not deter him
from providing William with an extraordinary initiation into the inner
world of political action and understanding. William had been given to
Their Noble Great Mightinesses, the States of Holland, to be instructed in
the laws, customs and predilections of his countrymen, and on their behalf
he would shape the youth who was moving so rapidly into manhood for the
tasks that would probably come to him.[25] De Witt undoubtedly set forth
the principles of the States government in the United Provinces and in
Holland, although we do not know how he treated the problem of the
presence or absence of a stadholder and captain-general; presumably he
did not repeat the arguments of the *Deduction* of 1654, and certainly he did
not diminish William's determination to become stadholder and captain-
general.

What the Prince also seems to have acquired, although we do not have
direct evidence for this but only his conduct in later years, was a knowledge
of how politics was done in the United Provinces, how persuasion was
combined with pressure and how States assemblies were managed.
Decades later, an English friend heard William speak of his admiration
for De Witt. He had learned more about the world from him than from all
his teachers, he said, and he described the lessons that the councilor pensionary had given him.[26]

Another product of this period of instruction and learning was a change
in the character of their relationship from the impersonality that had
marked it since William's infancy to an ambiguous mixture of personal
respect, perhaps with even a hint of liking, and continued and undimin-

---

25 Japikse, *Prins Willem III*, I, 151.
26 *Verdedigende Redenvoering Voor de Ere van de Doorlugtigen, Getrouwen en Doorsigtigen
Grondleggger der Nederlandsche Vryheid Willem den Eersten*, (Leiden, 1779), 62. This is a
reprint of the first Dutch translation, published in The Hague in 1734. The author of the
anonymous work, identified only as "a nobleman of Middlesex" (*een Edelman uit Middlesex*), was actually James Johnston, a "gentleman" but not a peer. The bibliographic origin
of the work is obscure: the passage involved is not found in Johnston's anonymous
*Panegyrical Essays upon the Prayer Lord, Pity the People: the only words of William I,
Prince of Orange*, either in the original edition (London, 1716) or later editions.

ished hostility in their political principles. De Witt had never been personally hostile to William, for purely personal considerations normally weighed little with him.[27] As for the Prince, he proceeded over the years with a cool deliberation, a readiness to take risks, and a steadiness of purpose that was so much like De Witt's that one is tempted to attribute a little of these traits to the councilor pensionary's instruction and example.[28] What certainly did not come from De Witt was William's immense pride of ancestry, the sense that he was both a Dutchman and a member of the royal caste of Europe, his certitude that he had been called by God to the leadership of the country. He was a "royal person" in a republic.[29]

Even while he played the teacher, De Witt continued to guide the destinies of the Dutch Republic with extraordinary success. During 1666 the tide of battle ebbed and flowed at sea, but by the next year the Dutch fleet was ready for a strategic campaign which De Witt had first envisioned during the First Anglo-Dutch War but was only able to put into effect after a long work of rebuilding, preparation and finding a fleet commander, Michael de Ruyter, who was both an admiral of genius and politically not an Orangist. Nonetheless the councilor pensionary arranged for his brother Cornelius to go with the fleet as deputy plenipotentiary of the States General to take the responsibility of risks that even the boldest of naval commanders did not like to assume. The fleet sailed into the mouth of the Thames in June 1667 and upriver to the Medway, where the great chain was broken and the ships of the English fleet, still at anchor, were either captured or burned where they lay. After setting fires ashore in the shipyards, the Dutch sailed their fleet safely home, taking off as a supremely insulting prize the flagship *Royal Charles*.

There had been no resistance by the stunned English. Only a month later Charles made peace with the United Provinces at Breda. De Witt's triumph was complete, but he tempered the Dutch demands because the French king, Louis XIV, had already opened the invasion of the Spanish Netherlands in what became known as the War of Devolution, and a Dutch–English coalition might well be required to forestall total conquest of the buffer country between the Dutch Republic and France. Charles gained no advantage over the Dutch. The exchange of fur-producing New Netherlands for sugar-growing Surinam was seen at the time as favoring the Dutch; the Navigation Act was relaxed to permit the Dutch to import some continental goods into England; and the Dutch rule for neutral shipping in wartime was accepted. De Witt and the regime of the "True Freedom" were more firmly established than ever.

27 Japikse, *Prins Willem III*, I, 134–36.
28 Japikse, *Prins Willem III*, I, 126; Geyl, *Oranje en Stuart*, 390–91.
29 Geyl, *Oranje en Stuart*, 391; Japikse, *Prins Willem III*, I, 145–46.

The conclusion of the peace at Breda was followed by the adoption of an "Eternal Edict" by the States of Holland on 5 August, less than a week later, abolishing the stadholderate in the province and interposing a veto on the election as captain-general by the States General of anyone elected as stadholder in any other province. All present and future members of the States of Holland and all persons holding office in the province were required to take an oath to the Eternal Edict. Another resolution provided, however, for William's entry into the Council of State.

The abolition of the stadholderate went beyond even the Act of Seclusion, which had been repealed in 1660. But the captaincy-general remained open to the Prince of Orange, provided he gave up all aspiration to the stadholdership elsewhere. William could become a servant of the Republic as the commander of its armed forces, but only shorn of all political power. The edict was therefore a victory for De Witt's doctrine that the political and military leadership should never be combined in a single person, lest he seize an opportunity to make himself sovereign.

The reaction of the country to the Eternal Edict was what might have been expected. The friends of the Prince of Orange denounced it as intolerable ingratitude and as constitutionally invalid, depriving him of what was rightfully his. De Witt's friends were delighted, although the more extreme opponents of the House of Orange were disturbed that the captaincy-general was not also barred to the Prince. De Witt tried to explain to them that the edict was a compromise between the ideally desirable and the practically attainable (in later terms, that politics is the "art of the possible").[30]

Almost everyone painted the councilor pensionary as the author of the Eternal Edict, but the accusation (or praise, as the case might be) was as untrue as it was plausible. The initiative had come from a leading Haarlem regent, Caspar Fagel, who was well known for his Orangist sympathies and had been implicated in the fringes of the Buat affair. Unlike two Rotterdam magistrates who were definitely tied in with Buat and fled to England in time to save their skins, Fagel stayed home and protected himself by the Eternal Edict proposal, which proved his patriotic fidelity. The councilor pensionary at first had demurred, but then went along. Only a handful of insiders knew the true story, however, and they had no reason to broadcast it. De Witt's denial of his authorship was no more successful now than it had been in the Seclusion affair, and for Orangists he remained daubed with an even thicker reputation as an opponent of the Prince who would balk at no trick to prevent his advancement. We have no indication that William himself was aware of Fagel's role, for he never ceased to see the Haarlemmer as one of his most faithful as well as most talented supporters.[31]

30 Geyl, *Oranje en Stuart*, 365.   31 *Ibid.*, 362–64; Japikse, *Prins Willem III*, I, 137–8.

Without aiming overtly at the stadholderate, William prepared to gain all the lesser offices open to him as well as the captaincy-general. Not yet seventeen years of age when the Eternal Edict was adopted, he was still younger than Maurice had been when he became stadholder of Holland and Zeeland in 1585, but if anything William was even more toughened by experience. He was taciturn, with intense emotions held under strict control and turned inward. He had few close friends, but to them he was deeply grateful and loyal. He won men over not by charm but by what he stood for and by his strength of leadership. His mind was sharp, but would show itself averse to abstractions. His will was strong, although channeled by the judgments of his mind; command, military and naval, came easily to him.[32]

His fate and fortune would be determined by events abroad, however, no less than by what he was in his own person. This had always been true with regard to England, but it became a crucial part of Dutch politics as it concerned him after 1662. In that year France and the States General entered into an alliance directed essentially against Britain. Each power had recognized that a league of the other two against it would present an immense peril; there was no other power that put any one of them in danger. Louis XIV would have preferred an alliance with England, but Charles II demanded a price in subsidies that the French king was unwilling to pay; the Dutch alliance gave him equal security at no cost to his treasury, although it hampered Colbert's program for strengthening French trade, industry and shipping at the expense of the Dutch. The mine that for five years lay unexploded beneath the alliance was the French ambition to acquire the Spanish Netherlands; agreement on some compromise satisfactory to both Louis and the Dutch could not be reached, and the alliance had been made possible by setting aside the issue of the Spanish Netherlands as if it did not exist. During these five years repeated efforts were made to find a solution, but what was too little to the king of France was always too much for the Dutch.

All the while Louis XIV and his ambassador at The Hague, D'Estrades, watched like hawks the stirrings of the Orangist party. William was Louis's first cousin once removed, but this relationship counted little compared to the uncle–nephew tie between Charles II and William. Restoration of William III would bring about of itself an alliance between Britain and the United Provinces in which the Dutch would be the junior partners. It was a threat to his own security and to his ambitions in the Low Countries that Louis dared not neglect, and he had pushed De Witt toward more rigorous opposition to the Prince of Orange than even the councilor pensionary

---

32 Japikse, *Prins Willem III*, I, 152–53.

believed necessary for the "True Freedom." It was Louis's suspicions of possible Dutch–English collusion that had made impossible any mercy for Buat after his conviction. Unlike his father or grandfather, then, William III never looked upon France as a natural friend.

After the death of Philip IV of Spain in 1665 and the refusal of the Dutch to concede the Spanish Netherlands to him while at the same time requiring him to enter the naval war with England, Louis finally lost patience and sent his armies into the Spanish Netherlands in May 1667. The invasion contributed to the willingness of both the Dutch and the English to make peace at Breda two months later, and they followed this with an alliance made at The Hague in January 1668 (called the "Triple Alliance" when it was joined by Sweden) to impose peace upon both France and Spain.

The Triple Alliance soon destroyed the already shredded remnants of the French–Dutch alliance of 1662, although the French did not bother to denounce it formally. Instead Louis XIV resumed negotiations with Charles II, and gradually opened the strings of his proffered purse wider and wider until in June 1670 the two monarchs entered into an alliance (the Treaty of Dover) to crush the Dutch Republic, to oust the government of De Witt and to install William III as ruler of what would be left of the United Provinces – sovereign in name, but in fact subject to the co-protectorate of Britain and France.[33] Louis XIV no longer had any trepidations about the advancement of the Prince of Orange who would obviously thenceforth be the puppet of his two royal masters. The French ambassador at The Hague had ceased to interpose the opposition of Louis XIV to measures on William's behalf as early as 1668, but now such actions were looked on benignly. There can be few greater miscalculations in history than Louis's change of attitude toward William III, but it would be some years before the painful lesson struck home, and it was always concealed beneath a cloud of silence in royal panegyrics.

Meanwhile the Prince of Orange acted decisively on his own behalf. In 1668 he proclaimed his own independence, as it were, by going to Zeeland without the knowledge of his grandmother, with whose caution he had become impatient, in order to accept the post of First Noble in the States of Zeeland, which he held as proprietary marquis of Veere and Flushing.[34] He was received at Middelburg with almost royal honors. The speech of reception by the secretary of the States of Zeeland is full of citations from classical antiquity and the Bible about kings, including the famous passage

33 The English side of the negotiation of the Treaty of Dover is studied in depth in R. Hutton, "The Making of the Secret Treaty of Dover," *The Historical Journal*, 29 (1986), 197–318, but it adds little to the Dutch side.
34 Japikse, *Prins Willem III*, I, 146–48.

in Psalm 82:6[35] depicting kings as like gods. The journey, bold and well-organized, was William's statement to partisan and opponent alike that he would claim what he considered his by right when he judged the time ripe. Amalia acknowledged the end of her guardianship, and William became his own man, choosing his own political path and administering his estates himself. The legal problem of Holland's law, which provided that the age of majority was twenty-three, was swept aside; he had come of age at eighteen.[36]

When William entered the Council of State in 1670, he received the ceremonial honors that had been paid to earlier Princes of Orange. Although its powers of final decision were few, the council was a good place to learn the details of military administration. But it was not where final and decisive power lay, which was in the States General and the States of Holland.[37] It was time to terminate the education committee along with Van Ghent's governorship, and this was done.[38] De Witt and the principles of the "True Freedom" were in retreat, although still in good order.

William meanwhile had received an invitation from Charles II to visit his mother's homeland, but his voyage was delayed by the squabbles over his entry into the Council of State. As a result, he was not present in Dover when the treaty for a joint English–French war upon the United Provinces was concluded in June 1670. When he did go to England in November, a mere hint from his uncle that Charles had Catholic sympathies (his conversion to the Roman faith was one of the provisions of the Dover Treaty) brought from William a blunt statement of his own stalwart Protestant convictions. The suddenly wary king therefore refrained from telling him what had been agreed to in June. The Prince for his part became aware of aspects of the situation in England which he had until then perceived only dimly. He was deeply impressed and greatly encouraged by his reception in England as a royal prince, fourth in the line of succession after James, Duke of York, and his two daughters, Mary and Anne, both still unmarried.[39]

By the time William returned home in February, it was already evident that France was planning war against the Dutch Republic. The realization that Britain too would be a belligerent, not just a neutral, did not come for another year, when the war was almost upon the Dutch. In the Republic

35 *La Chasse du Prince ou Relation de la Reception faite à S.A. Monsieur le Prince d'Orange Guillaume III. en la Province de Zelande. Et de son Installation là même en la dignité de Premier Noble. arrivées les 18. et 19. Septembre 1668* (N.p., 1668) (Kn. 9,668), 39–43.
36 Baxter, 49–50; Geyl, *Oranje en Stuart*, 383–84; Japikse, *Prins Willem III*, I, 148–50.
37 Japikse, *Prins Willem III*, I, 156.
38 Baxter, 52–53; Japikse, *Prins Willem III*, I, 150, 154–56; Geyl, *Oranje en Stuart*, 394–97.
39 Japikse, *Prins Willem III*, I, 159–65, 168–69; Geyl, *Oranje en Stuart*, 409–15; Baxter, 54–56.

the Orangists hewed to their belief, which even Charles's conduct in the Second Anglo-Dutch War had not dented, that all that was needed to restore the friendship and the protective alliance of the British king was to restore his nephew to all his forefathers' high offices; there was not even a whiff of anticipation that as captain and admiral-general William would have the task of directing hostilities against his uncle. On the other side, De Witt and his party dragged their feet when it became necessary to name a commander of the army in 1672. Unaware that William's English visit had strengthened his independence of Charles II, they feared to put the baton of command in the hands of one whom they saw as the king's all too obedient servant.[40]

It was not until 24 February that William was finally named captain-general by the States General, but for only one campaign and with severe constraints upon his freedom of action. He worried because his responsi-bilities were greater than his powers. The Dutch army, which had been badly neglected by De Witt, had been disgracefully beaten by the little army of the bishop of Münster, Bernard Christopher von Galen, in 1665, but England, which had inveigled him into the war, left him in the lurch and on his own. He was compelled by the Emperor and the Elector of Brandenburg to make peace with the States General, abandoning all his territorial gains. De Witt, so astute and resourceful when it came to build-ing a great navy, for a decade the best in Europe, did little to remedy the army's weaknesses of numbers, training and command. He thought a land army could be hustled together by quick recruiting and appointment of officers at the last moment. He utterly underestimated the time it took to assemble troops, to train them and to give them confidence in their com-manders.[41] Even as the war came close, the soldiers clamored for the Prince of Orange, now only twenty-one years of age, as their general-in-chief, rather than Wirtz, the aging Dane whom the councilor pensionary had brought in. William set to work at once and found De Witt an able, dedicated collaborator in the numberless tasks of getting the army ready. Fortunately, De Witt's careful guidance of Dutch public finances over two decades provided a full treasury and a deep well of ready credit.

William had not yet broken with Charles II. As late as January 1672, he sent a personal representative to the king indicating his intention of seeking the highest offices in the Dutch Republic. He would willingly be of service to Charles, but only in such things as were not directly against the very

---

40 Japikse, *Prins Willem III*, I, 174–75; Geyl, *Oranje en Stuart*, 415–21.
41 De Witt's misplaced optimism about the time and efforts needed to constitute an army was part of the general States party ideology. A pamphleteer twenty-two years before had made the same arguments. See *Het recht Derde Deel van 't Hollands Praatje, Aangaande de Wettige Souverayniteyt van de ... Staten van Hollandt* (n.p. 1650) (Kn. 6,842), 4–5, 8.

foundation of the Dutch state. He was "absolutely attached" to the interests of Charles II "so far as my honor and the fidelity which I owe this state permit" – a proviso which stripped his offer of service of all practical meaning.[42] In reply, the king informed him he would go about his business as he must, "in the usual and open way."[43]

The work of preparation in which William and De Witt collaborated was far from complete when the storm broke in April with a French declaration of war. Actually fighting had begun at sea a month before, with a surprise attack by an English squadron upon a Dutch merchant fleet off Cadiz, which was beaten off with small losses by the little force of convoyers. The Dutch navy continued to hold command of the high seas and the Dutch coasts. On land, however, the war went very badly for the Dutch. Louis XIV's army skirted the Spanish Netherlands and came down upon the United Provinces from the German Rhineland to the east. The French broke across the frontier in June, and drove the Dutch defenders back until they were west of Utrecht, half-way across the country, late in the month. There the Dutch flooded the low-lying polder country by opening the dikes, and the danger from the French was stemmed for the moment.

The more immediate peril became collapse from within. From the first news of the French crossing of the border, rioting had begun to break out here and there in the country, but it was not until late in the month when the military danger had already lessened that disorders resumed, so widespread and so violent that civil authority was almost overwhelmed in many towns in Holland. The simultaneous outbreak of so many riots seemed "strange" to one observer.[44] The rioters were not the rabble but the respectable citizenry.[45]

Eminently respectable, indeed, were the four young men who struck down De Witt in the streets of The Hague on 21 June. Although the councilor pensionary survived, he was bedridden with wounds and fever for weeks. The States party lost the steady hand at the helm it had known for almost two decades, just when the most difficult of political decisions – whether to seek peace on the victor's terms – had to be faced. The States General approved sending a delegation to Louis XIV, who by this time

42 *Correspondentie van Willem III and van Hans Willem Bentinck, eersten Graaf van Portland,* ed. N. Japikse (5 vols.; The Hague, 1927–37), II, pt. 1, 41; Baxter, 69; Geyl, *Oranje en Stuart,* 429–31; Japikse, *Prins Willem III,* I, 176–77.
43 Charles II to William III, 16/26 Feb. 1672, *Correspondentie van Willem III en Bentinck,* II, pt. 1, 43.
44 *d'Ontroerde Leeuw: Behelsende Een historisch Relaes van de merkweerdigste Geschiedenisse van tijt tot tijt voorgevallen sint de beginselen van desen Oorlog, tot nu toe* (Amsterdam, 1672) (Kn. 10,526), 28.
45 *Copie van een Brief, Geschreven uyt Rotterdam aen NN. Licentiaet in de Rechten tot Dantzich: Behelsende in 't korte 't Geene in de Vereenigde Nederlanden sedert den Jare 1648, tot den Jare 1672 voorgevallen is...* (Rotterdam, 1672) (Kn. 10,479), 18.

was encamped in Utrecht province, to offer terms that would preserve the integrity of the seven United Provinces while otherwise accepting great territorial and financial losses. The discussions with the king's chief ministers – they were never true negotiations, for the French made no counter-offers but waited for terms acceptable to the king, and these mounted as he became intoxicated with the prospect of total triumph – dragged on for almost a month.

Just when the French advance had stalled, and with the navy victorious against the English at sea, the rioting in the cities of Holland and Zeeland found its target in allegations that De Witt and his friends had sold out to the French.[46] Demands were raised that the Eternal Edict be torn up and William named stadholder. The Orangists were certain that this would bring peace – wasn't it the only reason Charles II had gone to war? One went so far as to demand that William be made Count of Holland.[47] With the civic guards in the forefront of the Orangist agitation and the regular army facing the enemy, there was no force available to put down the disturbances. Some cliques of regents out of office saw the opportunity to displace their rivals in power and encouraged or even organized riots.

Starting with Dordrecht, a movement for the reestablishment of the stadholderate swept over Holland; for Zeeland it was the chance to do what had not been politically feasible before. During the first days of July the States of the two provinces restored the stadholderate and gave the office to William. On 8 September, his captaincy-general was made a life appointment, and the restrictions imposed upon it were cancelled. William did not himself take the initiative in these events, but he did not act to prevent them either.[48]

By that time De Witt was no more. On 4 August, after he had recovered, De Witt resigned as councilor pensionary of Holland. But that was not the end of the story. During July, De Witt's brother Cornelius was accused by a barber-surgeon of having tried to recruit him for an assassination attempt upon the life of the Prince of Orange. The accuser, one William Tichelaer, was a notorious ne'er-do-well with an animus against Cornelius de Witt, who had found him guilty of attempted rape, and he had a local reputation as a pimp. He had gone to the army camp with a lady known for her easy virtue and had returned with new wealth in his pocket; but he had also seen

---

46 *d'Ontdeckte Ambassade van de Groot, Ambassadeur in Vranckrijck. Waer in 't geheym van sijn secrete Handelingh met sijn Complicen vertoont wert* (N.p., 1672) (Kn. 10,466).
47 *Waaragtig Verhaal van de Muiterij binnen de stad Rotterdam, die tegens de regeering ontstaan is* (N.p., 1785), 15; *Nodige Consideratien op den tegenwoordigen tijdt, en Een krachtige beweegh-reden, dienende tot opweckingge van alle Vaderlandt-lievende Ingesetenen van Hollandt* (N.p. 1672) (Kn. 10,597), 4.
48 Japikse, *Prins Willem III*, I, 207–9.

Zuilestein and the Prince's equerry. Cornelius was arrested, taken to The Hague, and put on trial for plotting the murder of the stadholder, a capital offense.

William refused to intervene on Cornelius de Witt's behalf, although he knew of Tichelaer's scoundrelly reputation. Let justice take its usual course, he had said, alluding to John de Witt's remark about the young man, one of the four who had attacked him on 21 June, who had been arrested, tried and beheaded. There was also the memory of William's adored Buat six years earlier. The course of justice was anything but "usual," however. Strong influences, which there is every reason to identify with Zuilestein and his friends, hovered in the background, and key provisions of the criminal law of Holland were violated during the trial, which dragged on for weeks. The gaping holes in Tichelaer's testimony were disregarded. Since his unsubstantiated assertions were insufficient for conviction, Cornelius de Witt was finally subjected to torture to obtain the necessary corroboration by confession; but even in the fiercest pain he would not admit any guilt.

On 19 August the judges nonetheless passed a sentence which was probably the strangest in all the history of Dutch legal proceedings. Cornelius was not found guilty, but he was not set free as innocent either. For unstated "reasons" he was deprived of his offices and condemned to perpetual exile from the province of Holland. Several of the judges were clearly coerced, as one admitted to his wife that night, but by whom he dared not say.[49] Meanwhile armed crowds had assembled around the Gevangenpoort, the little prison outside the Binnenhof, to prevent Cornelius de Witt's escape. The next morning, Tichelaer, who was released although the failure to convict Cornelius implied his own perjury, told the crowds outside that his release was proof of Cornelius's guilt. He called upon them to impose their own execution upon Cornelius de Witt as a traitor.

At the same time John de Witt, who lived about two blocks away, received a message conveyed by the jailer's maidservant that Cornelius wanted him to come to take him away, since he had difficulty walking after his torture. The message was apparently fictitious, for Cornelius was surprised when his brother came with his coach. Once in the prison building, John was prevented from going out with his brother. Only the presence of several companies of cavalry deterred the mob from breaking in, but rumors of a peasant attack upon the city led to their being sent to the bridges. William earlier in the day had declined to send troops to assure the safety of the De Witts, saying the soldiers could not be spared.

Late in the afternoon, encouraged by well-known partisans of the

49 See *Copie van een Brief, Geschreven uyt Rotterdam*, 28–30, for an Orangist critique of the sentence.

Prince, the mob broke into the prison, dragged the brothers down the stairs and outside, and slew them with muskets and pikes. Then the corpses, stripped naked, were hanged by the heels from the gallows nearby. The lynching had not really been the work of a mob in the ordinary sense, but of the civic guards acting with the rage of a mob and the discipline of trained men. Once they marched off, along with the distinguished personages and ordinary folk who had been looking on, the riffraff rushed at the cadavers. They slit them open, disemboweled them, removed their genitals and their fingers and toes. Not till past midnight did servants and friends of the De Witt family dare to come silently to remove the bodies for burial.

There is no evidence, or even hint of it, that William III himself was involved in the affair. To the contrary, he received the news of the De Witt's death with dejection.[50] Once the crime had been committed, the Prince had to act. He did not dare to take action to find the guilty lynchers, or to punish those whose part was general knowledge. It was not only that "everyone was guilty," as he was told, and therefore none could be tried; it was also almost certainly the knowledge that enquiry would lead to Zuilestein.[51] William was not a man of stern morality who put abstract principles of right ahead of all else. He was himself bound by his own convictions, but he was also a cynic who did not expect his fellow-men to obey them too.[52] He accepted the commands of "reason of state," the doctrine that in political life one must do what is needed for safety and success, whatever one's moral compunctions may be. And there was no question that the States party was beheaded now, as decisively as the Orangist party had been in 1650 when William II died.

The Prince went beyond merely refraining from enquiry, however. He rewarded Tichelaer and other participants in the crime with pensions and jobs, although he held them in contempt as verminous rascals. It may have been to pay them off as others had promised, or just to keep their tongues still. (Decades later Tichelaer on his deathbed admitted he had falsified the accusation against Cornelius de Witt), but either way the moral slime of the lynching stuck to William. It was not his finest hour. How strange, then, and how admirable, that for the next three decades he honored the memory of De Witt even while he condemned the principles of the "True Freedom," and that he gave his protection to the surviving family.[53]

Careful analysis of the downfall of De Witt and the stadholderless gov-

50 Baxter, 84–85; *Histoire de Guillaume III. Roi de la Grande Bretagne* (2 vols.; Amsterdam, 1692), I, 80.
51 [Adrien Baillet, pseud. Balt. Hezeneil de la Neuville], *Histoire de la Hollande, Depuis la Tréve de 1609, où finit Grotius, jusqu'à nôtre temps* (4 vols.; Paris, 1698), IV, 190–91; Japikse, *Prins Willem III*, I, 252–54.
52 Baxter, 274.
53 *Correspondentie van Willem III en Bentinck*, II, pt. 2, 744–45.

ernment reveals a course of events that was anything but predestined. The imposition of the Prince of Orange as stadholder and captain-general could not have been achieved by either the king of England or the domestic Orangist forces by themselves. It was only that alliance of the kings of France and England, the result of a stupendously gross miscalculation by Louis XIV, that caught De Witt in a trap not of his own making. It created the one situation against which his leadership was not proof: military disaster, especially on land. So long as Charles II and Louis XIV were joined in an alliance that ran against so many of their national interests, the councilor pensionary of Holland was essentially helpless. The military weight of the Dutch Republic was simply too small for such a task.[54]

What even the boldest of speculation that remains historically responsible cannot do is to anticipate what would have happened in the Dutch Republic had the two kings not made their alliance. Would De Witt have fallen, sooner or later, anyway? Would the Prince of Orange have ever gained the highest office he coveted? We cannot say, but to ask the question enables us to understand more clearly the course that events actually took.

54 Geyl, *Oranje en Stuart*, 226–27.

7

William III: stadholder and king

No Prince of Orange before William III had become stadholder at a more difficult and dangerous time. The French army had plunged ahead to the very center of the country, taking Utrecht late in June, and the way seemed open to Amsterdam and The Hague, only twenty-one and thirty-three miles away. In the North the bishop of Münster, von Galen, who hated the Dutch with all his heart for cheating him of his territorial gains in 1665, had the city of Groningen under siege; if he took it, he could make good his territorial claims in Drente and Overijssel. All of Overijssel, Gelderland and Utrecht provinces were occupied by the enemy, although far to the south the great fortress of Maastricht, which the French had bypassed during their march to the Rhineland, held out. In Holland and Zeeland, the core provinces, civil authority seemed shattered by the turbulence that had brought the Prince of Orange to the stadholderate. And William himself, unlike his great-grandfather exactly a century before, was a novice in both warfare and politics. It was, indeed, a time to try his soul and the souls of his countrymen.

The Dutch defenses, strained though they were to the utmost, held. William's gamble on his future paid off. Until well into July, defeat on the battlefield appeared certain. It was thought so by the French king, who followed on the heels of his army all the way to Utrecht, and by Charles II, even though a combined Anglo-French fleet was defeated by De Ruyter, the Dutch admiral, off the English coast. Actually, the French occupation of Utrecht was Louis XIV's last major victory on land against the Dutch in their homeland. The French army had been depleted by its very triumphs, for Louis had insisted upon putting strong garrisons into every captured town. Furthermore, his generals had not counted upon the defensibility of Holland west of Utrecht, where the polder country of diked and drained lands begins. It had been expected that by this time the Dutch defenses would have totally collapsed, with political turmoil completing what military defeat had not already done. The arrogance and greed of Louis XIV and his war minister, Louvois, in refusing the terms offered by the States General terminated the negotiation without achievement.

William III, 1650–1702

A new negotiation began between the chief English negotiators, the earl of Arlington and the duke of Buckingham, who came over in July to discuss peace terms, and William, who was authorized by the States General to talk on their behalf.[1] Arlington and Buckingham were surprised when they discovered that William did not think that the war was effectively over. He was impervious to the offer of sovereignty over a rump Dutch Republic that they brought with them. He preferred, he told them, to be a stadholder who was faithful to the country to whose service he had committed his life.[2] He countered with his own offer: a separate peace with England, provided the integrity of the United Provinces was recognized. He would accept sovereignty only if the Dutch themselves offered it to him.[3] Charles II replied with bitter anger: he would not break with France, and William must accept the protectorate of the two kings.[4] The talks continued through the next month, yielding the envoys only the unhappy realization that this young man was anything but a docile mannequin.

Accustomed to seeing the Prince of Orange as no more than the puppet of his royal uncle, Charles II and his ministers had not realized the strength of the Orange myth and the force of the Prince's personality. William's election as stadholder in Holland and Zeeland restored the confidence of the population, as was recognized by the more level-headed of the States party adherents themselves.[5] The events of July and August, whether deliberately plotted or the result of spontaneous outbursts of popular feeling, were put to effective political use. The immediate consequence of the slaying of the De Witt brothers was a political overturn in the cities of Holland that William had not imposed during the crisis of early July. In Amsterdam and elsewhere rioting broke out against the municipal governments, with demands that the sitting magistrates be replaced by others committed to the Prince of Orange. Even in cities with governments favorable to him, there were demands for a change, as in Haarlem.[6]

There was also an upsurge of a kind of primitive democracy, with "King

---

1 Geyl, *Oranje en Stuart*, 477.
2 *Ibid.*, 479; Baxter, 86–88; Abraham de Wicquefort, "Mémoire sur la guerre faite aux Provinces-Unies en l'année 1672," ed. J. A. Wijnne, *BMHG*, 11 (1888), 231–32.
3 *Correspondentie van Willem III en Hans Willem Bentinck, eerste Graaf van Portland*, ed. N. Japikse (5 vols.; The Hague, 1927–37), II, pt. 1, 80; Baxter, 89–90.
4 Charles II to William III, 31 July/10 Aug. 1672, *Correspondentie van Willem III en Bentinck*, II, pt. 1, 86.
5 *Copie van een Brief, Geschreven uyt Rotterdam*, 17. The same comment from the other side in *Den Bedrogen Engelsman Met de handen in 't Hair. Of t'Samenspraeck tusschen drie Persoonen, Daniel, een Fransman, Robbert, een Engelsman, en Jan, een Hollander. Nevens een vergelijckinge tusschen den Marquis d'Ancre, en Cornelis en Ian de Wit*. (N.p., 1672) (Kn. 10,480), 8.
6 Resolution of the *Vroedschap* (town council), 8 Sept. 1672, Gemeente Archief, Haarlem, Archief Stad Haarlem, Kast 27, no. 16, fo. 237vo.

Mob playing boss."[7] The rioters demanded not direct participation in government but the right to intervene to bring the Prince and his friends to power.[8] They expected that the stadholder would limit the arbitrary rule of the regents and assure a wider distribution of government jobs – *baantjes*, "little jobs," as the Dutch called them – that had been handed out by the burgomasters to their hangers-on.[9] They did not seek democratic government in the modern sense, but a savior, a magical, mythical figure who would "represent" them and restore the old privileges.[10] But, as a force that expressed itself through rioting, it was ephemeral and lacked any deeper unity than the Orangist slogan.[11]

William calmed the turbulence by a series of *wetsverzettingen*, the replacement of members of government in office before the normal election by cooptation, which in Amsterdam occurred in February each year. He acted upon the authority of the States of Holland, given on 27 August, a week after the De Witts' death. Those whom he named were all regents, exactly like their ousted predecessors, but ones who had favored him all along or who had accepted his advancement in time. An "out" faction replaced an "in" faction, using popular Orangism to its own advantage.[12] William saw to it that those he dismissed in 1672 did not return in later years.[13]

As for the popular elements, he had little compassion for their plight. He was as scornful of their ignorance and wild passions as De Witt had been,

---

7 [Johan Blasius], *Stok in 't Hondert, Op 't Burgerlyk Versoeck* ([Amsterdam], 1672) (Kn. 10,554).

8 See *Vrymoedige Aenspraek Aen alle Oprechte Liefhebbers van zijn Hoogheyt den Heere Prince van Oranje, haer wettelijcke Overigheyt, Ende Vaderlandt. Ofte een 't Samenspraeck, Tusschen een Oprecht Hollander, Soldaat, Bootsgesel, En Inwoonder van desen Staet* (The Hague, [1672]) (Kn. 10,291), *Apologie Of Verdediginge, van 't gene by de Gemeente in Zeelandt is gedaen, tot herstellinge van Sijn Hoogheyt den Prince Prince van Oranjen Willem-Henrick. In alle 't gesagh ende digniteyten van sijne Voor-Ouders Hoog-1. Mem.* (N.p., [1672]) (Kn. 10,261), and [J. de Rooy], *Stadhouders Eerste Geboorte-Galm* (N.p., 1672) (Kn. 10,635), 5, for explicit statements of this principle.

9 P. Geyl, *Democratische Tendenties in 1672* (Amsterdam, 1950), 313, 325, 336–37; Schöffer, "De Republiek der Verenigde Nederlanden," 198.

10 Geyl, *Democratische Tendenties*, 346–47; Schöffer, "De Republiek der Verenigde Nederlanden," 199. For a contemporary expression of this attitude, see *Tweede Deel van 't Wacht-Praetje, Over de oude Privilegien en Voor-rechten der Amsterdamsche Burgers, gehouden in der selver Wacht-huys aen de Weesper Poort den 10. September 1672. Tusschen een Sarjant, Adelboorst, en Schutter* ([Amsterdam], 1672) (Kn. 10,565), 8, 10.

11 See G. Hagius, *Afgeparste Waerheyt ofte Nodige en Naeckte aenwijsinge: Hoe dankbaerlijk de Magistraet, enige uyt de Vroedtschap, ende all de praesente Bevelhebbers van Leeuwarden tracteren hare Gecommitteerden, die sy, tot het instellen en bevorderen van de Reformatoire Poincten, op den 27sten. Septembris 1672. by d'Ed. Mog. Heeren Staten van Friesland gearresteert, hebben genomineert ende versocht* (Leeuwarden 1673), for interesting remarks about the structure and the character of the Dutch mobs in 1672.

12 M. A. M. Franken, *Coenraad van Beuningen's Politieke en Diplomatieke Aktiviteiten in de Jaren 1667–1684* (Groningen, 1966), 110–11.

13 William III to Fagel, 21 Nov., to States of Holland, 13 Dec. 1673, *Correspondentie van Willem III and Bentinck*, II, pt. 1, 315, 322–24.

and as ready to bring their rioting to an end, if need be by the use of force, once their violence no longer served his ends.[14] As early as 9 July, he had called upon the citizenry to halt their disorders, reminding them that it was his authority as stadholder that they were now challenging. Remedies for wrongs must be sought from him.[15] If "Orange democracy" began its rise during these years, it was not encouraged by its principal beneficiary.[16]

William's responses to the political challenges of these first months in office were as revealing of his character as any decisions he made at other, later critical times in his career. He was a man of intense feelings and a master of those feelings. He read astutely the chart of political affairs and chose his course with a keen awareness of consequences. He was neither a gentle nor a cruel man, but considerations of compassion did not deter him from making hard decisions. He practiced the principle of "reason of state," doing what needed to be done but not indulging in deception or worse for its own sake. He sought advice from a handful of close friends and confidants, but they did not manipulate him. He demanded loyalty and hard work from them and rewarded them well.

He left the details of domestic politics for the most part to Fagel, who had succeeded De Witt as councilor pensionary. Fagel was William's man, highly intelligent and diligent, without any compulsion to take the lead himself.[17] William worked well also during this first period of the war with former leaders of the States party, such as Van Beuningen and Van Beverningk, who had rallied to him in time.[18] William could also wait with at least the appearance of patience for years, then act with stunning rapidity. He was not a reckless gambler in politics, but as in warfare put his faith in well-planned and fought battles rather than in tedious sieges.[19]

The primary task of William III during the next six years was to wage the war against France. With the guidance first of field marshal Wirtz, the Dane whom he inherited from De Witt, and then of a German general of his own choosing, Waldeck, who became a close advisor and friend, he mastered the craft of war.[20] In a sense, he had other teachers, the very French generals against whom he fought, for Condé and Turenne, who

---

14 This was still his attitude in 1690. *Archives*, 3e Sér., III, pt. 1, 129.

15 *d'Ontroerede Leeuw: Behelsende een Historisch Relaes van de merkweerdigste Geschiedenisse van tijt tot tijt voorgevallen sint de beginselen van desen Oorlog, tot nu toe* (Amsterdam, 1672) (Kn. 10,526), 39–40.

16 Van Deursen, "Staatsinstellingen in de Noordelijke Nederlanden," 359; J. F. Gebhard, Jr, *Het Leven van Mr Nicolaas Cornelis Witsen (1641–1717)* (2 vols.; Utrecht, 1881–82), I, 151; Geyl, *Geschiedenis*, III, 738–39.

17 Franken, 34. 18 *Ibid.*, 106; Baxter, 110–11.

19 F. J. L. Krämer, ed., "Mémoires de Monsieur de B... ou Anecdotes, tant de la cour du Prince d'Orange Guillaume III, que des principaux seigneurs de la république de ce temps," *BMHG*, 19 (1898), 80; Baxter, 136.

20 Japikse, *Prins Willem III*, I, 197; Baxter, 92–94.

commanded the French armies at the beginning of the war, were the greatest generals of their age, and Luxembourg, who succeeded them, if more ruthless, was still very able. To claim that William was their equal, as does William's best biographer,[21] is to carry praise too far; the Prince displayed greater ability at organization and persistence in the face of difficulties than extraordinary tactical or strategic talents.[22] We might say that he carried mere competence as far as it could go.

His most brilliant military achievement during the Dutch War, as the conflict is known in history, was a bold winter sweep up the Rhineland to capture Bonn, the principal French arsenal.[23] As a result the French withdrew from their last positions in the United Provinces. The Dutch War became a European war.[24] In Germany the Imperial commander Montecucculi took the lead against the French, but in the Southern Netherlands, the other principal theater of operations, William III was the commander of the Dutch and allied forces. His dogged resistance to superior French numbers and skill limited the scope of French advances, although Maastricht was lost in 1673 and the armies of Louis XIV were creeping closer to the Dutch frontier in the final years of the war. French successes in Germany were more mixed, for the French allies, the electors of Cologne and Trier and the bishop of Münster, dropped out of the war in 1674, and neither side – neither the French with their sole ally, Sweden, nor the Emperor, especially after Brandenburg returned to the alliance following a brief peace with France – was able to gain a dominant position.

The crucial element in the situation was England. Defeated repeatedly at sea, Charles II faced a hostile Parliament demanding an end to the war and refusing to vote any new funds for its conduct. William turned the tables on his uncle, for he sent agents into England to stir up the opponents of the king, countering the commercial rivalry with arguments of the danger to Protestantism that Louis XIV's victory would bring, as well as the strategic peril to England from a French occupation of the southern Low Countries.[25] Britain dropped out of the war in 1674 with the Second Peace of Westminster. The nephew had defeated the uncle. The peace left unchanged the territorial provisions of the Treaty of Breda of seven years before, but in a momentous victory for Dutch maritime interests it granted the Dutch terms for the safe passage of neutral ships and cargos in wartime.

William now became a major force in English politics. His support was sought by both the king and his opponents, and he played his hand with an

---

21 Baxter, 94–95.   22 *Ibid.*, 282–83.   23 *Ibid.*, 100–2, 105–7, 135–36.
24 Carl J. Ekberg, "From the Dutch War to European War," *French Historical Studies*, VIII, (1974), 393–408; Carl J. Ekberg, *The Failure of Louis XIV's Dutch War* (Chapel Hill, 1979).
25 K. H. D. Haley, *William of Orange and the English Opposition, 1672–4* (Oxford, 1953).

extraordinary combination of caution and boldness. He avoided becoming Charles's enemy before the world, lest he throw away the rights he possessed in the line of royal succession after the duke of York and his two daughters. But he also kept in touch with the opposition and publicly stressed his own Protestant commitment, so patently in conflict with York's now fully revealed Catholicism. He ceaselessly reminded the English that, although they were now neutral, they would suffer like the continental nations from a French triumph in the war, and thus he undercut the king's secret subsidy negotiations with Louis XIV. William was therefore not just a royal highness in Britain who might one day come to the throne; he was also a prince whose interests were allied with those of the English Parliament and one who, as stadholder in the Netherlands, also displayed his ability to work within a parliamentary framework of government.

His presence in English politics became even stronger when he took as his bride his cousin, the duke of York's elder daughter, Mary, in 1677. Fourth in the line of succession in his own name, he now became second in his wife's, and, although James had taken a second wife, Mary of Modena, after the death of Anne Hyde, Mary's mother, none of the children to whom she gave birth survived. No living son came yet between Mary and the throne. Four years before, William had considered he might even precede Mary and Anne in the succession, but the marriage avoided the danger of a dispute.[26] For the Dutch, the marriage of the Prince of Orange to Princess Mary was an affair of great seriousness. It was a repetition of the binding in wedlock of the earlier William and Mary in 1641, and like that marriage was a matter of politics, not of affection. The prospect that the stadholder would also wear a royal crown came closer, greeted by William's own party with enthusiastic anticipation and, less loudly, by the revived States party with opposite feelings.[27]

In the Republic the progress of the Prince's cause during the war revived the fear that he might become overmighty. Within Holland, William had worked well at first with the new administration in Amsterdam, but that harmony dissipated as the immediate danger from France disappeared. Such statesmen as Valckenier and Van Beuningen, even when they collaborated closely with the Prince, were never his "creatures," and at best they could be persuaded, but never commanded, to do as William wanted.[28] When after 1674 the war continued all too obviously in the interests of William's grand vision of a European league to prevent French hegemony, with little or no direct and immediate gains for the trade-centered Dutch

---

26 [Constantijn Huygens, Jr], *Journaal van Constantijn Huygens, den zoon, gedurende de veldtochten der jaren 1673, 1675, 1676, 1677 en 1678* (4 vols.; Utrecht, 1876–88), III, 8.
27 Baxter, 148. 28 Brugmans, IV, 465.

economy, Amsterdam and most of the other cities in Holland began to hold back their consent to the Prince's insistent demands for funds.[29]

French diplomacy reestablished contacts within the United Provinces with some representatives of the States party. There might have been a sickening parallel to the Buat conspiracy had there been discussion of overthrowing William's stadholdership, but the talks went no further than proffered French terms for a peace that would be advantageous to Dutch commerce. The discussions yielded no results, for the States party still lacked effective leadership and remained more a matter of common moods and thoughts than of coherent organized action.

The departure of the French from the occupied provinces in late 1673 and early 1674 led to a strengthening of William's political position within the Republic. First came the decision of Holland and Zeeland in January and February 1674 to make his stadholdership in their provinces hereditary in the direct male line. It was followed by the decision of the States General to make the captaincy-general hereditary too. There then arose the question of the future status of the provinces of Utrecht, which had already been liberated, and Gelderland and Overijssel, from which the French would soon depart. Their deputies had been excluded from the States General in 1672: were they now entitled to return? Holland argued that the three provinces should be reduced to the status of reconquered lands, becoming "Generality Lands" like North Brabant and States Flanders, governed by appointees of the States General and lacking a voice in their own fate. William, for whom the provinces would provide a highly desirable counterweight to Holland in the States General, won their return to their former position. He reminded the Hollanders that some of their own towns had not defended themselves any better in 1672. It was at the Hollanders' insistence, however, that it was agreed that each of the provinces would have to accept "for this time only" a purge of their governments by *wetsverzetting*.[30]

William was elected stadholder in each of the three provinces, and they accepted from him a "regulation of government" (*regeringsreglement*) that placed in his hands in the future the appointment of the members of the town councils, the burgomasters and the high provincial officials, in consultation with those he named now. The details varied among the provinces. In Gelderland the town magistrates had formerly been named by the town councils from lists prepared by a board of citizens comprising guild masters and representatives of the burgher guards. Now this board was

29 Gebhard, I, 151.
30 Annie Henriëtte Wertheim-Gijse Weeninck, *Democratische Bewegingen in Gelderland, 1672–1795* (Amsterdam, 1973), 28–30; *Groot Placaet-Boeck*, 3 (1683), 47(misnumbered 37)–48.

selected by William himself, and he gave the offices not for life but for only three years. Deputies to the States General also required his approval.

The resulting situation may be taken as an expression of the Prince's vision of the best government in the towns. The authority of the States as the provincial sovereigns was not abolished, but the "members" (those towns and noblemen who had votes in the assemblies) had to reckon with serious consequences if they did not cast their votes as he wished. The nobles could not be dismissed, but if they forfeited his favor they could not expect appointments in the army, which most of them sought for themselves or their sons to supplement their relatively meager incomes from their estates. As for the officeholders in the towns, a good number were also nobles in their own right, while the burgomasters, who were elected annually, could feel the whip of his displeasure quite soon if they broke with the Prince. Retribution for members of the town councils who went astray would be delayed at most three years.

The domination of the stadholder over these provinces was large, therefore, but it was not, as is so often said, absolute. In law an absolute ruler does not need to persuade; command is his by right. Nor was the Prince's government "dictatorial"[31] by modern standards of arbitrary rule. The Prince found it easier than before to persuade the provincial assemblies to do his bidding, but their assent was not automatic. If the issue involved was important enough, they could balk, and he would have no legal way to compel them to act, only means of reprisal. Over the years the line of division between friends and foes tended to become obscured. There was in addition another cost to this method of political control. The regents who were sometimes treated shabbily and peremptorily by William's agents might not dare to resist or protest at the moment, but they did not forget their resentments.

There was no "regulation of government" in the province of Zeeland, where William's dominance resulted from his position as First Noble, but much the same situation as in the three inland provinces developed. William's lieutenant in Zeeland as stadholder and First Noble was his cousin, William Adrian of Nassau-Odijk, whose father had been an illegitimate son of Maurice of Nassau. Odijk's avarice and his hard-handed direction of affairs soon earned him the hatred, salted with intimidation, of the regents of the province, including most of those who had been long-time supporters of the Prince. This did not disturb William so long as Odijk kept the province obedient, and on those occasions when he did not follow William's wishes to the letter, he was sharply called to account.

In 1675 the Prince thought the situation ripe to make good an ambition

---

31 So termed by Wertheim-Gijse Weenink (p. 35).

which he must have harbored for years but had not revealed, or at least one to which he had been prompted by his friends and followers. This was to become duke of Gelderland (more precisely, duke in the quarters of Nijmegen and Arnhem and count in Zutphen, the fourth quarter of the province being still in Spanish possession). The initiative for specific action came from William himself, and the councilor pensionary of Holland, Fagel, was his principal agent.

The States of Gelderland made the offer unanimously on 29 January, but he decided it would be wise to sound out the other provinces before accepting.[32] He was stunned by the vigor and fervor with which it was opposed, not only by Holland but also by Zeeland, and not only among the regents but also among the common people.[33] The great majority of the articulate population, it turned out, had remained fervently republican; despite the sermons of the preachers and the rhetorical exaggerations of the poets, the stadholderate was still seen by the majority of its supporters as quite different from monarchy.

Utrecht and Overijssel were favorable, for which the Prince was grateful.[34] But that was not enough. The attitude in Holland and Zeeland was crucial. In this situation William displayed the flexible realism which characterized his policies no less than stubborn adherence to fundamental aims. Disappointed and angered though he was, he nonetheless declined the offer of the ducal crown and thereafter avoided confrontation with deep-held beliefs of the Dutch people.[35] But some of the magic of the Orange myth had been rubbed away.[36] The surprise had come because William had not intended any major expansion of his real powers as duke–count in Gelderland; he would have reigned as he had governed, in close and usually friendly collaboration with the States.[37] But he learned that a symbol or a slogan may be as powerful politically as a deed actually done.[38] Besides, he

32 *Conditien ende Verbintenissen, Waer op Sijnen Hoogheydt is opgedragen de Hooge Overicheyt over de Provincie van Gelderlandt ende Sutphen* (Arnhem, 1675) (Kn. 11,321).

33 *Resolutie van de E: Mog: Heeren Staten van Zeelandt, Rakende het Hertogdom van Gelder en het Graefschap van Zutphen* (Middelburg, 1675) (Kn. 11,324).

34 *Conditien ende Verbintenisse ...Extract* (Arnhem, 1675) (Kn. 11,323).

35 *Missive van syn Hoogheyt, Den Heere Prince van Orangie, Geschreven aen de Heeren Staten van Zeelant, Rescriberende op haer Ed. Mog. Missive van den 16. der voorleden Maent February 1675* (N.p., 1675) (Kn. 11,330), 3–7; Wertheim-Gijse Weenink, 32–33; Blok, *Geschiedenis*, III, 213–14; Japikse, *Geschiedenis*, II, 28–30; Baxter, 123–25.

36 Baxter, 131.

37 This was recognized by Nicholas Witsen, a burgomaster of Amsterdam, in a letter to Gillis Valckenier four years later. Gebhard, I, 157–1.

38 Brugmans, IV, 465–66; *Histoire de Guillaume III. Roi de la Grande Bretagne* (2 vols.; Amsterdam, 1692), I, 147–50. See *Presentatie van de Ridderschap ende Steden der Quartieren van Nimmeghen, Zutphen ende arnhem, aen syn Hoogheyt den Heere Prince van Orangien* (N.p., 1675) (Kn. 11,320); *Conditien ende Verbintenissen; Missive Aen den Heere &c. Behelsende eenige Consideratien over de Resolutien door de Ed: Mog: Heeren Staten van Zeelant Genomen den 24. Maant February 1675* (Middelburg, 1675) (Kn. 11,328), 3–4, 6–7.

failed to see that a duke of Gelderland could hardly remain a mere stadholder in the other provinces. The constitutional structure of the Republic would inevitably be bent and changed.[39] The débâcle was the last major political event observed by William's grandmother. Amalia van Solms died in September 1675, unaware that her highest aspirations for her grandson would be attained more than a decade later.

The ducal crown would have brought two advantages with it. The first would have been to make his place in the state hereditary, not elective. But this he achieved anyway, for Holland and Zeeland had already made their stadholderships hereditary the year before, and in the same year the captaincy-general was given the same permanence by the States General. The inheritance was limited, however, to his legitimate male heirs in the direct line only. There was no need for survivances such as his father had had. The second advantage would have been heightened dignity at a time when he began actively to seek the hand of his cousin Mary. Although there were other candidates for the honor, he rejected them after perfunctory consideration, for only she would give him strengthened status as a potential heir to the English crown. The wedding brought together a couple bound to each other at the beginning only by duty of state. It would take several years before deep love and strong mutual respect marked their marriage.[40]

A general peace had meanwhile been under discussion. A conference had met at Cologne in 1673 but failed because neither side was ready for compromise. Another peace congress assembled in 1676 in Nijmegen, but while the negotiators talked the armies continued to clash. William wanted a clear-cut triumph over the French but he could not override the desire of Holland in particular for peace, whatever the cost to the Dutch allies. The French endeavor to take advantage of the shift of the principal arena of battle from Germany to the Spanish Netherlands was nullified when Charles II, driven by a restless Parliament and nation, finally threatened in the Summer of 1678 to reenter the war on the Dutch side. A treaty ending the Dutch War was signed on 10 August, and it held fast despite the pitched battle initiated by William five days later at Saint-Denis in Hainaut, before he had received official notice of the signing of the peace. Like William's ambiguous reactions to the attacks upon the De Witts in the Summer of 1672, the battle of Saint-Denis became a blot upon his record, for it seemed a needless expenditure of blood.

Despite his disappointment, the Peace of Nijmegen was for the Dutch Republic an almost complete victory. It retained all its territory, including the restoration of Maastricht, and the replacement of the painfully high French tariff of 1667, the kingpin of Colbert's mercantilist program, by the

---

39 Franken, 137–39.   40 Baxter, 148–50.

much lower rates of 1664. The great loser was Spain, which had to make territorial cessions to France along the border of the Spanish Netherlands.[41]

The Prince retained leadership of the Republic, but his opponents still were able to block his more costly or risky ventures.[42] He could not carry the country along with his program of unremitting resistance to French expansion. His intellectual hostility to the policies of Louis XIV turned to personal detestation and even hatred when the king sent his troops into the principality of Orange in 1682, the one place in the world where William was indisputably a sovereign.[43] But this was an offense to the Prince of Orange, not to the stadholder in the United Provinces.

When France and the United Provinces resumed formal diplomatic relations after the Peace of Nijmegen, a new ambassador came from Louis XIV, Count d'Avaux. A subtle and persistent diplomat, D'Avaux was able to find a favorable response to his enticements in the cities of Holland, notably in Amsterdam, as well as in the northern provinces of Friesland and Groningen, where Henry Casimir II, William II's resentful cousin, was stadholder. They listened when he spoke of the advantages of remaining on neutral and friendly terms with Louis.[44] William might howl with rage when some of the private correspondence between D'Avaux and the burgomasters of the great city was intercepted in the Spanish Netherlands and came into his hands, but he could not get the States of Holland to inflict punishment upon the offenders.[45] It was not the Prince's doing but that of the king of France himself which finally turned the tide. The Revocation of the Edict of Nantes in 1685, followed by the flight of many thousands of French Huguenots abroad, and especially to the United Provinces, undercut D'Avaux's protestations of the benevolence of Louis XIV. The tension between William III and the States party diminished. The anxieties with regard to the resurgence of a militant Catholicism were greatly heightened when the duke of York became King James II in the same year as the Revocation. For the Dutch, James's accession meant a revival of the threat of the Dover alliance, and for William the possibility of the exclusion of his wife and himself from the royal succession – and Mary was still James's heiress presumptive. William maintained close contact

---

41 See *The Peace of Nijmegen 1676–1678/79 La Paix de Nimègue: International Congress of the Tricentennial, Nijmegen, 14–16 September 1978* (Amsterdam, 1980).
42 Baxter, 181; J. S. Theissen, "Iets over de verhoudingen in de Republiek in 1684," *BVGO*, 5e Reeks, 7 (1920), 188–89.
43 Baxter, 185–86.
44 Theissen, 82–83. A good discussion of the "parties" in the States General in [Claude de Mesmes, Comte d'Avaux], *Négociations de Monsieur le Comte d'Avaux en Hollande* (6 vols.; Paris, 1752–53), I, 25.
45 Theissen, 192–93; Baxter, 190–91.

with the forces of opposition to the king of England, encouraging them to stand firm but avoiding any open commitment to them.[46]

James managed the not inconsiderable feat of uniting Anglicans and Dissenters, Tories and Whigs, against him. This unlikely pairing proved disastrous to him when Mary of Modena became pregnant again and gave birth on 10 June 1688 to a healthy boy, named James after his father. The hope of the king's adversaries that they could be patient and undo his work after he died was made vain, while Mary and William saw their prospects for the crown receding far away. The English Protestants, making their needs the father of their thoughts, asserted that the infant was not really the Queen's but an imposter brought into her bed in a warming pan, and William and Mary believed (or affected to believe) the tale. William cast off his caution and accepted the urgent invitation of the most eminent of James's foes to intervene against the king. If you do not come, he was told by Admiral Russell in person, there will be a rising without you. William knew that if such a rebellion succeeded, the result would be a republic, or in any case a regime that deprived him and his wife of their right to the throne. For the Dutch nation it posed the prospect of the renewal of the difficulties that had come from the first Commonwealth.[47]

William's decision was therefore an act of desperation, not the culmination of a long conspiracy.[48] At stake were both the aspirations of the Prince of Orange himself and the possibility of creating a great alliance against Louis XIV, who plunged back into war in Germany in September to break up an alliance between the Emperor and the German princes (the League of Augsburg). It was another grand miscalculation by the French monarch concerning William III. Louis expected that the Prince of Orange would be tied up in a civil war in England while his own neat little operations in Germany would achieve quick success; then he could easily handle the conflict between James II and his enemies as he pleased.

Thanks to Louis's swashbuckling conduct, which aroused anew the fears that D'Avaux had worked for years to assuage, the States General, with Holland in the van, gave willing and vigorous support to William's English enterprise. The Prince had already acted to reassure the Amsterdammers, the key political and economic force, of his good will.[49] In November William set sail for England with the proclaimed purpose of restoring her laws and liberties. Whether he intended at the moment actually to overthrow James II he confided to no one; but it did not matter, for the king trapped himself in a hopeless position. In strictly juridical terms, the expe-

---

46 Baxter, 227–28.   47 *Ibid.*, 231.
48 For the conspiracy theory, see Lucile Pinkham, *William III and the Respectable Revolution: The Part Played by William III in the Revolution of 1688* (Cambridge, Mass., 1954).
49 Gebhard, I, 310–11, 322–25.

dition was an intervention in support of a revolt; in military terms, it was an invasion waged by a Dutch army carried over by a Dutch fleet.

The "Glorious Revolution" ran its course. James's inglorious flight was treated by Parliament and William as an abdication, and William and Mary were proclaimed as equal king and queen regnant in 1689. Their rank and station in Britain were far above those of a Dutch stadholder, although William sniffed disdainfully at the ceremonies to which he had to submit.[50] The overthrow of James II was politically the work of the English nation, and its representative, Parliament, gained the effective sovereignty. His position was therefore a duplicate of that which he held in the Netherlands, but with important differences. As stadholder, he was juridically a servant of the States, but he held numerous means of influence over the assemblies; as king, he was juridically a sovereign, sharing some of his powers with Parliament, but it was in reality far more independent of his influence than were the Dutch States. This was expressed in the celebrated quip that he was really stadholder in England and king in Holland.[51] In both countries he was able to maintain their participation in the war against Louis XIV, although protests began to arise against the great sacrifices and costs involved.

It would be exaggerated to say that the acquisition of the royal crown of England was a victory for William that turned sour, but it did not give him the joy he had anticipated. He found himself compelled by the same nauseating "reason of state" to accord a pension to Titus Oates, who had been the English Tichelaer during the Exclusion Crisis, and almost choked at what he did.[52] At the level of higher politics, he found that coping with Parliament presented unfamiliar difficulties, and he had no great body within the nation that was committed to him by historical memories and personal attachment. He had been in a sense a savior in both countries, but the English remained unhappy that their victory had been won for them by a foreigner. For, despite his fluency in English and although for decades he had been an acknowledged and honored member of the English royal house, he was never felt by the people to be truly one of themselves. He was called "Dutch William," and the nickname was truly bestowed, for his personal Dutchness never quit him and he was fully at home only in the Netherlands.[53]

England more and more imposed its dominance over him; it gave him more to worry about than his homeland, and in a bout of exasperation he

50 Baxter, 233–37.
51 Relation of Lorenzo Serandzo and Girolamo Venier, P. J. Blok, ed., *Relazioni Veneziane: Venetiaansche berichten over de Vereenigde Nederlanden van 1600–1795* (The Hague, 1909), 318.
52 Baxter, 250.   53 *Ibid.*, 398–99.

even thought about abdicating.[54] That he rewarded his friends from his Dutch days with English and Irish titles and estates – Hans William Bentinck became the earl of Portland, in the most notable of the creations – did not endear him to a jealous peerage. Queen Mary, who had always been English through and through although she lived in Holland for the first dozen years of her marriage, died in 1695 (1694 in the English "Old Style" dating). William was deprived both of the warmth of her personality and the stability that her willing sharing of the crown had given to their reign. Her insistence in 1689 that he rule jointly with her, not merely as her consort, assured that he would continue upon the throne until his own death. Otherwise, since no children had blessed their marriage, the crown would have passed at once to Mary's sister, Anne.

The barrenness of the marriage was of more significance in the Netherlands because it meant that the institution of hereditary stadholdership dwindled to almost nothing,[55] especially since William had been in frequent conflict with his cousin, Count Henry Casimir II, at Leeuwarden. Even before Henry Casimir died in 1696, however, William had established the count's young son, John William Friso, as his personal heir in 1695, but without obtaining for him the survivance for his political offices. The termination of the direct line of the House of Orange might not have mattered had William cultivated the good will of the regents.

He had indeed been a kind of "king of Holland," in the language of the jest, in that his attitude had been that of one who wanted to be obeyed. He was far too astute and familiar with the Dutch situation to use direct commands, but he had learned how to manipulate the system of States government with unusual effectiveness. What he had not done was to build up his own party, especially among the regents, establishing confidence that he wished to rule with them, almost as one of them, rather than as a quasi-monarch thwarted of his crown. As he displayed in a harsh conflict in 1690 with Amsterdam over his right to name members of the government there even while absent in England, he was punctilious about preservation of his own prerogatives while careless of those of the broad governing class of the country.[56] The dispute was settled by a compromise. William insisted, however, that Portland keep his place in Holland's order of Nobility despite his English earldom, and Amsterdam acceded.[57]

Such difficulties did not impede him in the conduct of either military operations or the diplomacy of the country, which became largely subordi-

54 *Ibid.*, 345–46.   55 *Ibid.*, 280–81.
56 William III to Portland, 16/17 Jan., Portland to William III, 3/4 Mar. 1690, *Correspondentie van Willem III en Bentinck*, I, pt. I, 67, 132–33; Brugmans, IV, 755–59; A. Porta, *Joan en Gerrit Corver: De politieke macht van Amsterdam (1702–1748)* (Assen and Amsterdam, 1975), 9.
57 Baxter, 260–62; Porta, 11.

nate to that of England, the senior partner in the alliance. He left most of the internal government of the Republic to the new councilor pensionary of Holland, Anthony Heinsius, after Fagel died in 1688.[58] Heinsius was less a party man than Fagel had been; he worked *with* rather than *for* William, because he agreed with his policies. William's trust in him was such that the government in the Netherlands, as distinct from his authority, slipped from the hands of the stadholder–king. It was becoming a government that did not need him.[59]

As in the earlier war, William proved his mettle in command by holding out against superior French forces and commanders. His diplomacy was fully the match of the French, however. When the French king recognized that, like his stubborn foe, he was not winning the war even if he was not losing it, the negotiation of a peace became possible. It was conducted at Rijswijk (Ryswick in the usual English transcription), near The Hague, and led in 1697 to a peace of mutual concessions. Louis XIV recognized William III as king of Great Britain but in turn obtained acceptance of the French territorial "reunions" of the 1680s. The Dutch Republic received from Spain the right to put garrisons into the most important fortresses in the Southern Netherlands. It was a peace that, if accepted by France in the spirit as well as in the letter, meant an end to the striving for domination of Europe that for a quarter of a century William had endeavored to thwart. For the next three years it seemed that the compromise might work, for France and the maritime allies agreed on two successive partition treaties for the Spanish monarchy designed to avert another war. Significantly, Heinsius, like the leaders of Amsterdam, was less eager than William for the treaties, which drew the venom of Vienna.[60]

The refusal of the Spanish nation and their king, Charles (Carlos) II, to accept division of their world empire between the Habsburg and Bourbon claimants destroyed the carefully wrought plans of partition. Charles died in 1700, leaving a testament that named Duke Philip of Anjou, a grandson of Louis XIV, as universal heir provided he accepted the bequest in its entirety; otherwise it would go to Archduke Charles of Habsburg, the Austrian claimant. Trapped between acceptance of the testament and with it the near certainty of renewed war, or allowing the Spanish monarchy to go to the Austrian without assurance that the maritime powers would fight to enforce the partition treaties, Louis XIV chose the more dangerous but potentially more rewarding alternative. Even then, the English and Dutch could not screw up their nerve to go to war simply to maintain the partition

58 [Anthonie Heinsius], *Briefwisseling van Anthonie Heinsius, 1702–1720*, ed. Augustus Johannes Veenendaal, Jr (3 vols.; The Hague, 1976–80), I, xi–xviii; Baxter, 258–59.
59 Baxter, 280, 326, 346, 369.
60 *Ibid.*, 367, 372; *Archives*, 3e Sér., II, 491–93, 593–97.

treaties. It was only when Philip V, as Anjou became known in Spain, proclaimed that he would not renounce his eventual rights to the French crown, and when French troops entered the Spanish Netherlands to eject the Dutch garrisons, that the die was cast for war. The declaration of hostilities came in May 1702 from England and the United Provinces.

William III was no longer there to witness the start of a third war against France. Two months before, he had died from injuries sustained when he fell from his horse at Kensington, one of his English residences. In the Netherlands the future of the stadholderate was again in the hands of the regents in the various provinces, except in the North where John William Friso had been stadholder in Friesland and Groningen since 1696.

In the three decades of his stadholdership, William III had consolidated the institution without changing its essential character. It became hereditary, but only in the direct male line. The powers and prerogatives of the stadholder were renewed in the other provinces, and in the three inland provinces the "regulations of government" were primarily confirmations in law of the practices of previous stadholders. The spirit of William III's government was less threatening to the regents than had been the few brief years of the administration of William II, but he had left behind resentment at high-handedness rather than the gross fear of tyranny that his father had inspired.

The combination of stadholdership and kingship created problems similar to those of personal union, but did not significantly change the internal political system of the Dutch Republic. What William and Mary did bequeath to the line of Nassau–Dietz was acceptance within the royal caste of Europe. How the new Princes of Orange would combine such acceptance, with what it implied of aspirations to a crown, with the consolidated practice of stadholdership after a dozen decades, lay ahead. William III also bequeathed to the future an image of the stadholder as a leader of immense strength, a master of politics and of himself.

8

The second stadholderless period: doldrums

In the absence of a direct male heir, the States in Holland, Zeeland, Utrecht, Gelderland and Overijssel refrained from naming a new stadholder. What Dutch historians call the "second stadholderless period" began.

The name is not strictly accurate, for John William Friso was already stadholder in Friesland and Groningen, although at fourteen years of age he was too young to exercise the office himself. Yet, without the stadholdership of Holland, he – or whoever acted for him until he came of age – had little in the way of real power, and the historical label for the period is essentially correct.

Those who decided against calling John William Friso down from Leeuwarden were not passionate believers in the "True Freedom" seizing an unanticipated opportunity, but men safely and securely in offices to which they had been named by William III or at his behest. The most important officeholder in the country was the councilor pensionary of Holland, and Heinsius was a gifted servant of those in power; but he was no leader, no master: he was cast in the mold of Cats, not of Oldenbarnevelt or De Witt. The "grief and consternation" into which he said the country was thrown by William's death[1] were certainly his own, and he took the lead when the States of Holland came as a body to the States General on 25 March to urge that the other provinces "join hands" in mutual trust and fidelity to "heal this deep wound", the deprivation of a "supreme head."[2] He did not, however, call for the remedy of a new stadholder. His supreme aim was to hold the United Provinces firmly within the alliance against Louis XIV. As long as he achieved this, he was willing, if not precisely happy, to go along with the regents who had been decidedly unhappy with their rough treatment by William and by his subordination of Dutch to general European interests.

The tie between the country and the House of Orange for more than a

---

1 Heinsius to Van Vrijbergen, 24 Mar. 1702, Heinsius, I, 25.
2 Blok, *Geschiedenis*, III, 309; *Verklaringen van de respective Provincien gedaen ter Vergaderinge van haer Hoogh Mog., tot onderhoudinge van Eendracht, tot bescherminge van den Staet, ende tot handthavinge van de Gemeene sake* (The Hague, 1702), (Kn. 14,748).

century did not extend to the abstract constitutional concept of a stadholder. At the intellectual level, it was recognized that the House of Orange had merged with its cousins of Nassau–Dietz, but John William Friso was not yet seen by the populace as "Our Prince." Whatever disorders occurred were not directed toward gaining his elevation to the stadholderate but against the holdovers from the regime of William III. In Zeeland, traditionally the most Orangist of the provinces, there was deep hatred for Odijk, William's creature who was notoriously corrupt and hard-handed in his government. On 3 April he was ousted by the States of Zeeland as deputy of the First Noble and the office was left vacant.

Nowhere were events in the wake of William's death more turbulent than in Gelderland. On 8 April 1702, the States of the province voted to abolish the hated "regulation of government." The right to elect their own members as well as to appoint lesser officials was given back to the town councils, but the town councilors (*vroedschappen*) would sit for terms of three years or less, not for life, as before. Those who had been named to the governments by William III would, however, remain in office.

The result was a conflict between the sitting regents, called the *Oude Plooi* (Old Crew) and those who had been expelled in 1675, or their descendants, called the *Nieuwe Plooi* (New Crew). Rioting broke out quickly among the common people in Nijmegen, the chief city of Gelderland, and the guilds were able to obtain the right to choose thirty-one *gemeenslieden* (men of the commons) to share in the municipal government with the regents. Similar movements occurred elsewhere, with similar success. The victory of the "New Crew" was not long-lived, however. In 1717 the States of Gelderland decreed that municipal offices would henceforth be held again for life; the burghers would keep only the right to present a double list of candidates to the councils. The "Old Crew" had won out at last.[3] Their triumph also implied that the appointments made by William III under the "regulation of government" were proper and legal.[4]

The testament of William III, which was opened at The Hague on 8 May 1702, in the presence of Princess Amalia of Anhalt, the dowager of Nassau–Dietz, and the English ambassador, Stanhope, named John William Friso universal heir. The States General, named general executors, avoided making a decision upon the rights of the rival claimants, and a temporary agreement was reached for the administration of the estates in the meanwhile. The dispute lingered on like a festering sore for three decades, until in 1732 an agreement was reached that gave most of the

3 Wertheim-Gijse Weenink, 35–43, 68–69, 74–77, 81–83, 88–89; W. F. Wertheim and A. H. Wertheim-Gijse Weenink, *Burgers in verzet tegen regenten-heerschappij: Onrust in Sticht en Oversticht (1703–1706)* (Amsterdam, 1976), 8–10.
4 Antoni Brants, *Bijdrage tot de geschiedenis der Geldersche Plooierijen* (Leiden, 1874), iv.

estates of the House of Orange outside the Netherlands to Frederick William I, who had succeeded to the Prussian throne in 1713, while those within the boundaries of the Republic remained with the House of Orange–Nassau, as the combined dynasty was now called.

The novel element in the situation had been the candidacy of a foreign monarch. King Frederick I of Prussia, the father of Frederick William I, had sought for himself both the private heritage of the House of Orange and its political place in the Netherlands. His claim as heir to the estate rested upon the testament of Frederick Henry, whose daughter had married his own father, Frederick William, the "Great Elector" of Brandenburg, whereas the grant of office was in the hands of sovereign States. Frederick I came to The Hague in person in 1702 not only to press his private claims but also to try to realize his political dreams. He hoped that the States of Holland would name him stadholder, an incredibly wild misreading of the possibilities. Indeed, Holland did not even permit him to enter the province in his official capacity but only incognito – a slap in the face he accepted. Thwarted in Holland, he made more vigorous efforts to gain political power in Zeeland, where three regents were implicated in a plot to obtain his recognition as marquis of Veere and Flushing. Whatever slim chances of success he may have had were foiled when the States General sent a delegation to Middelburg in February 1703 that took vigorous counter-measures.[5]

John William Friso's continuing ambition, which was not an outsider's aberration, was a more serious matter. He was unquestionably Dutch in birth, upbringing and attitude. He came of age in August 1703, when he turned sixteen years of age. He had completed his formal studies at Utrecht and began a different kind of education in the army. Once it became clear that the other provinces would not follow Friesland and Groningen in electing him as their stadholder, he put the political aspirations of his House aside until a more auspicious time and sought immediately the generalship of the army. Heinsius made proposals on his behalf, but they were repeatedly blocked by Holland, and he had to settle for a lesser rank and was promised a seat in the Council of State. When he attained the set age in 1707, Holland, supported by Zeeland and Utrecht, blocked his entry into the council because he was on active duty with the army.[6]

John William Friso, whose pride of rank made him haughty and harsh, strengthened his place within the European ruling caste by marrying Maria Louise, the daughter of the landgrave of Hesse–Kassel, in 1709. A woman of intelligence and sensitivity, she soon began to win the affection

5 Porta, 127–28, 130–31; A. J. Veenendaal, Jr, "De Republiek voor het laatst als grote mogendheid, 1702–1727," in: *Algemene Geschiedenis*, IX, 16–17.
6 Blok, *Geschiedenis*, III, 315–16.

of the populace in Friesland and Groningen, who bestowed upon her the fond nickname of "Marijke (or Maaike) Meu." They looked forward to the time when "Prince Friso's flame [would] bring forth a son."[7] John William Friso meanwhile continued to build his own reputation as a courageous and competent officer in the field to whom the supreme command that he still sought might some day be safely entrusted.[8] Fate intervened in 1711, however, when John William Friso, hastening to The Hague to support his claims in the continuing contest with Frederick I and the counts of Nassau–Siegen over the heritage of William III, drowned during a stormy crossing of the Holland Deep at Moerdijk. In strange parallelism to what happened after the death of William II, a posthumous son was born to Maria Louise six weeks later. He was given the name of William Charles Henry Friso, recalling in turn the stadholder–king, the restored Stuart, and Prince Frederick Henry, his own direct ancestor; as Prince of Orange he was William IV.

As during the first stadholderless period, Holland again was predominant among the provinces. If anything, the other provinces were readier than they had been in the years after 1650 to accept the policies proposed by Holland. Only Gelderland, after years of internal turmoil, began to edge into the Orangist camp. The attention of most regents turned inward again even more than in the past, leaving national and international questions to the handful of concerned officials in The Hague – the councilor pensionary of Holland, the deputies of the States General, and a few others, like the treasurer general and the secretary of the Council of State. Within their towns they ruled with iron hands for self-advantage. In the neat phrase of a modern historian, they were "little local absolutists" (*lokale absolutistjes*), although they abhorred absolutism in monarchical countries.[9] The absence of a stadholder meant that the constitutional system was again, as in 1650–72, a pure government by and of the States, controlled neither from below nor from above. The dispersion of power and decision-making became more extreme than ever, especially when the compulsion of war, which made action upon questions of national policy inescapable, was removed after 1713.[10] On the other hand, only war made a central national policy necessary.

During the War of the Spanish Succession (1702–13), Heinsius con-

---

7 P. Idema, *De Plegtelyke Intreede Van Syn Doorlugtige Hoogheyd den Heere Johan Wilhelm Friso, Door de gratie Gods Prins van Oranje en Nassau, &c. &c. &c. En Syn Dierbare Gemalinne Maria Louisa, Gebooren Princesse van Hessen-Cassel. Binnen Groningen den 12. Martius 1710* (Groningen, 1710).
8 Blok, *Geschiedenis*, III, 316; Porta, 134.
9 G. J. Schutte, "De Republiek der Verenigde Nederlanden, 1702–1780," in: *Winkler Prins Geschiedenis*, II, 212.
10 Boogman, 403–4.

tinued to direct Dutch policy with a skilled hand. Like William III before him, he hewed tightly to the alliance with Britain and, less tightly, with the Habsburgs who sought to recapture the throne of Spain for Archduke Charles. The conditions of the alliance had changed, however. The governments under Queen Anne in Britain had no compunction about using their upper hand in relations with the United Provinces, their country's chief ally. The English took the lead in the naval war, reducing the Dutch to a primarily land role. The Dutch leaders for their part now could think of almost nothing but assurance of their strategic security by means of a barrier in the Southern Netherlands, and they won this at Utrecht together with effective economic domination of the provinces, which passed under Austrian sovereignty. Nonetheless the Peace of Utrecht marked the definitive passage of the United Provinces from the status of a first-rate power to one of the second rank.

Peace also came to the Dutch Republic internally, if by peace we mean not so much the absence of conflict as that nothing of political importance was happening. Only the continuing turmoil in Gelderland between the "Old" and "New Crews" was an exception. As the years rolled into decades after the Peace of Utrecht, the changed economic situation of the Republic became at once more stable and more fragile. Economically the country fell behind in the competitive race with other nations, notably France and most of all England. In absolute figures the Dutch maintained the same level of activity in trade and shipping that they did the century before, but as compared to the great competitors they fell steadily behind. Fiscally the Dutch situation became steadily more difficult. Although private wealth remained very large and the per capita income was the highest of any nation in Europe, the revenues of the state did not grow commensurately and the burdens, especially the immense indebtedness from the great wars against Louis XIV, did not diminish. The state could sustain itself indefinitely at current levels of revenue, however, provided it did not become involved in another war.[11] Dutch industry was falling rapidly behind the more productive countries. Agriculture, always technologically advanced and highly productive, became more and more the one bright spot in the picture; but in a country of such small size it could not carry the principal burden of sustaining a great-power policy.

Politically the situation slipped into a new ambiguity. The domestic power of the regents remained strong, perhaps more so than it had ever been before because of the absence of any effective challenge. Popular riots were less troublesome than disputes and rivalries among the regents themselves, and these were largely kept under control by the method of "con-

11 James C. Riley, *International Government Finance and the Amsterdam Capital Market, 1740–1815* (Cambridge, 1980), 78.

tracts of correspondence," agreements among cliques of regent families about the distribution of offices across the decades. It was a high price to pay, however, for acceptance of rule in any form is always eased by the belief that the ruler (or rulers) serves the interests of the ruled. This confidence was eroded during the second stadholderless period, and the hope for good rule was shifted from the regents to the Prince of Orange. The belief that the Prince was somehow immune from the human quality of self-interestedness grew greater as the experience of actual government by stadholder disappeared from memory or was limited to the flaccid leadership of the Prince of Orange in the provinces where he was already stadholder, especially after the death of John William Friso.

In 1716–17 another "Great Assembly" of the States General was held, repeating that of 1651, at the initiative of Overijssel. It provided a theater for the efforts of Simon van Slingelandt, the secretary of the Council of State, to urge reforms that would make the central government more effective. His key idea was to abolish the practice that all important decisions before the States General had to be referred back to the provincial States for decision; he hoped that the resident deputies from the various provinces, more familiar with events and confronted more directly with their urgency, would yield to argument and come to agreement. His zeal for more effective government was shared by few, however, and the second "Great Assembly" yielded no reforms.

Such leadership as existed in The Hague remained in the hands of an aged and tiring Heinsius, and after his death in 1720 in those of a new councilor pensionary who was just a technician, carrying out the bidding of Their Noble Great Mightinesses of Holland without trying to lift them to any higher vision of policy than the provincialism and localism which triumphed everywhere. Van Slingelandt, retaining his reformist fervor despite his setback at the "Great Assembly" and his rejection as Heinsius's successor, wrote treatise after treatise to urge upon the regents of Holland and the other provinces the necessity to make national decision-making more effective. He did not consider replacing the federal structure of the Dutch constitution by a unitary regime after the model of England or France; he argued that all that was necessary was to give the States General the power to enforce their decisions, particularly in the realm of fiscality, upon tardy and recalcitrant provinces. He also put forward, although more hesitantly, arguments in favor of the restoration of the stadholderate in all the provinces, providing an "eminent head" who would be both an arbiter among the provinces and a source of initiative in policy-making. Despite his intellectual boldness, he did not print his writings but allowed them to circulate in manuscript. When they were published later in the century, the debate over the stadholderate had been reignited and flamed higher than ever.

Van Slingelandt's "memoranda," as he called them, were unusual in that he was a member of a family that had been closely related to the De Witts but after 1672 had come to terms with William III. They are important in the history of the stadholderate because they express the ideas of a man intimately familiar with the operations of the Dutch political system, yet not bound dogmatically either to the "True Freedom" of the first stadholderless period or to the House of Orange through thick and thin.

He paid a price for this attempt to look at the Dutch constitution in an original way. A quarter century had passed since the death of William III, and the dominant forces in the Republic, especially in the province of Holland, had come to feel not merely that they could govern well without a stadholder, but that stadholderless government was a positive good. When the councilor pensionary's post fell open again in 1727, the States of Holland at last chose Van Slingelandt in recognition of his abilities, but put this admittedly brilliant and committed public servant in fetters. He was required to promise to make no proposal for restoration of the stadholderate. Aged sixty-three years, fatigued and discouraged about achieving his higher aims, he gave the promise. He spent the next nine years until his death carrying out his ordinary duties, his dream of improvement of the state set aside.[12]

It was not only the personal career of Van Slingelandt that became listless in these years, but also the larger political life of the nation. There were almost no major differences of policy or even of interest among the ruling groups of the Republic; politics became more relentlessly local than ever, the combat of pygmies in tiny arenas. The old parties, just spongy coalitions of local factions bound together by tactical concerns and a thin overlay of principles, memories and emotions, remained just barely visible. Even the authority of the States of the provinces was almost a fiction, for their various Mightinesses could not enforce their decisions upon their "members" – towns and Nobilities – as had still been possible in De Witt's day. The blinkered self-interest of the towns, always characteristic of Dutch politics since the foundation of the Republic, was less hampered by provincial and national concerns than ever before.[13]

After Van Slingelandt died in 1736, the same promise not to seek the restoration of the stadholderate was exacted from his successor, Anthony van der Heim, who was Heinsius's nephew. His election was a silent confession of weakness on both sides: the States party had no person of high

---

12 Japikse, *Geschiedenis*, II, 102–3; Geyl, *Geschiedenis*, IV, 995; Schutte, 211–12; J. A. F. de Jongste, "Een bewind op zijn smalst. Het politiek bedrijf in de jaren 1727–1747," in: *Algemene Geschiedenis*, IX, 44–47.

13 P. Geyl, *Willem IV en Engeland tot 1748 (Vrede van Aken)* (The Hague, 1924), 8; G. Groen van Prinsterer, *Handboek der Geschiedenis van het Vaderland* (3rd edn; 2 vols.; Amsterdam, 1863–65), II, 441, 435.

competence able or willing to take the key position in the Republic, the Orangists could not shake their opponents' domination, not even when the fierce winters of 1740 and 1741 brought food riots in Holland.[14] There was still no sign of popular dissatisfaction with the regents so deep and widespread that it put their government in peril. The common folk accepted the established regime even if they did not love it, and their traditional sympathy for the House of Orange persisted, but without effect.[15]

Only the growth of William Charles Henry Friso – William IV as Prince of Orange – toward manhood kept the old conflict and the old parties alive, if almost moribund. The course of events would be shaped largely by the kind of man he would become, the kind of leadership he would provide to the Orangist party, and the circumstances that might make it possible for him to gain the stadholdership in the provinces that continued to deny it to him.

Maria Louise saw to it that her son was well prepared for his future role. She imbued him with her own sense of what made a "good prince." He studied at Franeker, where Friesland had its tiny university, and then at Utrecht, learned law and what today we call economics, and became fluent not only in Dutch and Latin but also in English, French, Italian and German. Unlike his father, however, he had no taste for a military life, all the more because he had a somewhat deformed shoulder and a weak body (but such bodily frailties had not hampered William III as a soldier). He acquired the virtues of a civilian gentleman, courteous manners, sensitivity in personal relations, fluent speech, but not the forthrightness of a military man or the wilful character of a statesman. He learned well what his rights (or what he considered to be his rights) were, but not how to get them.[16] He was, therefore, a new phenomenon as a Prince of Orange, one who did not know how to take the helm of state and impose his own will upon the country. But until he came of age in 1729, his cause was in the hands of his mother and those about her in the little court of Leeuwarden, away from the center of power in the country.

The road back to power for the House of Orange began in Groningen, where William IV was designated stadholder in 1718. The moving spirit behind the action, which had primarily symbolic value, was not a native but a Frieslander, Sicco van Goslinga, who urged his friends in the sister province to follow the lead of Friesland. He reminded them of the popular "veneration" for the House of Orange–Nassau (was he merely stiffening their resolve, or using a very gentle threat?) and argued that supporting the restoration of the stadholderate did not violate republican principle and

---

14 De Jongste, "Een bewind," 47–48; Japikse, *Geschiedenis*, II, 105; Dekker, 118.
15 De Jongste, "Een bewind," 50.   16 Blok, *Geschiedenis*, III, 364–65.

that a stadholder was essential to overcome the endemic quarrels among the factions in Groningen.[17]

The next step was taken four years later. The election of William as stadholder of Drente mattered only as a sign, for the province had no seat in the States General. It was more significant when the movement for his designation spread to Overijssel and Gelderland. Holland, with Zeeland's strong backing, was able to thwart the efforts of Marijke Meu and her adherents in Overijssel, but in Gelderland they won out. Yet the States of Gelderland, in granting William designation as stadholder and captain-general of the province to take these offices when he reached the age of eighteen, bound the hands of their eventual "illustrious head" (*doorluchtig hoofd*). His instructions put severe restrictions upon the power that he would assume as military commander and political leader. Less important to Holland, however, than these limitations upon the Prince's powers was the principle enunciated by the States of Gelderland in rebuffing Holland's protest against their action. It was beyond dispute, they held, that the Prince of Orange was "the only born resident of this state who can be elected to the High Dignity."[18]

The danger to the rule of the regents remained slight so long as William was content to affirm his rights but remained ready to wait until these were granted to him by the sovereign States in the recalcitrant provinces, Overijssel along with Holland, Zeeland and Utrecht. Friesland, Groningen and Gelderland could not agree on common action on his behalf in the States General. Finally, in 1742, Holland was able to drive through the States General over their opposition a decision to name twelve lieutenant-generals, with William among them. He wanted only the captaincy-general and refused to accept the next highest rank in the army. His aspiration for the top post was blocked in 1745 with the appointment of a supreme commander.[19]

The dispute between the House of Orange and the States of Zeeland over the marquisate of Veere and Flushing had been going on for decades, but William let his cause flounder; he repeatedly reaffirmed his indefeasible rights but sustained them by no effective action. In 1702, after the death of William III, the States of Zeeland had refused investiture to John William Friso on the grounds that he was still a minor, implying the continued existence of the marquisate and the Prince's possible investiture. In 1722, however, when Zeeland joined Holland in attempting to thwart William

17 Goslinga to Van Slingelandt, 7 Oct. 1718, *Briefwisseling tussen Simon van Slingelandt en Sicco van Goslinga, 1697–1731*, ed. W. A. van Rappard (The Hague, 1978), 164.
18 Blok, *Geschiedenis*, III, 356–58; Wertheim-Gijse Weenink, 92; Geyl, *Willem IV*, 3; '*t Leven van Willem den IV. Prins van Oranje en Nassau* (Amsterdam, 1752), 27.
19 Blok, *Geschiedenis*, III, 365–66; De Jongste, "Een bewind," 53–55.

IV's election as stadholder in Gelderland, the States of the province considered outright abolition of the marquisate. His guardians, the Princess Dowager and her father, the landgrave of Hesse-Kassel, protested to the States General, who were executors of William III's testament, but to no effect, since the two towns were not under the authority of Their High Mightinesses but of the province of Zeeland. Nonetheless the States in Middelburg delayed for more than a decade taking the final action of abolition.

They were driven to a decision in 1732 when the marquisate was awarded to William IV as part of the settlement of his long controversy with King Frederick William of Prussia over the succession of William III. The States thereupon voted "by virtue of their sovereignty and indisputable power to relieve these cities of their vassalage forever." The sum of 250,000 guilders would be paid to William IV in compensation for his loss of property. He protested vigorously and refused to accept the payment, which was then deposited in the Bank of Middelburg in escrow to his credit. Fagel, the *griffier*, urged William to accept the marquisate as a fief of Zeeland, not as his "lordship" in freehold, but he declined even such a compromise. The Prince's position made sense in law, if not in political reality. If the marquisate was not his property, he asked, why offer him money for it? If it was, it was not for sale. The States of Zeeland replied that they were expropriating it for reasons of general political interest.[20]

The episode illustrated a number of significant points in the development of the stadholderate. Not only did William IV hold himself aloof from revolutionary action, he accepted without question the republican system *with himself in the traditional posts of stadholder and captain-general.* He was a wholehearted constitutional conservative, and he viewed the anti-stadholderians in power in the four provinces as the violators of fundamental law. Decades of accusations from the States party leaders and writers that the Princes of Orange had sought to become monarchs had bit into his mind and soul: he wanted only the rights and prerogatives that the Princes of Orange had held since the emergence of the Republic in the sixteenth century, those and no more. He wanted their restoration by the free will of the States, whose sovereignty he did not deny or contest; he did not want to regain them from the hands of the mob. He would not even play up to the Calvinist preachers, whose grip upon the populace was so strong. However, a Prince of Orange so devoted to law, order and legitimacy posed no real threat to the regents in Zeeland or the other provinces where the States party held the helm of state. They had nothing to fear as long as their strength was not shattered by some external event. "External event" is a pallid word, how-

20 Geyl, *Willem IV*, 3–4, 17–18; G. Groen van Prinsterer, II, 469–70; Blok, *Geschiedenis*, III, 366.

ever, for a possible repetition of what had happened in the "disaster year" of 1672; foreign invasion, the defeat of the Dutch army, followed by popular rebellion sustained rather than suppressed by the burgher guards, so that the government lacked the military force to maintain itself.[21]

The chances for such an "external event" were not small, however. The United Provinces continued to be located at the heart of European "grand policy," the fierce rivalry of the powers sustained by the twin means of diplomacy and war. For England in particular, the Republic was the one essential ally on the continent. For their part, the Dutch, even with the States party preponderant, continued to treat the English alliance as a permanent and unvarying part of their foreign policy. The anti-stadholderians thereby opened a door for a renewal of the interference of England in their internal affairs which had been so crucial during the decades of De Witt's administration.

English involvement acquired an aura of *déjà vu* in 1734 when George II gave his daughter Anna in marriage to William IV. Discussion of a renewal of the dynastic tie between the British royal family and the House of Orange had begun more than a dozen years earlier with a British initiative. It was expected in London that the Dutch Republic could not deny the stadholdership to the husband of the king's daughter. Anna, a young woman so strong-willed as almost to be called unruly, was ambitious for a position in which she as a wife could be more her own person, less dependent especially upon her intelligent and equally strong-minded mother, Queen Caroline; she even studied Dutch history and government to be ready for her new position. For Maria Louise and her son, this marriage would bolster his standing as a member of the royal caste in Europe.

By 1733 the discussions were moving toward accomplishment. The English government tried to overcome the recalcitrance of the Hollanders by a combination of reassurances and threats: the marriage, they were told, would be a "private and family affair" that did not in any way concern the Dutch government; but they should keep in mind that King Frederick William of Prussia had held forth the possibility that he would give one of his daughters to William IV, and the Dutch knew how such a tie would threaten their independence. How an English alliance would protect it was not explained. When Anna departed for her new home, her father said to her in French, "Va, cherche fortune" (Go, seek your fortune).[22]

The king gave official notice of the marriage to the States General, but

21 Geyl, *Willem IV*, 91–93, 101, 106.
22 *Ibid.*, 6, 20–25; N. A. Bootsma, "Prinses Anna van Hannover," in: F. F. J. M. van Eerenbeemt *et al.*, *Voor Rogier: Een bundel Opstellen van oud-leerlingen van de Hoogleraar bij zijn afscheid aangeboden* (Hilversum, 1964), 132; Groen van Prinsterer, II 470; Porta, 197–99.

their response did not bode well for the hope that the recalcitrant provinces would cease to block William's advancement. Their High Mightinesses replied with proper courtesy to George's expression of expectation that they would receive his daughter in a way worthy of her and himself, but they turned his words around. Since he had chosen a "free republic" as a home for his daughter, they hoped that she would be happy in the country's present constitution, whose preservation they took to heart.[23] Clearly the anticipations in England had been oversanguine. Far from easing William's path to the stadholderate, the marriage was stiffening the resistance of the party of "True Freedom."

The newlyweds made their home in The Hague for several years before taking up residence in Leeuwarden and at the palace of Het Loo built by William II. Anna grew even further away from her family, especially after the death of Queen Caroline in 1737, and she embraced more than ever her husband's aspirations as her own.[24] These ambitions were held with absolute fixity by the couple, but William could not bring himself to rise above their querulous assertion to concrete activity on their behalf. Members of their little court tried to spur him to deeds, but he preferred to follow the advice of the new councilor pensionary of Holland, Van der Heim, and the *griffier*, Fagel, who urged upon him the importance of patience. With extraordinary lack of self-understanding, he wrote in 1742 that he had made it a principle to do nothing that smacked of ambition or impatience. In exasperation he thought of taking up residence in Germany, where his power in the Nassau lands was not contested, but Anna dug in her heels against going to a little German town to dwell in isolation from the world of great affairs, and the couple stayed in the Republic.[25]

The "external event" which might make possible the full restoration of William IV came closer with the onset of the War of the Austrian Succession in 1740. The diplomatic situation of the Dutch Republic became extraordinarily complicated. It was allied with Great Britain and bound by treaty to provide it with assistance in such a case, yet there was no direct Dutch interest involved, certainly not in the conflict between France's ally Prussia, where William IV's cousin was now on the throne as Frederick II, and England's ally Austria, which ruled, lightly and benignly, in the Southern Netherlands since the Peace of Utrecht. Nor was there any pressing reason why the Dutch Republic should take a side in the conflict between England and France. They fought primarily over colonial domination in America and Asia, where the Dutch had their own positions to maintain. Alone against either France or England, the Republic had long

23 Geyl, *Willem IV*, 26.
24 *Ibid.*, 33; Blok, *Geschiedenis*, III, 369–70; Bootsma, "Prinses Anna," 138–39.
25 Blok, *Geschiedenis*, III, 370; Geyl, *Willem IV*, 59; Japikse, *Geschiedenis*, II, 106.

since ceased to have adequate strength for its own defense. Neutrality was the only safe course. Furthermore, neutrality, with its accompanying principle of "free ships, free cargos," was necessary if Dutch merchants and shippers were to use the opportunity of the war to expand their trade. Neutrality, too, was the policy that seemed inescapable to those who understood how weak the Dutch fleet and army were now, just a quarter of a century after the War of the Spanish Succession in which the Republic still took part as a great power.

The Orangists saw events more simply. To them the English alliance was beyond question, and it was the duty of the United Provinces to come to the aid of England in its present hour of need. The government at The Hague shilly-shallied, conceding a little to England when it had to and watching fearfully as the French armies under Marshal Maurice de Saxe carried the war into the Austrian Netherlands and up to the Dutch frontier. If and when French troops crossed into Dutch territory, the "external event" that could reshape the Dutch political scene would be present. Whether the "revolution" – the restoration of the standholderate and the transfer of power – that the English envoy Trevor saw coming as early as 1741[26], would actually come to pass would depend then upon the Orangist party, for revolutions do not just happen, they are made.

The Orangist party wakened out of its slumbers in these years, revived not by the ever placid William IV but by a supporter who embodied in his person the connection between the Netherlands and Britain. This was William Bentinck van Rhoon, the second son of Hans William van Bentinck, whom William III had made earl of Portland. Born in England in 1704, Bentinck van Rhoon was at the height of his vigor, intelligent, strong-willed, with vision and courage, at home both in his native country and in the Netherlands, where he came at the age of sixteen to be educated by his guardian, Wassenaer van Obdam, who was a staunch republican. Bentinck settled permanently in Holland in 1733. His unusual ability to apply understanding of English politics to the Dutch scene became important in 1737, when he was named one of the deputies of the province of Holland to the States General. In 1740 he imposed himself on the Prince of Orange's court, learned to know the Prince well and began to seek for him the victory that William himself refused to wrest from events. A Whig to the core in English politics, he adapted to the Dutch situation the Whig vision of government by king and country together, with leadership in the hands of a party leader such as Walpole. Like William, he believed that a government of stadholder and State together was the true constitutional form of the United Provinces and a political necessity.[27]

---

26 Geyl, *Willem IV*, 87–88.   27 *Ibid.*, 74–75; Porta, 211–12.

He understood that William's elevation in the stadholderless provinces could result only from the opportunity that would come in the event of a French invasion, but that an uprising of the people would need leadership by the Orangist party that the Prince would not give. He cast himself in the role of organizer and leader of the eventual seizure of power.[28] His first major step was a demonstrative visit to William IV at Het Loo in December 1743. Then he went to Amsterdam to talk with a number of important merchants who were hostile to the ruling faction: he discussed with them, as he wrote his mother, things that he did not dare to put on paper.[29] But he also envisioned open English intervention on behalf of the Prince of Orange, which would obviate the need for a rising of the people, which might never come. He urged the English government to compel Zeeland to reestablish the marquisate of Veere and Flushing by threatening seizure of Zeeland merchantmen by British warships. This was a flirtation with treason that did not jibe at all with William's emphasis upon legality and the free will of the regents.[30]

By mid-decade the revival of the Orangist party was evident. There was hearkening back to the lynching of the De Witt brothers in 1672,[31] and one Holland regent, François Teresteyn van Halewijn, a Dordrechter, began to fear for his life.[32] In March 1746 a group of Zeeland Orangists who were close to Bentinck urged William to come to Zeeland to demand his rights in the Veere–Flushing matter (they hardly needed to remind him of how much William III had done for his cause by such a visit in 1670). But he refused, reaffirming both his abhorrence of violence and his eagerness to be restored to the stadholderate.

He wrote to Bentinck in a letter that stated his attitude quite clearly:

However I am aloof from seeking my advancement from a revolution caused by a popular revolt, in which moderation and justice would always be cast aside and it often happens that innocent victims are sacrificed to the intensity of an unleashed passion which in its relentlessness cannot distinguish them from the guilty.

Such a movement was therefore always to be avoided if possible as odious. He never wished to encourage such movements directly or indirectly. He would not fail to appear when the country's need called him, however, and he would not be deterred by fear. He did not want to profit by public

28 [Willem Bentinck van Rhoon], *Briefwisseling en Aanteekeningen van Willem Bentinck, Heer van Rhoon (tot aan de dood van Willem IV 22 October 1751) Hoofdzakelijk naar de Bescheiden in het British Museum*, C. Gerretson and P. Geyl, eds., (Vol. I, all published; Utrecht, 1934), I, 81–82; Geyl, *Willem IV*, 110.
29 Bentinck to Countess of Portland, 11 Feb. 1744. Bentinck, I, 94.
30 Bentinck, I, 81–82; Geyl, *Willem IV*, 116, 121–22.
31 *The Present State of Holland, or a Description of the United Provinces* (London, 1745), 13.
32 Geyl, *Willem IV*, 64.

disturbances or to foment popular rioting. He would not respond to pamphlets and vague clamoring by a few burghers or common folk, but would remain tranquil in his solitude. If, however, a number of important and sensible people who thought like Bentinck, responding to the voice of the people, wanted him and invited him to come, he would not hesitate to show himself and to let them know that he was filled with zeal to serve his country usefully.[33]

Since the States party remained firmly in power in Holland, Zeeland and the other two antistadholderian provinces, this was a letter that left Bentinck and the other activists in the Orangist party in a dilemma. William wanted the fruits of a revolution without the revolution itself; but only the uprising of the populace in the wake of the disastrous "external event" could bring about the change. This seemed so unlikely that when Van der Heim died in July 1746, the new councilor pensionary elected to replace him, Jacob Gilles, had no qualms about taking an oath not to seek changes in the established political order.[34] Neither Gilles nor the States party leaders could solve their own dilemma, however – how to maintain the neutrality of the Republic in the face of contrary demands from England and France. The bastion of the States party, Amsterdam, remained firmly in the hands of those opposed to William's elevation to the stadholdership. The election of burgomasters in February 1747 indeed brought a coalescing of feuding clans under the leadership of the able Gerrit Corver.[35] But the deluge was about to break over the regime of the "True Freedom."

33 William IV to Bentinck, 19 Mar. 1746, *Archives*, 4e Sér., Supplément, 57–58; Geyl, *Willem IV*, 178–79.
34 Porta, 171–72.   35 *Ibid.*, 157–58.

9

William IV: neither revolutionary nor reformer

By the Spring of 1747 the French were no longer willing to acquiesce in the tremulous neutrality of the Dutch. All of the Austrian Netherlands was now in French hands, and the French army stood at the Dutch frontier. The Dutch were neutral, to be sure, but with a patent bias toward the English and Austria. That was no longer tolerable. On April 17, 20,000 soldiers of Louis XV's army crossed the border into States Flanders (the part south of the Schelde River held by the United Provinces since the early seventeenth century), and prepared to move northward into the heart of the Dutch Republic. The Dutch army was hardly an obstacle; it had offered almost no resistance to the invaders.

The "external event" that could transform the political situation in the Republic had occurred. One leader of the States party stammered to the French ambassador, "You're ruining us, you're making a stadholder."[1] The French invasion provided the occasion for a revolution that bestowed upon Prince William IV the stadholderate in the recalcitrant provinces, Zeeland, Holland, Utrecht and Overijssel, and made him captain-general of the United Provinces. It was a revolution with almost no violence on behalf of a Prince of Orange who was not a revolutionary, and it wrought an absolute minimum of change in the institutions of the country.

It began in Zeeland – where English ships lay off shore ready to provide assistance if needed – during the night of 24–25 April. The popular emotions had been stirred by tales of French atrocities, and panic was rampant. The paranoia that explained defeat by treason broke out again, as in 1653 and 1672, as if somehow the domination of the States party would be reinforced by French invasion. But there was method amidst the madness. The disorders that broke out in the towns of Zeeland, starting in Middelburgh, were coolly organized and efficiently led. There was just enough violence to shatter the last remnants of courage among the regents who had ruled the roost for decades for the States party and its "True Freedom." In ordinary times the burgher guards would have put down the riots without

1 Geyl, *Willem IV*, 213.

William IV, 1711–1751

difficulty, but the States party leaders preferred not to test their fidelity and stepped down. Veere was the first to proclaim the restoration (for so it was conceived, not as a new grant) of the stadholderate to William IV, and was followed in other towns, sometimes after the regents of known republican convictions were roughed up. After a few days of such incidents, the States of Zeeland voted on 28 April to name William Charles Henry Friso, Prince of Orange, as stadholder and captain-general.[2]

The organizers in Holland were ready to follow up at once upon Zeeland's breakthrough. The great event occurred two days later. The initiative was taken by Rotterdam, where the magistrates faced riotous crowds. In The Hague the mob poured into the Binnenhof, making similar threats to the deputies of the States of Holland. The deputies would have acted at once but had to wait for the approval of their principals, and Bentinck calmed the crowds with assurance that the election would take place five days later. This was duly done on 3 May. The States of Utrecht followed suit that same day, although there was reluctance to accept reestablishment of the "regulation of government" of 1675 as well;[3] Overijssel took the step a few days later. All the decisions had been unanimous.[4] William IV was stadholder at last in all seven provinces. On 4 May the States General completed the restoration by naming the Prince captain and admiral-general of the Union.

The *Staatsgezinden*, to the amusement of their Orangist opponents, began to wear orange ribbons and cockades. Even Cornelius de Witt, the grandson of the councilor pensionary's brother slaughtered with him in 1672, walked the streets of Dordrecht with orange trappings on his apparel, lest he be pitched into a canal, as had happened to others less cautious. There were not many like the Amsterdam merchant called "the Patriot" in a pamphlet about the events of 4 May who refused to be scared by such threats.[5] The "True Freedom" met its second demise not with a bang but a whimper.[6]

---

2 J. A. F. de Jongste, "De Republiek onder het erfstadhouderschap, 1747–1780," *Algemene Geschiedenis*, IX, 73; Blok, *Geschiedenis*, III, 435.

3 [Dirk Woertman], "Korte notitie van't geene gebeurt is bij occasie van't afsterven van de Heer Boudsen, Raad in de Vroedschap der stad Utrecht, en mijne bevordering in desselfs plaats, met het geene van tijd tot tijd daerop gevolgt is," *BMHG*, 1e Reeks, V (1882), 286–91.

4 Geyl, *Willem IV*, 216.

5 *Koffie-Huis-Praatje, Tusschen een oud Amsterdamsch Koopman, een Fries, en eenige anderen. Gehouden, des Nagts van den 4. May, 1747 in het Koffiehuis van Monsieur N. te Amsterdam* (Amsterdam, 1747) (Kn. 17,612), 16.

6 Geyl, *Willem IV*, 215–16; Blok, *Geschiedenis*, III, 436; H. Pallardy and I. Sacrelaire to (A. Tremblay), 2 May 1747, Willem Bentinck, I, 256.

It was a victory: but whose? The people's or that of the man behind the scenes, Bentinck van Rhoon, and behind him, the English government? Lord Chesterfield, the English secretary of state for the North, in whose bailiwick the Republic lay, wrote as soon as he heard of Zeeland's action to William IV. A "certain person" – obviously George II – is supporting the Prince's interest. If more was needed to "melt the great bell," secret means would be made available to his adherents.[7] But Bentinck and his friends could have done little or nothing if there had not been deep hatred and suspicion of the regents on the part of the mass of the population, at least in the towns. (As is usual, we really do not know the political views of the peasantry, but even if they had such, theirs was a voice that no one heard.)[8] What was different from 1672 was how little violence was needed to bring about the change.

What was different, too, was the character of the man whom the revolution put in power. William IV was no William III. He was still the man who had told Bentinck a year earlier that he did not want the stadholdership from the hands of a popular revolt but would accept it if he were invited by the right people. Still in Leeuwarden, far from the scene of events, he repeated this policy in a letter to the States of Zeeland on 25 April, just as rioting peaked. He offered his services, but would not go until the States invited him, for they were the legitimate sovereigns. He rebuffed appeals to come to The Hague without delay to strike while the opportunity was good. At this time of decision, he began to doubt his own abilities, and he wanted no spilling of blood, but not to the point of actually rejecting the proffered posts.[9] He would never have understood Lenin's use of the French political epigram that you can't make omelets without breaking eggs. He was not at all guilty, as a misinformed Frederick II believed, of using a means that could some day become very dangerous to him. But he was at heart a timorous as well as an ambitious man, as the Prussian king had seen when he had met him years before.[10]

On 1 May a delegation from Zeeland went to Leeuwarden to bring him the invitation he wanted, soon followed by another from Holland with the same mission. W. Z. Van Haren, one of his closest advisors, wrote a desperate plea for him to come to Holland without delay; the people were thirsting for vengeance and might well get out of hand. Anyone who dared to assert that the country could not throw out the French invaders was in

---

7 Chesterfield to William IV, 17/27 Apr. 1747, *Archives*, 4e Sér., I, 1–2.
8 G. J. Schutte, "De Republiek der Verenigde Nederlanden, 1702–1780," in: *Winkler Prins Geschiedenis*, II, 228.
9 William IV to Van Haren, 4–6 May 1747, *Archives*, 4e Sér., I, 9.
10 G. Arntzen, "Waren Willem IV and Frederick de Grote Vrienden?", *TvG*, 64 (1951), 320–23.

peril of being *Alewiné* ("Halewijnized").[11] The "neutralists" – as he called councilor pensionary Gilles and his associates even after the outbreak of war – had "lost their bearings"; the time to act had come.[12] William rejoiced that events had not cost any lives; they were "a work manifestly marked by his [God's] seal." He would not go anywhere except in conformity with the law, displayed in a resolution or official letter from the States.[13] Not until 10 May did the Prince, his insistence upon the last tittle of legality met, leave with Princess Anna for The Hague, where they arrived two days later. There he was greeted by the full panoply of ceremonies, the symbolism of power that he so coveted. Only on 17 May did he journey on to Zeeland, where his restoration had begun.[14] Apart from taking measures for defense against the French, he had to show himself in person there to calm the people; otherwise they would not believe he had been made stadholder.[15]

It was, however, one thing to take power from the hands of men who had lost the nerve and the means to keep it; it was another to use it. As so often happens when disparate forces combine for victory, once triumphant they did not see eye to eye as to what should be done. For the simple folk who had taken to the streets and done the dirty work of intimidation, the reply to this question was strongly felt but vague in specific definitions. They saw the Prince of Orange as their protector and friend against the regents, who had ruled so hard and so unfairly over them;[16] now he could redeem the promise of improvement which they had read into his mind and which he had never made. It would be a little while, however, before they would discover that they had misread his affections and his intentions.

For the most astute of the Orangist leaders, Bentinck in particular, the time had come to reform the government along the lines he had earlier urged upon William. It was not redistribution of powers in the Republic that he envisaged, but reorganization of the national leadership now that it was exercised by the Prince of Orange. But William himself saw only one task, apart from assuming the offices duly and properly bestowed upon him. This was to wage the war of resistance against the French in alliance with his father-in-law, the king of England. For all of them – people, Orangist leaders, the Prince himself – after the exultation of triumph would come confrontation with obdurate reality and deep disappointment.

---

11 Van Haren to William IV, 6 May 1747, *Archives*, 4e Sér., I, 10–11.
12 W. Z. van Haren to William IV, 2 May 1747, *Archives*, 4e Sér., I, 4–5.
13 William IV at Leeuwarden to Bentinck van Rhoon, 4 May 1747, *Archives*, 4e Sér., I, 7–8.
14 Geyl, *Willem IV*, 217–18.
15 Bentinck at Middelburg to Countess of Portland, 16 May 1747, Bentinck, I, 259.
16 *Brief van Claudius Civilis Aan den Heer Justus Batavus. Wegens de noodzakelijkheid en de Redenen van de Burgeren van Gouda, om by Request te verzoeken, dat alle Ampten verkocht worden ten mitte van het gemeene Landt* ("Krysopolis," 1747), 10.

Like William III before him, William IV came to the task of military leadership which was now given to him without prior experience of command. He assured the States General that he had had "long experience of the theory of war." But the long immersion in abstract principles without opportunity to test them and to integrate them into habit of mind and will, the long years of impatient waiting when he did little and little that he could have done would have worked, had sapped his readiness to become another Frederick II, like his cousin in Prussia.

He believed that the restoration of the stadholdership in itself transformed the situation, that nothing had been essentially wrong but the cowardice and ineptness of the States party regents. In this regard Bentinck and the Prince differed at the very core. Bentinck was an activist, seeking change, William a passive man who sought no change other than the restoration of the offices of his forefathers. The Prince rejected Bentinck's entreaties to cast the old officeholders out of their posts and to rebuild government, high and low, with the new men devoted to him. Once the regents had given him what he deemed was his by right, he ceased to be their enemy. He shared with his wife confidence that they could be managed by playing upon their narrowest self-interest and encouraging their division into cliques; what had worked in Leeuwarden, with its minuscule politics, ought to work in the larger political world of The Hague. Even Bentinck, whose commitment to the cause of the House of Orange came from strong intellectual and emotional commitment, to his indignation was treated as if he were after nothing but a rewarding job. Nor did William understand the longings of the common people, their expectation of action on their behalf as the true aim of the revolution.[17] Popular enthusiasm was all to the good, but he found that it did not extend so far as to back up hatred of the French and the regents with readiness for heavier sacrifices. Had not the preachers, the people's mentors and guides, taught them that the mere name of Orange would fend off the French like an exorcism? Such expectations were a dangerous dream. The restoration of Dutch strength could not come as the result of a battlefield triumph over a far more powerful enemy, but from laborious improvement of government and perhaps of society at home.[18] Victory did not yet pit popular Orangism and the Orange dynasty against each other, but it was beginning to expose the differences between their purposes.

Bentinck was aware of the problem and tried to alert William to it. Late in July, after he had observed the dilatoriness and slackness of the Prince's management of the affairs of state that were now in his hands, he wrote a lengthy memorandum for him. It was, he warned, of "utmost consequence," since William's future authority and prestige would depend upon

17 Geyl, *Willem IV*, 228–29.   18 *Ibid.*, 218–21.

his decision. He must cease his soft policy toward the old regents, whom Bentinck called the "French cabal" that had used its usurped power to oppress and rob the people and grow fat on the Prince's blood. To save them, was William ready to lose the love and veneration of the people and become the object of their scorn and even hatred? Was he ready to allow his old friends and servants to become confused because they were treated no differently than those who had brought the country to its sad state? The Orangist feelings of the people must not be taken for granted. They were not fixed upon him as a person, but upon the deliverance that was hoped for from him. If he failed them, there would be no more shouts of "Long Live Orange"; discontent and murmuring would take the place of joy and acclamation. The point of this almost hysterical plea was that William had retained councilor pensionary Gilles and another States party official in their posts; they must be dismissed.[19]

Vengeance and reprisal were not, however, what the Prince wanted. He wrote to Gerrit Corver, the influential burgomaster of Amsterdam who had dominated the city's government for years, to reaffirm his pleasure in Corver's friendship, promised to discuss important matters with him in confidence, and sought his advice on how to raise revenues without reducing the zeal of the people.[20] It would not be easy for Bentinck to persuade a man of such good will towards his erstwhile adversaries to sweep them out of office and power.

The English envoy at The Hague rooted the problems in William's personality. He had the best of intentions, wrote this perceptive observer, but lacked independence of judgment and depended upon good advice. Of this, however, there was a bad shortage: the Prince had fewer able men about him than he had ever seen in such a case.[21] An even more devastating portrait was given by Hardenbroek, an Utrecht nobleman who came to The Hague at this time as a deputy to the States General and became part of William's circle. Hardenbroek found him "terribly trivial" (*schrikkelijk bagatellier*), making jokes when serious matters were put before him. He did not work hard although people thought so, leaving documents unsigned for long periods. He was good-hearted to the point where he promised anything without thinking twice, and gave away 10,000 guilders of the country's money, in Hardenbroek's phrase, as if it were a penny piece (*dubbeltje*). He was not at all fitted for the great post he held.[22]

19 Memoire of W. Bentinck for William IV, 26–29 July 1747, Bentinck, I, 274–76, 279–80, 301–2.   20 William IV to Gerrit Corver, 26 Aug. 1747, *Archives*, 4e Sér., I, 68–69.
21 Geyl, *Willem IV*, 268.
22 [Gijsbert Jan van Hardenbroek], *Gedenkschriften van Gijsbert Jan van Hardenbroek, Heer van Bergestein, Lockhorst, 's Heeraartsberg en Ammerstol, President der Utrechtse Ridderschap, Gedeputeerde ter Generaliteits-Vergadering enz.*, ed. F. J. L. Krämer and A. J. van der Meulen (6 vols.; Amsterdam, 1901–18), I, 32–33.

It was not long, however, before the military threat that the restoration of William IV to the stadholdership was supposed to remove was revived and expanded. On 16 September, French forces which had crossed the river barrier of the Schelde took the fortress town of Bergen op Zoom, opening the way either westward into Zeeland or northward into Holland. The outcries of betrayal that had swept the country in April were repeated. The proposed remedy was to strengthen the House of Orange even more, by making the stadholdership hereditary in both the male and the female lines, like the crown in England. Since the only child William and Princess Anna had was a daughter, Caroline, it would avoid the situation of 1702, when the stadholderate in Holland and other provinces had not passed to William III's cousin at Leeuwarden because it was hereditary only in the direct male line.[23]

A plan was worked out by Bentinck, who took the initiative, in collaboration with Henry Fagel Sr, the *greffier* of the States General, and two other leading Orangists, and then steered through the States of Holland with the assistance of Gilles, the councilor pensionary who until the events of April had been a steadfast foe of the Prince.[24] The States of Holland adopted the proposal on 16 November. A female stadholder would be called a "gouvernante," and she might marry only with the approval of the States. If she married, her husband would represent her as captain-general and upon the Council of State; otherwise, she could choose a representative. Zeeland followed suit quickly, and Gelderland, Overijssel and Utrecht somewhat later. These last three provinces also agreed to reenact the "regulations of government" that had been introduced under William III and which the regents had come to abhor as deprivation of their dearest independence. The heart of these "regulations" was the provision by which the stadholder appointed and dismissed magistrates in the towns. It was his most important right as the "representative" and the "advocate" of the sovereign, who of course continued to be the States.[25] In Gelderland the resistance of the regents to making William hereditary stadholder had been broken by guildsmen and the burgher guards, although usually the threat of violence was enough.[26] The States General also acted to make the captaincy and admiralty-general similarly hereditary in both lines, but not until December 1748.[27]

23 Geyl, *Willem IV*, 245.
24 N. Japikse, "De Staten-Generaal in de achttiende eeuw (1717–1795)," in: Fockema Andreae, 116–17; Arnoldina Kalshoven, *De diplomatieke verhouding tusschen Engeland en de Republiek der Vereen. Nederlanden, 1747–1756* (The Hague, 1915), 26.
25 *Rechtsgeleerde Verhandeling over eene Gewigtige Preëminentie, den Heeren Stadhoudeeren omtrent de Regering der Steden eigen.* (Rotterdam, 1747) (Kn. 17,606), 3, 6–7.
26 Wertheim-Gijse Weenink, 97–99.
27 Japikse, "De Staten-Generaal," 121; Blok, *Geschiedenis*, III, 438.

Here and there the Orangists had to call up the instrument of intimidation by popular riots, indicating the persistent unhappiness of many regents with what they had to do.[28] William and his entourage had hoped it could be done more cleanly, without the involvement of the populace. They did not want him to be called "the Prince of the Mob," the sarcastic name given him by the English Whigs, who recognized that the Dutch regents were really their own kind of people.[29] In any event, the precaution of making the stadholderate hereditary in both lines proved unnecessary, for a son, named William like his father and given the title of Count of Buren, was born to Anna on 9 March 1748.

Politics to William IV was more a matter of form than of effective power. This was displayed when he demanded that he receive joint command of the Anglo-Dutch army facing the French with the duke of Cumberland, who was a son of the king. George II refused; he would not grant William anything more than command of the separate Dutch corps stationed at Breda.[30] Princess Anna was furious. To her it was a family matter, and why should her husband be subordinated to her much younger brother? Her protests, supported by councilor pensionary Gilles, were to no avail; the English terms for agreement had to be accepted.[31] It was evident even to the more percipient and candid of William's own adherents that he was not fit for supreme military command, lacking all experience either in the field or in sieges. He admitted that the English considered him a poltroon, and he responded by calling them a nation of devils and enemies. Yet he allowed Cumberland to overrule him in the most humiliating way.[32] Not that it mattered much when it came to the actual conduct of the war. The principal scene of combat shifted to Germany and Italy from the Low Countries until peace was finally made at Aachen (Aix-la-Chapelle) in October 1748. The laurels of victory escaped William, and he had to confront domestic problems that did not go away, but only changed their shape somewhat with the advent of the stadholderate.

The stadholder's ability to act effectively in difficult and complex circumstances depended upon himself and his government. If any man were to play the role of advisor that Sandwich, the English ambassador, saw was essential for William IV, it was Bentinck van Rhoon, who again found himself trying to drive the Prince forward in ways that he did not want to go. But it proved one thing to conduct a revolution on his behalf almost despite him, and another to take steps which only he could take to create an

---

28 H. A. Weststrate, *Gelderland in den Patriottentijd* (Arnhem, 1903), 5–8; Hardenbroek, I, 4; Schutte, 228.

29 I. Sacrelaire at The Hague to Countess of Portland, 9 Oct. 1747, Bentinck, I, 302; Geyl, *Willem IV*, 249.

30 Geyl, *Willem IV*, 255–56.   31 *Ibid.*, 259–61.   32 Hardenbroek, I, 32.

effective administration of government at the center. The Prince and Princess of Orange had known for years that Bentinck was a fervent advocate of their cause, but they found him uncomfortably independent in his judgment, too eager to make things happen instead of waiting patiently upon events, and too ready to tell them what they needed to know and should do rather than soothing their sensibilities with honeyed phrases. He was now more than ever their principal advisor, but when he tried to persuade the Princess to support his strong line, he found himself often opposed and even thwarted by her friends from the years in Friesland, in particular the group around the Van Harens, whom she found more pliant than the impetuous Bentinck.[33]

What he had in mind was really a merger of the English system of cabinet government with functional ministries on the pattern of the French monarchy. But William and Anna – for the woman who had married beneath her to escape passive subordination at home for an effective role in life, if not full independence, began to play an ever larger part in his government – resented what they saw would be a limitation upon their free judgment. They saw, even if they never said it in so many words, that Bentinck was casting himself in the role of Sir Robert Walpole, England's first prime minster, although without the name, and William IV in that of an acquiescent George II – a comparison that the proud daughter of the English king would hardly have relished. They let the memorandum in which Bentinck made his proposals repose in the files, unacted upon and waiting for its reemergence as a historical document long afterwards.[34]

The form of government after the revolution of 1747 may have been constitutionally a return to the traditional collaboration of Prince and States, but in practice William IV did not know what to do with the leadership that had passed wholly into his hands. He did not know it, however, and sought to do everything, trivialities no less than grand policy. A memorandum of "Considerations" dated 11 July 1748, written by Bentinck and presented to Princess Anna, is so significant for our understanding of William's situation as head of Dutch government that it must be set forth here in some detail.

Internal reorganization of the government is absolutely necessary, he wrote, if the state is to escape danger; but it is also the Prince and all his party who are in peril. "The foundation of all government is the confidence which the people places in those who govern them. This confidence is now utterly extinguished here." All complaints are heaped upon the Prince. He has been given authority and power greater than that possessed by any of his predecessors, despite the resistance of the city magistrats; indeed, it

33 Kalshoven, 24.   34 Geyl, *Willem IV*, 265–67.

was precisely in order to put a brake upon their ambition and avarice that the Nation had given him such power. The Nation (the capitalization is Bentinck's) sees that the Prince is not using the power as had been expected of him. Almost none of the old officeholders have been dismissed; worse, they and their relatives and friends continue to receive favors from the Prince, somtimes even in violation of the law. He cited an instance: the command of a company of burgher guards in Amsterdam was given to a child, to wide astonishment and indignation. This is, Anna commented in the margin, "so great a trifle that it would be better to be a sergeant than a stadholder if he cannot give pleasure in such a matter without being responsible to censors, who must find something wrong since they insist upon such minutiae." The contrast could hardly be sharper between her essentially private and personal view of the state and Bentinck's political vision.

Bentinck went on to warn her against the continued use of regents who belonged to the "old cabal" and had not changed their character despite their willingness to wear orange ribbons. There was a general notion that they embarrassed the Prince by giving him problems and preventing him from doing all the good that he wished to. Informed persons believed some of this, the less informed much more, and the little people, who were the least informed of all, said the Prince needed more power to reform the abuses and hence ought to be made count of Holland. This was an idea that must be combatted by everyone attached to the Prince. He had enough power; it was up to him to use it. He had said as much to a deputation of burghers from Rotterdam that very day who said the public outcry was to make the Prince count of Holland. They had replied that he must have at least the power to "change the government" (the famous *wetsverzettingen*) that William III had had. In any case, the responsibility fell upon the Prince.[35]

With this last point, if with no other, Anna agreed. The Prince, she affirmed, "would rather leave the country than be Count of Holland, and he does not at all desire a more extensive power."[36]

Bentinck's warnings were to no avail. The traditional lethargic pace of Dutch decision-making slowed down to interminable delay, and confusion was endemic. In England Lord Chesterfield, who not long before had thought the Prince of Orange "must have great self denial, or great timidity if he is not very soon as absolute over the seven provinces as Louis XV is in France,"[37] became so pessimistic that he thought the Prince "escaped deposition."[38] It would take a half century of history, however, before it would come to that.

35 W. Bentinck, Considerations presented to the Princess of Orange, 11 July 1784, *Archives*, 4e Sér., I, 220–33.   36 Japikse, *Geschiedenis*, II, 124.
37 Kalshoven, 18 n5.   38 Geyl, *Willem IV*, 264–65, 282–83.

What came within a year was the reemergence of the people upon the scene as a force with its own identity. The populace remained overwhelmingly friendly to the House of Orange, but with an increasing sense that it had to look out for itself. The shift of attitude was indicated in a poem entitled *Impromptu Thoughts In Reconsideration of Present Circumstances* published in Groningen in 1748, in which these lines occur:

> There's none, we see,
> To make us free
> But we ourselves,
> The common folk.[39]

The target of the popular movement, as it had been for a century, was the rule of the regents. Their overthrow was an aim more easily expressed in slogans, vituperation, and occasional inflicting of bodily harm on particularly loathed magistrates, than in conceiving of an alternate regime and bringing it into being. It was an aim, furthermore, that ran directly counter to the desire of the Prince of Orange to tame the regents, to make good Orangists out of them, and to work with them, rather than to root them out or put simple citizens in their place. He was willing to accept modest reforms that did not cut the heart out of the regents' oligarchy. During 1747 he obtained a ban on the sale of offices by magistrates (the purchase price did not make the offices hereditary, as in France, and was paid to the magistrates, not to prior officeholders) and requiring officeholders to perform their duties in person. The cities of Holland were persuaded to turn over their post offices, the profits from which had gone mainly to the burgomasters' private purses, to the province. And the next year the collection of indirect taxes was taken from tax farmers and entrusted to municipal tax collectors. But he acted reluctantly, and rejected more extreme demands.[40]

Neither the birth of the count of Buren nor the signature of preliminaries of peace brought civil peace, however. Disorders erupted in Groningen over the issue of the farming of taxes, becoming violent in December 1747 and continuing until the next summer. Although the form of government was democratic, the reality was an oligarchy of a few families far narrower than Holland's regime. The party in power found itself isolated, with the Orangists able to draw upon both the burghers in Groningen city and the peasantry in the surrounding countryside to put backbone into their demands. The regents buckled under the pressure, seeking personal security

---

39 *Invallende Gedagten, by het Overdenken der tegenwoordige Tyds Omstandigheden* (Groningen, [1748]), 5. (Kn. 17,928) Maer noemt my een, / Buiten 't Gemeen, / Die ons oit kan bevryden.
40 Japikse, *Geschiedenis*, II, 118, 124–25.

rather than standing together.[41] The supporters of the Prince sought to keep the movement within safe limits, although William held back from the employment of troops, as the States requested. William wanted no violence; indeed, he gave his protection to a fiercely hated regent, John Geertsema, against the fury of the populace, even after he was charged with crimes.[42]

The troubles soon spread to Friesland, and there too the States of the province found themselves forced to dicker with a popular movement. A delegation from Harlingen brought a program that included not only the abolition of farming for harbor dues and internal taxes, but also the reestablishment of old laws which gave suffrage rights to a wider electorate, an explicitly democratic demand, and the declaration that the stadholderate in Friesland, as in Holland, be made hereditary in both the male and the female lines, which was a narrowly dynastic issue. With the threat of popular violence hanging over them, the States of Friesland on 4 June declared the stadholdership hereditary in both lines and with the same powers as in the other provinces. Controversy continued, however, over exactly how wide the extension of the suffrage should be.

By August the situation was so difficult that troops were sent up from Overijssel to bring the disorders to an end.[43] The States pleaded with William to return to Friesland to calm the populace, which he finally did months later. While there he was spoken to boldly by the people. "We are the sovereigns and recognize neither States or Prince," he was told, according to Hardenbroek. Their attitude, according to this worrisome informant, was encouraged because they did not fear the soldiery, who had orders to act softly.[44] Fagel told Bentinck that many in Friesland "no longer recognized the Prince as anything but a private person" and claimed that "sovereignty has fallen back into the bosom of the people."[45] The only net result, apart from the decision on the stadholderate, was the abolition of the tax farms. Bitter disappointment followed.[46] The grumbling of the burghers was accompanied, however, by heightened anxiety among the traditional governing class, including zealous Orangists like William van Haren, that the "rabble" were out of control and turning against them.[47]

The troubles in Friesland brought quick imitation in Holland. Riots against tax farming broke out in Haarlem in June, soon followed in Leiden.

41 J. E. Heeres, "Stad en Lande tijdens het erfstadhouderschap van Willem IV," *BVGO*, 3e Reeks, 4 (1888), 253–54.
42 *Ibid.*, 271–72, 277–80, 296–97, 303–11; Blok, *Geschiedenis*, III, 448–50.
43 Blok, *Geschiedenis*, III, 448.   44 Hardenbroek, I, 15–16.   45 Kalshoven, 35 n2.
46 F. G. Slothouwer, "Friesche troebelen gedurende het jaar 1748," *BVGO*, 3e Reeks, 2 (1885), 408–12, 417–18, 428–29; Blok, *Geschiedenis*, III, 446–48.
47 William van Haren to William IV, 1 July 1748, *Archives*, 4e Sér., I, 217–18.

In The Hague the homes of tax farmers were plundered. William did not want to use troops against the rioters, saying he lacked such authority; but finally disturbances in Rotterdam could be put down only with military forces. The movement against tax farming then traveled to Amsterdam, where the disorders were halted by the civic guards and two ringleaders were hanged. The Prince finally acted, appearing unexpectedly in the States of Holland on 25 June to propose the abolition of tax farming, proposing instead a capitation tax to replace the lost ten millions of revenue; it in turn aroused opposition because it would fall heavily upon property owners, but not upon either the poor or foreigners.[48]

The great challenge came in the Summer of 1748 in Amsterdam, after the rioting had ceased elsewhere. It was a movement called the "Doelisten," after the hall, the Kloveniersdoelen, a former target range ("target" in Dutch is *doel*, plural *doelen*), in which it met. It was not a spontaneous movement but was prepared in advance, with Bentinck the chief organizer and his chief collaborator an outstanding journalist, Jean Rousset de Missy, who combined passionate Orangism, involvement in the secret world of freemasonry, and leadership in the world of what has been called the "radical Enlightenment."[49]

It had begun in September the year before when a porcelain merchant of Amsterdam named Daniel Raap took the lead in a movement that combined Orangism and a primitive democracy. In the name of his fellow-citizens, some of whom accompanied him, he presented four demands to the burgomasters. First, a call upon them to support making the stadholdership hereditary in both lines, which was pure Orangism. Second was a proposal that municipal offices be taken from the grant of the burgomasters and sold at auction to the highest bidder. The intention was democratic, because it would overcome the narrow favoritism of the oligarchs by opening up opportunities for public employment to families that possessed money but had been excluded from the circle of the regents. Nonetheless it was not the democracy of wide suffrage and popular elections. The closest Raap's program came to that was in the proposal that officers of the burgher guard companies be elected by the guards, not by the burgomasters, and in another that the ancient privileges of the guilds (themselves bastions of guildmasters' dominance) be restored, giving them the influence in town government that they had supposedly possessed before the pro-Spanish government had been overthrown in 1578 in the so-called "Alteration."[50]

Soon two currents, one moderate and the other radical, developed

48 Blok, *Geschiedenis*, III, 450–52.
49 Margaret C. Jacob, *The Radical Enlightenment: Pantheists, Freemasons and Republicans* (London, 1981).
50 Brugmans, V, 78–81, 91–92.

among the democrats in Amsterdam. The leader of the moderates was Raap, upon whom the Orange court counted to keep the movement in check. He was invited to The Hague, where he was first received by Bentinck and De Back, the private secretary of the Prince of Orange, and then by Princess Anna herself in Huis ten Bosch. Anna had to assume much of the responsibility during this period because William was in the grip of illness, at times to the point of delirium. When she was urged by Charles Bentinck, Fagel and De Back to act vigorously to crush the rioting, she offered to send in troops, but they declined such heavy responsibility and she refused to take it upon herself.[51]

The radicals were not catered to in the same way as the moderates, and they began to act independently. They met on 9 August in the Kloveniersdoelen and established a kind of parallel municipal government of elected representatives, which competed with the town council, so that it has been compared to the Soviets in the months before the October 1917 revolution in Russia.[52]

What emerged from these events was a clarification of mutual attitudes between popular Orangism and the House of Orange. The democrats began to realize that the Prince of Orange was not, and did not want to be, their savior against the regents. But they had no explicit vision of another order, political or social; it was not revolution that they wanted, but new persons in power and the restoration of an idealized past. As for the Prince, he could not be budged from his commitment to the existing social and political order, of course with himself at its head.[53] He made this clear late in August when delegates came from Amsterdam to plead with him to come to their city. It was an unusual early morning meeting at Huis ten Bosch, where they were brought by Bentinck, for the Prince had to be wakened from his slumbers to receive their urgings. It was decided that he would have to go to prevent tragedy, but only at the formal request of the municipal authorities as well as of the citizenry and in order to present his good offices to the burgomasters, but leaving them to judge what was advisable. A massacre was his worst fear.[54]

William arrived in Amsterdam on 1 September, an unready and unwilling savior sent by the States of Holland to investigate the grievances, to propose remedies, and if all else failed, to "change the government." He could master the grand gesture, as when he left his personal guards at the gate, saying that he needed the protection only of the burghers. Three thousand ships' carpenters, shouldering the *bijltjes* (little axes) from which they received their nickname, led him to the town hall and there they paraded before him. The burgomasters, town councilors and aldermen

51 Hardenbroek, I, 13, 16.   52 Brugmans, V, 92–93.   53 Schutte, 230.
54 Notes of Bentinck, [c. 27 Aug. 1748), *Archives*, 4e Sér., I, 241–42.

(*schepenen*) who awaited him as he descended from his carriage repeated in person their readiness to resign their posts into his hands if he restored order. He insisted that the contending forces combine their petitions into one, but this was difficult to obtain. He met the leaders of both the moderates led by Raap and the bolder democrats with Gimnig at their head.

He wanted almost anything but a *wetsverzetting*, he wrote his wife, but did not see how he could avoid it. He was particularly disturbed in his legalistic punctiliousness because the burghers were demanding replacement not only of the burgomasters and town council, which was authorized by the resolution of the States, but also of the "Old Council" (*Oudraad*), in which former aldermen sat, which was not. How could he pick new regents wisely, he wondered, when he did not know people and their talents, qualities and relationships? He called on God to guide him in his choices.[55]

On 4 September, he met the same delegation for the third time, finding them bolder to the point of seditiousness. They demanded that the government be changed the next day, warning that the *Bijltjes* were becoming impatient. The citizenry were offended because he dined with the burgomasters, they told him, and there were threats to chop the offending officials to bits if it happened again. Raap – the moderate – said he would rather see him eat with a cobbler. Once they left, he called in the burgomasters to tell them of the "insolent" remarks he had heard and the danger they faced if he ate with them. He was especially concerned about burgomaster Corver, "poor Corver" as he called this stalwart of the States party. But he would go ahead with their dismissal.[56] This he did the next day, weeping when he had to tell "good and honest Corver" that he was no longer a burgomaster.[57]

Once William "changed the government," he found himself confronted by the people in person, intruding upon him once more to present their demands. The most dramatic, and at the same time comic, meeting occurred when a delegation of "Doelisten" demanded and obtained entry into his quarters at 3 o'clock in the morning. While he was still lying in bed, the angrier of the visitors told him that they could no longer conceal their displeasure with him because he was politically and personally friendly with unworthy persons. Others were ready to forgive him if he did what was needed. His reply was the essence of passivity. My life is in God's hands, he said, and I will await what happens. He related the episode to friends a day and a half later, with tears filling his eyes.[58]

He announced the names of the new burgomasters during the morning of 6 September, sure that "persons of standing" (*gens de façon*) would

55 William IV to Princess Anna, 2, 3 Sept. 1748, *Archives*, 4e Sér., I, 245–46, 248–49.
56 *Ibid.*, 4 Sept. 1748, *Archives*, 4e Sér., I, 250–52.
57 *Ibid.*, 5 Sept. 1748, *Archives*, 4e Sér., I, 252–53.   58 Hardenbroek, I, 14.

approve his choice. He was not swayed by the desires of the Gimnig party, one a Bicker (descended from the family of De Witt's in-laws) for reasons he would not put on paper, and the other a "simple burgher" who should be satisfied to become a town councilor and colonel of the burgher guard. He was pleased that Raap and his group were acting well.[59] The approval for Raap lasted only overnight, for the meeting at the Doelen the next day came up with proposals he had difficulty persuading them to drop, while Gimnig, whom he saw as intimidated by his "philippics" of the day before, won his praise. The article which he found most difficult to accept was one creating a council of war for command of the burgher guards. He explained to the new burgomasters that he refused it because it would deprive the government of the authority it needed; yet he did not want to incline too much toward the regents lest the old abuses take root again. With God's help he hoped to find a "happy medium" (*juste milieu*) that would strengthen the "soul of republican government"; but the principal danger at the moment was from "popular government" (the term "democracy" was not yet current except among scholars), especially in a commercial city like Amsterdam.[60]

The strength of his commitment to the existing political orders was indicated by those he chose. Some of those he named to the town council were members of families famed for their States party activity over the past century, including a De Witt, a De la Court and a Deutz. New councilors included a banker, George Clifford.[61] He apologized in writing to one of the dismissed burgomasters, P. C. Hasselaer, for taking an action "which is very much against my character" but had been forced upon him by "a desperate situation." He assured Hasselaer that he saw in him an "honest and bold patriot" whose friendship he would cultivate in the future.[62]

The problem of the Old Council which had worried him solved itself when the sitting members decided to quit on the morning of 9 September. What did not go away as easily was the demand of the Doelisten for the war council in Amsterdam, which became so vehement that such leaders as Raap and Gimnig were suspected of insufficient zeal. William met four of the Doelisten's new deputies and found them hard to persuade and persistent in their endeavors to put limits on his powers of action, indeed desiring to prescribe him laws. He warned them against forcing him to a decision one way or the other on the matter, assuring them that he wanted their friendship (*amour*). One of them replied that they trusted the Prince himself because he wanted to give them justice and full freedom, but was dissuaded by his advisors. Shocked, William wrote his wife that "I wash

---

59 William IV to Princess Anna, 6 Sept. 1748, *Archives*, 4e Sér., I, 254.
60 *Ibid.*, 7 Sept. 1748, *Archives*, 4e Sér., I, 257–59.   61 *Archives*, 4e Sér., I, 260.
62 William IV to P. C. Hasselaer, 7 Sept. 1748, *Archives*, 4e Sér., I, 256.

my hands of them."[63] A visit by sergeants of the civic guard the next day turned out even worse. They demanded action on the war council, and he told them that if they did not leave him a free hand, he would gladly renounce the whole affair; and this was the position he stated in a printed statement to the burgher companies decided upon in a conference with the burgomasters.[64] The next few days passed in further futile conferences, his attempts to persuade the Doelisten to disband their assemblies falling on deaf ears.[65]

He returned to The Hague on 15 September, exasperated and puzzled by the course of events. He had wished to do what was necessary and desirable, as a faithful servant of the Republic that he was leading, but was unwilling to grasp supreme power, an ambition attributed to him by the rumor mills.[66] When he went to Utrecht a few weeks later to conduct another "change of government" there, he spoke with feeling about what his forebears had done for Dutch freedom, which he said he had imbibed with his mother's milk. If he had spoken to the deaf in his meetings with the Amsterdam Doelisten, he spoke in Utrecht to the unhearing on the other side, for a former burgomaster boldly and angrily proclaimed his own republican vision in the town council. Prince William I had not freed them from the Spaniards so that they might be enslaved now. By slavery he meant William IV's few hesitant actions to quiet the Amsterdammers.[67]

Whatever "revolutionary" potential there had been in the Revolution of 1747, it was dissipated by the events of 1748. "Orange democracy" began to disintegrate, and those who had put their faith in the Princes of Orange to protect the common people from the oligarchic regents had to face the consequences of their deep disappointment. Their program had been directed more at tying the hands of the regents than in creating forms of effective popular participation in government, and there was little thought of direct popular elections of officials. On the other side, the regents found that they had been ousted from their seats of power by a Prince of Orange whose elevation to the stadholdership they had had to accept in the face of popular disorders (with the knowledge that the English were not far away if needed by their foes). The fact that he was a Prince who, when faced by the reality of hard decisions, preferred compassion, decency and courtesy in human relations to the sharp, decisive actions of a hardened politician,[68] did not win him their affection, however.

63 Anna, 9 Sept. 1748, *Archives*, 4e Sér., I, 264–66.
64 *Ibid.*, 10 Sept. 1748, *Archives*, 4e Sér., I, 267.
65 *Ibid.*, 13, 14 Sept. 1748, *Archives*, 4e Sér., I, 272–73, 275–76.
66 Hardenbroek, I, 16.   67 *Ibid.*, 17, 45.
68 See W. Bentinck, notes, 4 Feb. 1749 (*Archives*, 4e Sér., I, 295) for a meeting of William IV with Amsterdam Bijltjes in which he showed himself the apostle of reconciliation among the contending parties.

Calm, at least most of the time, returned to Amsterdam and to the country as a whole. Only in Groningen did troubles flare up again in January 1749, aroused by dissatisfaction over the failure of three plenipotentiaries of the Prince to carry through the "change of government" as soon as they arrived the month before. Rioters who took command of the streets compelled the sitting magistrates to resign their offices so that William IV could name new men in their place, which he delayed doing, asking them to stay for the time being. A flood of petitions were sent to him proposing various reforms, but he would not go beyond the abolition of tax farming in favor of direct collection, and the taking of a census. Finally, late in November, he came up from Holland, amid general rejoicing so intense that one poetaster compared it to the way a bride head over heels in love awaits her beloved bridegroom on their wedding night(!),[69] and finally replaced the magistrates in the city and the officeholders in the provincial government. To the States he presented a "regulation of reform" (*reglement reformatoir*), which was adopted on 28 November, restoring to the commoners in Groningen city rights of participation in the municipal government and confirming the guilds in their charters and privileges, according the stadholder the right to approve new members of the municipality, and dividing legislative, executive and judicial functions, an innovation.[70] The assembly in turn formally declared the stadholdership hereditary as had been agreed to the year before.[71]

Bentinck, disappointed and almost despondent over the way events had gone since 1747, analyzed the situation in January 1749 in preparation for a discussion with the Prince and Princess. We do not know how much of his bold thoughts this impatient man actually presented to them, but his notes are important nonetheless because they are based upon a deeply political judgment, not the narrowly personal one of William and Anna. Bentinck saw the House of Orange in peril, indeed on the edge of a precipice. Amsterdam was returning to its old ways now that they saw they had little to fear from the Prince; yet, until he could be certain that Amsterdam would not thwart him, the Prince would not have a sure hold on anything.

In the country at large he had to provide effective leadership for the state, with a single large coherent vision and purposeful activity. He could not count upon the affection of the people no matter what happened, yet without it he had only the army to support him, and without money to pay its wages it would melt away and the foreign officers go home. He would become the object of scorn, which is worse than hatred because that passes and is accompanied by respect (shades of Machiavelli!). The key to a change was getting rid of the councilor pensionary of Holland, the selfsame

69 Heeres, 252–53.   70 *Ibid.*, 321–23.   71 Blok, *Geschiedenis*, IV, 460.

Gilles who had been in office before the 1747 overturn and had still to be mistrusted despite his apparent change of party. Yet the Prince relied upon him and protected him.[72]

Despite the frantic, almost hysterical tone of these notes, Bentinck was bringing out two crucial facts. First, if the restoration of his stadholdership was not to be an empty achievement, the Prince had to exert a clear and positive leadership, working with people committed not only to him personally, but to a political program. Second, it could no longer be assumed that the population, in their antipathy to the regents, would always turn to him as their savior. Their grievances had to be met in some way.

Bentinck turned to the Princess, whose judgment, he knew, carried so much weight with William. He repeated his arguments for the dismissal of Gilles, whom he accused of cowardice or malice in his easy compliance with whatever the Prince wanted. Anna denied that there were any complaints against Gilles except in Amsterdam, and things were quiet there now. Bentinck repeated his warning that the reality was very different, that the Prince was losing, indeed had already lost, the respect and confidence of the nation. If something untoward happened to her husband, she would be sent away with her children and her friends ruined and lost. The only way to prevent this was for William to exercise his power while it was still in his hands to remedy affairs and bring the complaints to a close. What complaints? she asked. In general, he replied, that everything is going on as it did before or worse in all the government boards and the admiralties. The admiralties will be acted upon when there was time, was her answer. But nothing is being expedited, he expostulated. At this she lost her temper. The Prince is an unfortunate man, she said. His friends, those in whom he has most confidence, instead of helping him make matters more difficult. He was working himself very hard, from morning until late in the night, giving no time to pleasure, which for him meant life with his family, so that he was wasting away. His humor was turning bad where once he had been such a good and sensitive person.[73]

These, indeed, were the traits that William displayed when Bentinck discussed the status of Gilles again with him early in March. He admitted Gilles's flaws – coldness, slowness, and even indifference in some important matters – but he believed nonetheless that simple humanity ought to prevail. Yet, if a replacement could be found, such as the pensionary of Leiden, Van der Straten, he would replace Gilles. But the candidate, diffident about the necessary close dependence upon the stadholder, declined the post, suggesting Peter Steyn of Haarlem instead.[74] When Bentinck

72 W. Bentinck, notes, 18 Jan. 1749, *Archives*, 4e Sér., I, 280–82.
73 *Ibid.*, 5 Feb. 1749, *Archives*, 4e Sér., I, 299–301.
74 *Ibid.*, 4, 6 Mar. 1749, *Archives*, 4e Sér., I, 340–42.

refused to continue as William's advisor unless Gilles went, the Prince, knowing how much he needed him despite his impertinent forthrightness, dismissed Gilles and named Steyn, who was a financial expert but a political nullity.[75]

Bentinck, himself so thoroughly a political man, did not realize the inner tragedy of the Prince and Princess. William IV and Anna were committed by their birth and upbringing to the ideal of rulership, but when it came into their hands (for their partnership was close and real), it did not yield the joys that they had expected. The Prince in particular did not share the delight in the "craft of kingship" (*le métier du roi*) that Louis XIV had described in his memoirs. In the case of this Prince and Princess of Orange it can be truly said that private virtues became, if not public vices, at least grave political weaknesses.

Yet these virtues, narrowly private, had their limitations. Discussing with the Prince and Princess the satires printed in Amsterdam that took them as the target, Bentinck found an attitude that he had difficulty accepting as honorable. It was quite right, they thought, that inferiors (like Bentinck) should be faulted for the deeds of their betters. Anna compared that principle with the practice in England, where ministers assumed all responsibility and the king none. Bentinck explained that this was because the king did nothing and the ministers everything; without their counter-signature, the king's orders would be treated as null. The Princess of course had seen the outer appearance of the English system of ministerial responsibility, Bentinck its core. He realized that the Princess was ready to shove upon those who served the Prince the fault and blame for whatever went wrong, whether or not they had advised it or taken part in it. It was a "false" principle with "awful" consequences.[76] In this matter, it was Bentinck who was the idealist and the Princess of Orange the cynic, belying our ordinary understanding of their personalities.

Bentinck, unable to make William over into a clear-minded and hard-handed politican, turned to an endeavor to make his government more effective. In February he began to set down his ideas for a government modeled essentially upon the French system in which the king's inner council was his cabinet and its members headed branches of government with distinct functions, although this comparison was not made explicit. Four departments were needed, for foreign affairs, military affairs, finances and domestic affairs, including the choice of magistrates. The task of foreign minister, if not the title, could be left where it had been traditionally, in the hands of the councilor pensionary of Holland, provided that he was trustworthy. The ministry of war would be immensely more difficult to

---

75 Kalshoven, 102, 104.   76 Bentinck, notes, 1 Apr. 1749, *Archives*, 4e Sér., 1, 368–70.

achieve, but Bentinck thought it could be achieved by bringing in Duke Louis of Brunswick-Wolfenbüttel, a member of the House of Hanover who was in the service of Maria Theresa in Austria. With him the Prince could make decisions, with all others excluded. Finances – the area in which the Dutch skills were formidable – could be left in the hands of any person of high ability. Most novel was Bentinck's notion for what today would be called a ministry of the interior.

With the experience of English party government clearly in mind, he saw the desirability of an organized system of leadership and guidance throughout the country. In each province the Prince should choose the best persons and then work with them, but not permitting them to interfere in the affairs of other provinces. Above these ministries there should be a council to which all matters of importance were brought for consideration and decision, so that the departments would work in unison. "There is not a Prince in the world who does not have such a council," he wrote. "The idea of governing a state without it is impracticable."[77]

On 25 March Bentinck submitted his proposals to William in a long memorandum, in which he also reviewed the political situation since 1747. William found one suggestion of Bentinck's to his taste, the proposal to bring Duke Louis of Brunswick-Wolfenbüttel to the Netherlands to become a general in the States army and to help provide leadership in the Dutch state. There was also an element of insurance for the House of Orange in the scheme. If William IV, whose health was not strong, should die before either of his children came of age, then the duke could aid Princess Anna in the governance of the country.[78] Bentinck himself was sent to Vienna to obtain his release from the service of Maria Theresa. William wrote in his own hand to the Empress Dowager to seek the duke's release "to succor" him in the command of the army.[79] His release was granted, and he arrived in the republic in December 1750 to accept the post of field marshal. It was a post, however, that was of importance only in wartime, with few powers and duties during peace.[80] William refused, however, to give him a civil position with clearly defined powers and functions. It would be a violation of the constitution, he said.[81]

The accident to which Bentinck had referred so often in his pleas to the Princess to accept his advice came on 22 October 1751. The man who had been hailed as a savior four years before departed this world without the tears of the populace. Deputies came from the States to express their

---

77 *Ibid.*, 19 Feb. 1749, *Archives*, 4e Sér., I, 306–8.
78 *Ibid.*, 23 Sept. 1749, *Archives*, 4e Sér., II, 9–11.
79 William IV to Empress Dowager of Austria, 17 Dec. 1749, Koninklijke Bibliotheek, The Hague, Hs 72 d20/10, holograph.
80 N. A. Bootsma, *De Hertog van Brunswijk, 1750–1759* (Assen, 1962), 22.
81 *Ibid.*, *Brunswijk*, 15–16.

condolences, but they were not accompanied by guards or troops, except for Holland's. "There is no consternation in the world," recorded the Utrecht deputy Hardenbroek in his diary. Anna accepted the death of her beloved husband with much phlegm and firmness, he informs us, and took the oath as guardian-governor for her son, who was just three years of age.[82]

In the eyes of the world, in his own time and in the retrospective judgment of historians, William IV had failed. He had not met the task that "History", that is, later generations in their special wisdom, thought he faced. It is doubtful that he would have thought himself so gross a failure. He had attempted a reconciliation with the regents as well as one between the regents and the people, and if, high and low, they balked, they would have to face the alternative. Where nonetheless he did fall woefully short was in his understanding of the nature of the conflicts within the Dutch polity and Dutch society. He reduced them to matters of good will, of which he had a full store himself, and did not understand why his soft words did not restore calm. He cannot be fairly faulted for not having played the role of a revolutionary, which he did not want; but he did not understand that his restoration was the work of a revolution, organized by his own supporters and fostered by the English for their own purposes.[83]

The stadholderate did not change much during these brief four years. For the first time there was a single stadholder in all seven provinces, but otherwise the government remained as steadfastly provincial and particularist as it had always been. There was no longer any need to seek election, for the office of stadholder in each of the provinces was now hereditary in both male and female lines. The division of powers between the stadholder and the States remained as vague and ambiguous as always, a constitutional swamp that could easily swallow up the political debate in the country.

82 Hardenbroek, I, 75.   83 Blok, *Geschiedenis*, III, 471.

10

William V: the era of Anna and Brunswick

There was no repetition of 1672 or 1702 upon the death of William IV. No effort was made to take advantage of the novel situation – the hereditary stadholderate in the hands of an infant – in order to overturn the institution and return to stadholderless government. William V's mother, Princess Anna, was accepted as regent in the child's name and on his behalf. Bentinck and the councilor pensionary of Holland, Steyn, acted quickly and vigorously to assure that she was given her place as Princess Gouvernante. For the reviving States party, allowing her to take over as Gouvernante was preferable to inflaming anew the conflict with the burghers in the towns. The regents recognized that they no longer had the power to abolish the stadholderate.[1]

One of the Princess's privy councilors, C. H von der Lühe, defined the situation sharply for her in a *mémoire* dated 2 December, which he may have drawn up at the instructions of the dying William IV. None of the functions of the stadholdership must be allowed to lapse or be taken over by the States, he urged, even for a period, lest a new Act of Seclusion result; these tasks must be assumed by the Prince's guardians. It was important, too, that his education remain in their hands and not be assumed by the States; there must be no repetition of the "Child of State" episode of William III's youth.[2] Bentinck, with a wholly different political vision, saw to the contrary that William V, even in his infancy, was a public personage and that the States, as the sovereigns, could not be excluded from his guardianship out of hand. He did not waver in his conception of the stadholderate as government *with* the States, not over them.[3]

The issue was not an idle one, for the various provinces were not able to agree easily about guardianship. The States of Holland proposed that each province exercise a distinct and separate guardianship, but the States of Gelderland vigorously opposed such multiple guardianships, favoring a single board of guardians with common and uniform representation of the provinces.[4] The Frieslanders feared that what would actually come would

1 Kalshoven, 114–115; Japikse, *Geschiedenis*, II, 131. 2 Bootsma, *Brunswijk*, 71.
3 *Ibid.*, 72. 4 *Ibid.*, 82, 93.

William V, 1748–1806

be another stadholderless period, something that they had never experienced.[5] The issue was not finally settled for another four and a half years, when all the provinces at last agreed to "regulations of guardianship." The right to appointment of municipal magistrates was the key issue in dispute, and the Princess's friends won it for her.[6]

Anna was intelligent, but the years of isolation in Leeuwarden had taken their toll on her. In the little capital town in the northern province, so far from the center of power in the Republic, she had been doomed to virtual idleness, although she supported her late husband's scattered followers when she could. Her grasp of the Dutch political system was imperfect, especially in the way it actually worked rather than in its purely constitutional and juridical aspects.[7] Even during the not quite four years of William IV's administration (only preachers and poets given to rhetorical recklessness called it a "reign"), she had found herself frequently thwarted by contradictory demands upon her. Now, a widow, she had to take upon her shoulders the task of leadership of the state.

She did not have to carry it alone, however. Duke Louis of Brunswick, who had come two years before to enter the Dutch military service, now gave the Princess the political support which Bentinck had had in mind when he first recruited him. The promises of a formal political role which William IV had made to him were not fulfilled, but he was persuaded to remain as an advisor to Anna in addition to keeping his military post. Like the Gouvernante he adhered to the political ideas and attitudes that he imported from his German homeland to the strange soil of the United Provinces, although he tried to apply them in ways that would work in the new conditions.[8]

Together with Bentinck and a few other close counselors of the Princess, Brunswick formed a so-called "conference" on foreign affairs which was a kind of informal cabinet. The councilor pensionary of Holland, Steyn, was also a member of the "conference." This was an acknowledgment of the granite fact that Holland was the heart of the country and its chief officer the most important official in the state after the stadholder himself. Steyn wanted conflict neither with the House of Orange nor with the States of his own province; indeed, he was as staunch a traditionalist as Anna herself.[9] Bentinck saw Steyn as an ally through whom the province of Holland, in which resided "the whole strength of the Republic," could be held for the stadholder, "whatever little dabbling politicians may say to the contrary."[10]

Unlike the "secret committee" (*secreet besogne*) of Frederick Henry's time, the "conference" was not a committee of the States General but a

---

5 *Ibid.*, 82–83.   6 *Ibid.*, 140–41.   7 Blok, *Geschiedenis*, III, 471–72.
8 Bootsma, *Brunswijk*, 155–56, 231.   9 *Ibid.*, 85.
10 Bentinck to Newcastle, 29 Aug. 1752, *Archives*, 4e Sér., II, 240.

part of the Princess's court. It read dispatches and discussed policies, but, although it had no power of decision and execution, it was potentially the instrument for the unification of leadership by the stadholder that Bentinck, and before him Van Slingelandt, had had in mind.[11] Its success depended, however, upon the willingness of the Princess to follow its advice and the firmness of her will. She continued to misread the political situation in the Netherlands, especially in her relations with Amsterdam, and she was like her father, George II, in her resentment against domination by others – and with such forceful personalities as Bentinck and Brunswick as her closest supporters, that was not an empty concern – while being quite unable to chart and follow an independent political course on her own.[12] It was more comfortable for the Princess to take the advice of favorites, who had no independent status but were totally dependent upon her, and, worse, were open to bribery by those who wished to benefit by her decisions.[13]

Bentinck and Brunswick, however uncomfortable with her attitude toward them, were strong men who were not shaken by it; the opposite was true of Steyn. To her the conflict that broke out in 1755 between Steyn and Brunswick over Dutch foreign policy was not simply a choice between alternatives in which diverse, even contradictory, interests were represented: whether, as Brunswick favored, the Republic should stand by the "Old System" of opposition to France, or, as Steyn, prompted by the needs of the Dutch economy, urged, it should seek to remain neutral in the visibly approaching event of a renewed war between France and Britain. She had her secretary demand of Steyn whether he was pro-Amsterdam or pro-Princess, to which he replied that he had already proved his devotion to the House of Orange but had to bear the weight of Amsterdam's financial and political power.[14]

She confronted him later in the year in even blunter fashion. As Bentinck and Brunswick, whom she ordered to be present, watched, she told the councilor pensionary that she respected his office but he must not play at being stadholder. If he worked loyally with her and respected her function as Gouvernante, she would be reconciled with him. Steyn at first sought to defend his policy, but at last lost his poise and capitulated.[15] Her triumph was a pyrrhic one, however, for Steyn had served William IV and then herself as a pliant instrument for influencing the policy of Holland; he

11 Japikse, "De Staten-Generaal," 104–5.
12 N. A. Bootsma, "Princes Anna van Hannover," in: *Voor Rogier: Een bundel Opstellen van oud-leerlingen de Hoogleraar bij zijn afscheid aangeboden*, ed. F. F. J. M. van Eerenbeemt, A. F. Manning and P. H. Winkelman (Hilversum and Antwerp, 1964), 142–43.
13 Blok, *Geschiedenis*, III, 477–78.
14 Bootsma, *Brunswijk*, 237–38; Bentinck, notes, 21 Feb. 1755, *Archives*, 4e Sér., II, 464–67.
15 Bootsma, *Brunswijk*, 295–96.

was a councilor pensionary in the tradition of Cats, not of De Witt, and by demanding unconditional fidelity to herself, she undercut his ability to bring about an accord of interests between herself and Holland.

From the beginning of her governorship Anna's policy was essentially to hold on to the power and prerogatives of the stadholderate. But she could not prevent the States of Holland from taking the choice of magistrates in the towns from her and giving it back to the municipal governments, as had been done after the death of William II in 1650. Their Noble Great Might-inesses of Holland also made themselves masters of the future of William IV, deciding in 1752 that he would not attain majority until he reached the age of eighteen years. They decided too that his education would be super-vised by a committee that would be named by the Princess, so that the boy would be a "Child of State."[16] If the party of the regents in Holland was being very cautious, they were far less so in the eastern province of Over-ijssel, where in the town of Zwolle as the dominant faction, once bitterly anti-Orangist, they now expected the backing of the Princess. At the same time the landed nobility began to assert their independence of the House of Orange and to flaunt republican principles, although a competition for jobs lay behind the high-flown words.[17]

In this they were following the example of Amsterdam, where the town council decided early in 1752 to go ahead with the election on 1 February of States party burgomasters in flagrant disregard of the recommendation of the Princess, a prerogative that rested upon the oral promises made during the troubles of 1748 and not upon any legal requirement. The novelty of the situation was that the magistrates had the majority of the population behind them in this virtual insult to the Prince's mother and guardian: the disappointment over William IV's conduct in 1748 was ex-acting its price.[18] In this contest of wills, the Amsterdam regents no longer felt the hot breath of an angry populace. When Daniel Raap died in January, the burial ceremonies brought crowds on to the streets to shout their hatred for him and their new antipathy to the House of Orange.[19] In the whole relationship to Amsterdam, the Princess displayed a lack of tact in her conduct toward the great city, a desire to command rather than to persuade, qualities of which she was not bereft in other circumstances.[20]

In the year 1754, despite her general reluctance to accept any change in the political system, she brought up the idea of splitting the stadholder-ship, so that her daughter would become stadholder in Friesland and

16 Blok, *Geschiedenis*, III, 473.
17 Bootsma, *Brunswijk*, 104–5; Charles Bentinck to Princess Anna, 24 Feb., May 19, 1753, *Archives*, 4e Sér., II, 253–54, 275–77.
18 Brugmans, V, 219–20, 224.   19 Blok, *Geschiedenis*, III, 479.
20 Bootsma, *Brunswijk*, 52–53.

Groningen with the title of "Gouvernante" and her son would keep the post in the five southerly provinces.[21] Bentinck thought it a "wild" notion, conceived by persons who played upon Anna's affection for her daughter; it was doubly dangerous, he warned the English ambassador, for it called the fixity of the existing constitution into question. It would create a new party in the country, which had enough of parties. He was equally critical of her desire to make Caroline her brother's guardian in the event of her own death. This was to decide a fundamental question of state without the States.[22] The idea of dividing the stadholdership had arisen because plans were already afoot for Caroline's eventual marriage to Prince Charles Christian of Nassau-Weilburg, a distant cousin, even though she was still only ten years of age.[23]

The next year the Gouvernante put her signature on a testament that established Brunswick as first guardian of the Prince of Orange after her death, despite her personal antipathy (Bentinck called it hatred) for him.[24] The States of Holland, Friesland and the other provinces thereupon decided to set the terms for Brunswick's military command as acting captain-general, but rejecting any possibility of split stadholdership.[25]

By 1756 it was becoming evident to insiders whose principles made them Orangist but who had not become courtiers and flatterers that the Princess Gouvernante was shaping the young Prince in her own image. At the age of six he was acquiring the traits that would probably be his throughout life ("the child is the father of the man"), and these troubled the Utrecht deputy Hardenbroek. The little Prince was "surly" and given to outbursts of temper, especially toward those who he was told were not his friends, like the Amsterdammers. Of such people he said, "Once I'm in power, they'll learn to shit better." He spoke of hanging as if it were a trifle.[26] Two years later there were still anxieties among thoughtful observers about his attitude. He respected no one, it was reported, not even his sister, of whom he said, "She's a beast" (*C'est une bête*).[27]

When war broke out again between Britain and France in 1756, the issue of neutrality or alliance for the United Provinces could no longer be put off. George II recognized that outright Dutch entry into the war was not in the cards, but he nonetheless demanded that the Republic send him an auxiliary corps, called a *secours*, of 6,000 men, according to the provisions of the treaty of alliance. Bentinck worried about whether the Princess would remain loyal to the "Old System," because of her lack of assiduity

21 *Ibid.*, 130–31.
22 Bentinck to Yorke, 3 May 1754, to Newcastle, 31 May 1754, *Archives*, 4e Sér., II, 388–92, 406–9.
23 Bootsma, *Brunswijk*, 122–23.
24 Bentinck, notes, 15 Apr. 1755, *Archives*, 4e Sér., II, 513.
25 Bootsma, *Brunswijk*, 94, 99, 129–30.   26 Hardenbroek, I, 133.   27 *Ibid.*, 143.

and her ignorance of important matters.[28] Nor was he happy when English ships came to pick up the *secours* before the Dutch government had come to a formal decision. He reminded the Duke of Newcastle that the matter had to pass through "all the formes, which every affair of importance is subjected to in this country." There was no way to avoid differences of opinion in "popular and mixed governments."[29] Bentinck forgot for once that the Whig vision of British politics was one of "popular and mixed government," and that the key difference between the British and Dutch governments was less the difference between the absence or presence of a crowned head than the tight centralization of the island monarchy and the unconquerable provincialism and localism of the Republic.

The course of events impelled Bentinck to turn his mind once again to the deeper causes of the problems of the Dutch state. His analysis may be marred by his strength of feeling and his never-failing confidence in his own judgment, but he had a knack for seeing what was wrong. Whether his cure would have worked, we cannot say, for it was never really tried. What he saw in October 1756 was the lack of effective leadership in the country. He bemoaned the absence of what he called a "formed party," by which he had in mind a coalescence of factional interests and broad principles in the person of recognized leaders. There was no leader in any of the cities to whom a national leader could address himself (or, at the moment, herself) and receive a reply that bound its government. Formerly there had usually been such persons.

The national leadership belonged to the stadholder and the councilor pensionary of Holland working in tandem, he held, because they were able to get the States of Holland to accept their policies, if not at once and not always without resistance, at least in general and in the long run; but it required knowing the interests involved and the forms of Dutch politics and maintaining the unanimity of the stadholder, the order of Nobility, and the councilor pensionary. Together they could overcome the vitiating faults of the Dutch constitution and do great things, such as had been done in the past, to the astonishment of Europe. The problem was that leadership was in the hands of the Princess Gouvernante, and she was using it only to spread mistrust and confusion, undercutting the interests of the very stadholdership she was trying to protect. She did not respect the councilor pensionary, who was crucial in the committees of the States, where real leadership was exercised. At the moment Amsterdam happened to have no true leader of its own, but one would come and then she would face difficulties far greater than the present problems.[30]

28 Bentinck, notes, *Archives*, 4e Sér., II, 60–61.
29 Bentinck to Newcastle, 2 Mar. 1756, *Archives*, 4e Sér., III, 70–71.
30 Bentinck, notes, 6 Oct. 1756, *Archives*, 4e Sér., III, 319–25.

His fundamental insight was that the key function was leadership, and he was emotionally and intellectually tortured by his awareness that this was precisely what Princess Anna, like William IV before her, did not provide. Her concern, indeed, was almost the exact contrary. She told Steyn in 1758 that the Amsterdammers were trying to lay upon her alone, "being at the head of the Republic," the responsibilities for the disasters that could arise out of the existing circumstances (clearly the foreign policy tangle of the country).[31]

In mid-December of 1758 the Gouvernante became so ill that there was fear for her life. Bentinck and Brunswick, concerned lest the States party attempt to repeat the experience of 1650 and 1702 as they had not done when William IV died, were reassured when Steyn told them he would stand firm against either outright abolition of the stadholdership or any violation of the terms of the resolutions on guardianship, although Bentinck continued to worry that the councilor pensionary would not stay firm.[32] The Princess herself, trying to undo her own policy of preventing unity of the cities in Holland, now sought to bring them together in support of the preservation of the stadholderate.[33]

On 11 January, she sent letters to each of the provinces informing them of the projected marriage of Princess Caroline to Prince Charles Ernest of Nassau-Weilburg. She asked that they recognize the rights of the eventual children under the succession resolutions of 1747 and 1748; the resolutions required that the Princess marry only an adherent of the Reformed faith, but, although Nassau-Weilburg remained a Lutheran, the children would be brought up in the mother's church.[34] It was just in time, for the next day she was dead. She had accomplished the fundamental task which had been entrusted to her, to maintain the stadholderate intact.[35]

On the very day of the Princess's death, the States of Holland met to carry through their resolution of 1752 upon the guardianship. The other provinces followed suit. The duke of Brunswick became the young Prince's guardian and at the same time was named as acting captain-general. Unlike Princess Anna, who as Gouvernante had exercised the functions of the stadholder, he was barred from a political role. His instructions from the various provinces restricted his official duties to the strictly military. Nonetheless it was not long before he was making his political influence felt. Within the Orangist party he became its head and spokesman, and the States party, itself still without effective leadership, was not ready for an assault upon the stadholderate. Brunswick was therefore able to

---

31 "Precies van eene conversatie tusschen H. K. H. en desen Heere RP Stein in 't Huis d'Orangezaal," 26 Aug. 1758, *Archives*, 4e Sér., III, 554–55.
32 Bootsma, *Brunswijk*, 474–75.   33 *Ibid.*, 475.
34 *Archives*, 4e Sér., IV, 42 n1.   35 Van Deursen, "Staatsinstellingen," 360.

devote himself more to the preservation of the prerogatives of the stadholder for the future than to their vigorous present use.[36] Yet he was not wholly satisfied, for he would have to serve as commander in the customary Dutch manner, with the States and Delegated Councilors having the right of final decision upon the proposals he submitted to them. This, he complained, was not what he had been led to hope in 1752.[37] But the need of the moment was not complaints but action, for which he was ready.

The first task was to bring to completion the arrangements for Caroline's marriage. Yet all did not go as smoothly as Brunswick and Bentinck desired. Weilburg's insistence on remaining Lutheran provided Delft and Amsterdam with a basis for urging that the States stick to the letter of their resolution; if Weilburg did not convert to the Reformed faith, the States should withhold their consent.[38] The negotiations for the marriage moved slowly, but at last all obstacles were overcome, and Caroline and Charles Ernest became wife and husband on 5 March 1760.

In the years that followed, Brunswick acted his various roles as fully as he could. With the United Provinces neutral, his military duties were few, although he remained always an advocate of increasing the number of troops. His political role was constricted by the absence of explicit powers, and the most important prerogatives of the stadholderate were exercised by the States, pending their resumption by the stadholder when he came of age. A third stadholderless period came into existence, although not in law and without the name.[39] But Brunswick's most important task was to bring the boy of eight years who was in his care to full intellectual and moral growth, able himself to perform the tasks and exercise the prerogatives of the stadholdership.

The duke permitted only pages to see the boy, so that he remained stiff and awkward in social intercourse. He did not go out very much, not even to visit his sister and her husband. What kind of man would come of this child who knew only the company of pages and servants?[40] Even when William was fifteen, he was disturbingly childish. He was weak both in body and character, perhaps not even destined for a long life, it was thought. He was proud of his rank and place. "That is my property, this king is one of my relations, I can do that," were remarks that fell from his lips.[41]

Brunswick rejected a proposal of Bentinck and Steyn to have the Prince take the seats in the States General and the Council of State to which he

36 Bootsma, *Brunswijk*, 94, 476–77; Blok, *Geschiedenis*, III, 493.
37 Louis of Brunswick to Bentinck, 30 Jan. 1759, *Archives*, 4e Sér., IV, 25–26.
38 Bentinck, annotations on meeting of States of Holland, 9 May 1759, *Archives*, 4e Sér., 109, 111.
39 Groen van Prinsterer, II, 532; Japikse, "De Staten-Generaal," 125; Schutte, 244.
40 Hardenbroek, I, 174–75, 195, 203, 207.   41 Hardenbroek, I, 273–74.

would have a right when he came of age on 8 March 1763. His argument was that he would not be entitled to a place in the States of Holland until he was eighteen, and the arrangements in the States General should be kept parallel with those in Holland. The three years should be allowed to pass tranquilly, without continual intrigues and cabals, while the Prince continued to learn more of what constituted the welfare of the government and more about himself. When that was completed, he would be ready to undertake the government himself.[42] It was a curious argument. At that same age William III was old enough to learn statecraft from John de Witt, and statecraft was an art that was better learned in the council chambers of government than from books or bookish tutors.

William was old enough, however, for the question of his marriage to be raised. Reports that an English princess was being sought as his eventual bride stirred the Prussian envoy, Thulemeyer, to propose Princess Wilhelmina, the niece of King Frederick II, for the honor. Brunswick found all the talk premature and thought the Prince ought to be allowed to make his own choice when the time came. He did reassure the Prussian monarch, however, that William would not require the consent of the States for his marriage, as had been true for Caroline if she wished to retain her rights as heiress apparent.[43]

As the Prince's eighteenth birthday approached, it became evident that Brunswick had met the first of his tasks, to assure the entry of William V into the offices of his forefathers. The regents had learned to work with Brunswick, trusting him if not loving him because he did not intrude on their rights. He had avoided Princess Anna's peevish relationship with Amsterdam, and he had not tried to make the Republic a submissive vassal of its ally, England. The thanks offered to the duke as his ward came of age and took over the government in his own name were usually sincere, if not quite anticipated.[44]

The prospects for William's administration looked good. He assumed his multiple offices without dispute. When he took his seat in the Court of Holland, an advocate could rejoice in the fact that, unlike his two predecessors, William III and William IV, he had become stadholder strictly according to law, not thanks to riots, and hence did not have the people to thank but only those who had governed well during his minority.[45] Indeed, on Brunswick's advice, he asked the various provincial States to give him their own acts of appointment, even though in view of his hereditary stadholdership this was not strictly necessary. The States party was

42 Louis of Brunswick to Bentinck, 30 Jan., 14 Feb. 1763, *Archives*, 4e Sér., IV, 473–74, 476–79.
43 Louis of Brunswick to Steyn, 2 Aug. 1764, *Archives*, 4e Sér., IV, 513–17.
44 Blok, *Geschiedenis*, III, 504.   45 Groen van Prinsterer, *Handboek*, II, 539–40.

pleased with the gesture, which acknowledged the principle of the sovereignty of the States.[46]

Yet events would soon prove that the picture was too rosy. William V was almost a clone of his father. He replaced strength of character and independence of judgment by stubbornness and dissimulation. His bookish learning was displayed in a detailed knowledge of Dutch history and constitutional law, but he was not at home in the complications of general European politics. In a deep sense, he did not understand politics, the formation and execution of policies and the handling of people. He thought that he could simply command within the framework of his prerogatives and obedience should follow without argument – a notion that absolute monarchs if they were wise might uphold in words but did not adhere to in their deeds. He made no effort to hold the affection of the people, indeed looked almost pridefully disdainful when he appeared in public. He defended his prerogatives with fierce intensity, yet did not work hard. He was a vacuum at the head of state, for he failed to provide the strong leadership that was all the more requisite in the Dutch Republic because of the ambiguity of its institutions.[47]

The Prince did take one immensely important political step, however, although he kept it secret not only from the public but even from most of his intimates. On 3 May he put his signature on a document called the Act of Advisorship (*Acte van Consulentschap*); the duke of Brunswick was the other signatory. A "consulent" was a legal advisor, but here it meant something wider, both literally and in its implications. The Act opens with an admission that Brunswick had been called to the Republic by William IV not merely to become a field marshal, as had been given out to the public, but also "in reality" to help him in the supreme military command and to become a "trusted friend and relative" who, in the event of his death, could be a counsel and friend to Anna and her children. This had been done in 1751. Anna then made Brunswick the executor of her own testament and the guardian of her children after her death, as had also happened.

Now William V wished to continue for some time to have the assistance of Brunswick, to whom he was bound by the strongest bonds of tender love and filial affection. Brunswick therefore promised to assist William in military and all other branches of government under his authority, and to advise him in personal and political matters, showing neither favor nor disfavor to any province, city, body or person. The duke would stay with

---

46 Blok, *Geschiedenis*, III, 504.
47 *Ibid.*, 504–5; Thulemeyer to Frederick II, 1 Apr. 1766 [F. W. von Thulemeyer], *Dépêches van Thulemeyer, 1763–1788*, eds. Robert Fruin and H. T. Colenbrander (Amsterdam, 1912), 17–18.

him at all times, even during his travels. In return William accepted the obligation to hold Brunswick responsible only to himself and to provide him with indemnity against all others.[48]

This document is astonishing in both its strictly political and its more broadly human dimensions. Brunswick himself shredded the intended veil of secrecy. He gave the Act to Bentinck two days later to read, after he had already shown it to at least one other person. If you had asked my advice beforehand, Bentinck told the duke, I would have been glad to tell you what I thought, but now it is too late and there would be no point to my comments. Brunswick understood that this was a polite criticism, but did not enter into a discussion with his friend.[49] We know what Bentinck thought from the remarks he set down soon afterward, which sum up the political meaning very well. It was a "kind of safeguard, a better safe-conduct" against what might happen as a result of the duke's advice. But what indemnity could William really give? In what capacity was he acting? What cases were covered? It removed Brunswick from the purview of the laws, which was in violation of the constitution and of the Prince's own commissions as stadholder. Furthermore, Bentinck wrote in his reflec-tions, the protection of the laws should be sufficient for Brunswick; any-thing else is dangerous in a free country, where all instructions, commis-sions and documents relating to the state, and the duties of all persons in the employ of the sovereign, must be and always have been public.[50]

Bentinck in these remarks revealed again the difference between his political vision and that of the heads of the House of Orange that he served so sedulously and faithfully. They saw the public power in essentially private terms, he in those of public service. The historian may detect in Bentinck flaws of conduct and even self-deception (what human being avoids them totally?), and he certainly resented being displaced by Bruns-wick as William's principal confidential advisor,[51] but the sincerity and loftiness of his conception of his duty as a statesman cannot be denied.

The Act also reveals in almost blinding clarity the kind of human being that Brunswick had molded in William V. If there was ever a document that called for the skills and insights of a psychohistorian, this was it.

48 William V, "Acte van Consulentschap," 3 May 1766, *Archives*, 5e Sér., I, 21–26; [Louis, Duke of Brunswick-Wolfenbüttel], *Kort voorstel van het geene omtrent den overgang van Zyne Hoogheid den Heere L. Hertog van Brunswyk, In den Dienst van de Republicq der Vereenigde Nederlanden en deszelfs Conservatie in den gemelden Dienst is voorgevallen, en vervolgens aanleiding heeft gegeeven tot het passeeren van Zeekere Acte, Tusschen Zyne Hoogheid den Heere Prince van Orange en Nassau, en gemelde Zyne Hoogheid den heere L. Hertog van Brunswyck, Op den 3. Mey 1766 aangegaan* (The Hague, [?1781]), 17–20.
49 Bentinck, notes, 5 May 1766, *Archives*, 5e Sér., I, 28–29.
50 Bentinck, reflections upon the Acte van Consulentschap, undated (after 3 May 1766), *Archives*, 5e Sér., I, 27.
51 Bootsma, *Brunswick*, 96.

Without going so far, we may note that the French envoy, D'Avrincourt, wrote a penetrating judgment in a letter to his own court, of which Bentinck obtained a copy; he worked out the cipher himself and kept the copy in his own hand. D'Avrincourt thought that Brunswick had spoiled William's education by indulging him in frivolities and dissipations. The duke would become in effect the prime minister, leaving the stadholder with only the appearance of power. All the same nothing would get done, the envoy anticipated, until the Prince married, and then his wife (probably Princess Wilhelmina of Prussia) would take umbrage and no doubt encourage him to throw off this yoke.[52]

Two facts probably explain Brunswick's initiation of the advisorship. First were the uncertainties about his position in a republican state to whose institutions and character he never wholly adapted, always assuming as he did the identity of the interests of state and dynasty, the political principle in which he had been brought up and lived until he came to the United Provinces.[53] Second were the inadequacies of the duke's conception of fatherhood (for William V would repeatedly call him his "second father" and his feelings for him were patently filial). Wishing to protect the child and youth, Brunswick had sheltered the Prince from life itself, from which he could have learned to know, understand and work with people. Fearing the mistakes William would make, he had kept him from making the mistakes from which he could learn. It was a classic instance of the father (or the surrogate-father) who will not allow his son to grow up, to become his own man. At the same time he had taught William (and the flunkeys at the court did the same) that he held high rank, was a member of the royal caste of Europe, that all others in the country were his inferiors. Admitting all this, we must add that bringing up crown princes was notoriously one of the most difficult and treacherous of tasks, one in which the best of intentions could have untoward consequences in the character of the person destined for power. None of this might have mattered much in a private person, except for himself and those about him, but a stadholder's character shaped the character of his government no less than did the structure and the events of politics.

Bentinck continued to be concerned about the Prince's disregard for established and proper procedures in the work of government. His high posts did not make him a sovereign who could do whatever he wanted.[54] Yet, over the years, he began to take his work more seriously and to do it better. With his extraordinary command of the details of the constitutional framework of Dutch politics, he could effectively insist upon his prerogatives in appointments, which in skilled hands could be the key instrument

---

52 *Archives*, 5e Sér., I, 31–32.   53 Bootsma, *Brunswijk*, 98–99.
54 Bentinck, notes, Sept. 1766, *Archives*, 5e Sér., I, 56–60.

in mastery of the system. But he was neither a good administrator nor a good politician; he treated questions large and small with equal attention, but on matters of policy he swung this way and that, avoiding coming to a decision. His continuing dependence upon Brunswick was all too evident, and it was worsened by the duke's own unmethodical methods and his failure to keep in close and steady touch with the principal officers of government, like councilor pensionary Steyn.[55] William was at his best as a patron of culture and science, and was probably the most intellectual of all the stadholders.[56]

Bentinck was deeply disturbed by the way the Prince went about his projected marriage with the Prussian princess, Wilhelmina, acting without careful discussion with his own chosen advisors. He saw that once William had entered the path of negotiations there was no going back. The consequences for both the Dutch Republic and the House of Orange could be immense and varied.[57] There would be no political advantage gained by the marriage, for so far as he could see the king of Prussia had no interests in common with the Republic of the United Provinces, and many in conflict. If the Prince and the duke had asked his advice, he would have told them to seek the hand of the English princess Mathilda; but she had in the meantime become queen of Denmark.[58]

Bentinck had read the situation correctly. The English ambassador, Yorke, had to ask the Prince outright what was happening, and William admitted he would have preferred Mathilda, but now he had no choice. If I marry the princess of Prussia, he added, I will not therefore be marrying the king of Prussia or his principles; I will always remain firm in friendship with England, whose interests are the same as those of the Republic and my own. William timidly told the envoy that he very much wanted to visit England, but was "not yet enough his own master" to do so; he hoped he would be able to come after his own marriage.[59] Time would show whether taking a bride would make him in fact his own master. After all the talk, the marriage of Prince William V of Orange to Princess Frederika Sophia Wilhelmina of Prussia finally took place in Berlin in October 1767. For Wilhelmina, as for her husband's mother whom she had never met, marriage was an escape to relative freedom, a chance to be on her own after an unhappy childhood.

Brunswick and Bentinck had a falling out in 1769, ending their long friendship. Even in their collaboration, there had been a rivalry for domination over the Prince of Orange. The particular occasion for the conflict

55 Bentinck, notes, 28 May 1767, *Archives*, 5e Sér., I, 63.   56 Schutte, 244.
57 Bentinck to Fagel, 13, 20 Aug. 1766, *Archives*, 5e Sér., I, 44–45, 48–49.
58 Bentinck, minute of letter without addressee, 26 July 1767, *Archives*, 5e Sér., I, 71.
59 Bentinck, notes, 22 June 1767, *Archives*, 5e Sér., I, 65–66.

was a dispute over the right of the Prince as captain-general to transfer from a civil to a military court the trial of an "invalid" (a veteran soldier, as in France) who had murdered his wife. When Bentinck upheld the rights of the civil authorities, Brunswick was gleeful, for William could then see who was his "true friend."[60] On the duke's recommendation, the prisoner was taken from Woerden, where he was being held for trial by the civil court, to The Hague, where the High Council of War would sit in judgment upon him. If Bentinck comes to protest, Brunswick suggested to William, tell him a little drily that you know what is yours by right, what belongs to civil justice and what to military, and that you will not sacrifice the latter to the former. To the duke's delight, this is just what happened.[61]

The price that had to be paid for this little victory was that deputies to the States of Holland from various towns went to Steyn to protest the transfer as a violation of the fundamental laws of the Republic. Unless the councilor pensionary could assure them that the prisoner had been returned to Woerden, they would inform their towns. Steyn replied that William had given the order not as stadholder but as captain-general, and he would not change his opinion on what he believed was his right. The pensionaries of Amsterdam came the next day to press their case. If William persisted, they said, the form of government would have been totally changed; instead of a stadholder they would have a despotic sovereign and the Dutch would be in a worse position than they had been under the Spaniards. "The usual piddling notions," was Brunswick's dismissive comment to William.[62] The comparison with the rule of Philip II, which echoed a common theme in States party pamphlets, was obviously grossly exaggerated, yet it revealed a direction of feeling that could be gravely dangerous to the stadholderate. The affair ended when the High Council of War condemned the murderer to death, but the Prince commuted the sentence to life imprisonment.[63]

Bentinck was confirmed in his judgment that William was inexperienced and did not know the world, but that it was useless to try to persuade him so long as he was led by Brunswick. The duke had broken with those who had brought him to the country, and the actions he took, by causing blame to be heaped upon the Prince, were endangering the political system of the Republic[64] – which meant the stadholderate. The conflict between the two men, who embodied contrary visions of the Dutch constitution and the

---

60 Louis of Brunswick to William V, 15 Aug. 1769, *Archives*, 5e Sér., I, 150–52.
61 Louis of Brunswick to William V, 16, 18, 21, 23, 26 Aug. 1769, *Archives*, 5e Sér., I, 156–63.
62 Louis of Brunswick to William V, 31 Aug. 1769, *Archives*, 5e Sér., I, 165–70.
63 *Archives*, 5e Sér., I, 181 n1.
64 Bentinck, notes, Sept. 1769, *Archives*, 5e Sér., I, 132–33.

place of the stadholder within it, sharpened. Brunswick called Bentinck's conduct "abominable," and he told the Prince that he must not abandon the least of his rights, lest all be lost. He must uphold in worthy fashion the role that Providence had given him as his portion.[65]

Bentinck began to think back to the Act of Advisorship, for it embodied for him the source of the irregularity, inconsistency and unconstitutionality of the way the business of the government had been handled since William had become stadholder in his own name.[66] He urged Steyn, to whom he made these remarks, to stay on as councilor pensionary instead of retiring when his current five-year term expired. The post was in danger of being debased unless Steyn acted more vigorously. It was all the more important because the Prince was so ineffectual in the stadholderate and was earning the disapproval of the enlightened public abroad and at home. Without naming Brunswick, he put the blame on him for depriving William of the opportunity to hear men give a variety of opinions in each other's presence.[67] In his endeavor to extract the Prince from the dependency upon Brunswick, Bentinck found an ally in Wilhelmina, as the French ambassador had anticipated before her marriage. Without opposing Brunswick outright, she wanted her husband to reduce the duke's powers and to assert himself in the conduct of government. She was afraid of what such continued tutelage would do to his character.[68]

The habit of thinking deeply and speaking candidly, at least to himself but often to William, was too ingrained in Bentinck to be easily abandoned. He continued to try to teach the Prince. His model, he told William, should be the Glorious Revolution in England. It had been the result not of the private ambitions of William III and Mary but of the need to prevent arbitrary government and papism from being established in England. Under their reign the country remained free, that is, governed by laws.[69] Clearly, he was attempting to instruct the Prince of Orange in the principles of Whiggery, but faced the contrary influence of Brunswick, who formally accepted the republican institutions of the United Provinces, but with a leaning toward giving the stadholder greater authority to act on his own, more like an absolute than a constitutional king.

Bentinck made another attempt to capture the Prince's understanding. The occasion was a remark by the Prince with regard to a dispute being discussed by the Delegated Councilors of Holland. It was of little importance, said William, whether they understood the matter on which they

---

65 Brunswick to William V, 1 Sept 1769, *Archives*, 5e Sér., I, 172.
66 Bentinck, notes, Nov. 1769, *Archives*, 5e Sér., I, 136–37.
67 Bentinck to Steyn, Nov. 1769, *Archives*, 5e Sér., I, 140–43.
68 Johanna W. A. Naber, *Prinses Wilhelmina, Gemalin van Willem V, Prins van Oranje* (Amsterdam, 1908), 38–39.
69 Bentinck to William V, Aug. 1769, *Archives*, 5e Sér., I, 109–11.

were voting so long as the vote went well. Debate was only a formality; the result alone counted. This was a pernicious and ruinous maxim, Bentinck warned him, especially in a Republic. When William, who considered the practice in conformity with stadholderian principles, asked him for his reasons, Bentinck wrote another long letter. The stadholderate existed because of the country's need for effective executive power in the state, but it did not change the fundamental law.[70] But what Bentinck dared not tell the Prince to his face he wrote in his own notes in March 1770. "No one in the States of Holland, or in any other province for that matter, has any confidence in the Prince of Orange because of his great deference to the judgment of the Duke in favor of Bleiswijk."[71]

Peter van Bleiswijk was the pensionary of Delft, a steady partisan of the House of Orange on the pattern of subservience the duke liked. He was able to swing his election as the new councilor pensionary of Holland after Steyn died in November 1772.[72] Although the stadholder and Brunswick lost in Steyn a collaborator who had generally worked hand in hand with them, they did not bemoan his loss, for they felt that he had forgotten his obligations to the Prince; specifically, he had sought to carry out his duties as the minister of the States of Holland and to conciliate Amsterdam as far as possible.[73]

The year 1773 was marked by the emergence of a new figure upon the Dutch political scene, an Overijssel nobleman named Joan (a form of the name John) Derk van der Capellen tot den Pol. He drew attention to himself by opposing proposals for increasing both army and navy. His statement in the States of Overijssel drew Brunswick's ire. He was hostile to the present form of government, the duke warned, and William should never give any commissions to this "ungrateful and unworthy subject."[74] Brunswick's choice of noun was revealing: the people of the Dutch Republic were not "subjects" of the Prince but of the provinces, and a member of a provincial States assembly like Van der Capellen ("tot den Pol" was his baronial title) was therefore both a subject and a member of the sovereign. The duke's choice of target was to the point, however. Van der Capellen became the principal voice of a new political force that was beginning to take shape, an opposition to William V that took the name of "Patriots."[75] For the next two decades political debate and struggle in the

---

70 *Ibid.*, Nov. 1769, *Archives*, 5e Sér., I, 137–39.
71 Bentinck, notes, 18 Mar. 1770, *Archives*, 5e Sér., I, 191–92.
72 Thulemeyer to Frederick II, 4 Dec. 1772, Thulemeyer, 100–1.
73 *Ibid.*, 23 Oct., 10 Nov. 1772, Thulemeyer 93–94, 96.
74 Louis of Brunswick to William V, 4 Sept. 1773, *Archives*, 5e Sér., I, 308–9.
75 For the Patriot movement, see P. Geyl, *De Patriottenbeweging* (Amsterdam, 1947) and Simon Schama, *Patriots and Liberators: Revolution in the Netherlands, 1780–1813* (New York, 1977), chs. 3, 4.

Dutch Republic would focus on the conflicts between the Orange party and the Patriots.

Yet, within the Orangist movement, the domination of Brunswick was giving rise to discontent. Bentinck had lost the last shreds of William's friendship by this time and would die on 13 October 1774. The Prince did not realize that Bentinck had sought the good of the country and the House; what he saw and remembered was a restless personality and an almost arrogant intelligence that only intensified his own feelings of inadequacy.[76] Whether, if William V had accepted the guidance of this counselor rather than that of the Duke of Brunswick, events would have turned out more happily, remains a matter of speculation; what is certain is that his counsel was followed only intermittently and very incompletely. In that sense Bentinck's service to a cause we might call "Dutch Whiggery" ended in failure.

His criticism of the policies of the Prince and the duke was being echoed now, however, by others who felt the need to guide and lead the country more effectively, and in particular to make sure of the assent of the provinces in general and in Holland of Amsterdam in particular before declaring a policy. Yet Amsterdam was concerned not only for its economic interests, to which Brunswick was willing to cater, but also for its freedom from the overriding political power of the stadholder.[77] It was not long before Van Bleiswijk's subservience to the Prince and Brunswick gained him the distrust of Amsterdam, without which no councilor pensionary of Holland could lead effectively.[78] The duke lost interest in conciliation. When Amsterdam continued its resistance to Brunswick's proposal to expand the army and navy, he took up what he called the battle against the city's "tyranny and despotism."[79] He considered himself to be protecting the "undivided sovereignty" of the province of Holland against the caprices of Amsterdam's burgomasters.[80] Capricious or not, they were able to exert such pressure that Van Bleiswijk, like his predecessor, began to show signs of acting independently.[81]

William's staunch constitutional conservatism guided his comments on a draft article that was being written for a new edition of the Diderot–D'Alembert *Encyclopédie* being printed at Yverdon (actually, a pirated edition)[82] by one of *griffier* Fagel's friends. At the author's request Fagel sent

76 William V to Van Bleiswijk, 25 Aug. 1774, *Archives*, 5e Sér., I, 351.
77 Thulemeyer to Frederick II, 16 Nov., 3 Dec. 1773, Thulemeyer, 123, 125.
78 Thulemeyer to Frederick II, 3 Dec. 1773, Thulemeyer, 124–25.
79 Brunswick to William V, 8 Dec. 1773, *Archives*, 5e Sér., I, 316.
80 William V to Van Bleiswijk, 29 July, 2, 9 Aug. 1775, *Archives*, 5e Sér., I, 381–82, 388, 395.
81 Hardenbroek, I, 373–74.
82 Robert Darnton, *The Business of Enlightenment: A Publishing History of the Encylopédie, 1775–1800* (Cambridge, Mass., 1979), 19.

it to William for his approval, and the Prince went through it rapidly but did not attempt to do all the research he thought adequate comment required. He found the article in general competent but sometimes inaccurate in detail, and in any case he could not take it as a code establishing the rights and prerogatives of the stadholderate. It erred in saying that the Prince was a political officer in the provinces and a military officer only in the Generality; he was also captain-general in each province individually, a "very delicate" point. In many of the offices, he had the right of recommendation but not of appointment, as he did in the army. Although he was called "Prince of Orange," the principality was now in the hands of the king of France.[83] The comments are revealing in the absence of any remarks about his *duties* as stadholder and captain-general, which we may fairly take as a weakness of political vision. The finicky concern for accuracy down to the the last tittle would honor an erudite scholar but was scarcely what an active statesman needed.

More to the point than erudition was effective leadership of the state. Hardenbroek was reminded of the situation in France when Louis XV gave the reins of government to Cardinal Fleury, his former tutor. Fleury, it had been said, did everything well but one thing: he failed to bring up a king capable of ruling in his own person by knowing what a monarch needs to know in order to govern and lead his people.[84] Hardenbroek noted, however, that Brunswick's hold on the Prince was being challenged by Princess Wilhelmina. In her presence the English ambassador, Yorke, took up a question he had already raised with the duke. William said he would consider it (obviously, in order to discuss it with Brunswick), and the Princess interjected, "It's not necessary to speak about it with the Duke. I accept it."[85]

The quarter-century after the death of William IV was therefore a period in which little had really happened. There were no great events, no great struggles. There had been in effect a stalemate in the country, a balance of strength between the House of Orange and its rivals; the contest was so muted that one cannot call them "enemies." It was something happening far away, across the ocean, that began the transformation of the stalemate into a sharp, bitter conflict in which the opposing parties became in the course of a few years unwilling to live with the ambiguity that had been the soul of Dutch politics since the emergence of the Republic almost two centuries before.

83 William V to H. Fagel, 4 Dec. 1774, *Archives*, 5e Sér., I, 360–62.
84 Hardenbroek, I, 365–66.   85 *Ibid.*, 371.

William V: the Patriot challenge

The event which released the latent conflicts of Dutch political life was the rebellion of Britain's American colonies in 1775, which at once divided Dutch sympathies and interests. William V unhesitatingly found the English government in the right and the colonists in the wrong; it was obvious, he thought, that a sovereign had the right to put down rebels. He had a copy of the American Declaration of Independence in his hands by 20 August 1776, and he read it with boiling indignation. It was a parody of the Dutch Act of Abjuration of 1581: how could the tyranny of Philip II be compared to the rule of George III?[1] It was the mere fact of rebellion that he loathed. In a conversation with Hardenbroek, who raised the parallel with the overthrow of James II by William III, he said, "In that event, I am a Jacobite."[2]

For all their hostility to the American rebels, William and Brunswick were anything but happy with English threats against the Republic if it did not halt the smuggling between the Dutch island of St Eustatius in the Caribbean and the Americans. The English were particularly indignant because a Dutch warship off St Eustatius had returned the salute of an American warship, in effect recognizing the independence of the new United States of America.[3] Brunswick found the demand of the English ambassador for immediate punishment of the governor of St Eustatius "unparalleled," indeed impossible for a state that wished to keep its sovereignty and independence. Of course the governor should be punished, but only according to constitutional forms.[4]

William wanted the Republic to maintain its neutrality nonetheless, even if war came between England and France, which was already aiding the insurgent Americans. The House of Orange had nothing to gain in war, he wrote the councilor pensionary. If the Republic became involved in war,

1 William V to Fagel, 20 Aug. 1776, *Archives*, 5e Sér., I, 449.
2 Hardenbroek, I, 380–81.
3 The best account of the role of the American rebellion in Dutch events in J. W. Schulte Nordholt, *Voorbeeld in de Verte* (Baarn, 1979) (translated into English as *The Dutch Republic and American Independence*, Chapel Hill, NC, 1982).
4 Brunswick to William V, 21, 22 Feb. 1777, *Archives*, 5e Sér., I, 455–59.

the common people, who always judge by the outcome of events, would place the blame upon him if things did not go well.[5] The effort of Amsterdam to gain establishment of an unlimited convoy seemed reckless to him unless the Dutch navy was brought up to strength; it could lead to a war for which the Republic was not prepared.[6] In the Dutch public, however, the antistadholderian party was already cheering on "the brave colonists of North America," and calling on the Dutch people to emulate their republican spirit.[7]

By this time, the sole dominance of the duke of Brunswick over the Prince was beginning to give way as Princess Wilhelmina won her husband's increasing confidence and he discussed important papers of state with her.[8] Their relationship was briefly disturbed when he dabbled in a flirtation with a young noblewoman, *juffrouw* ("Miss") Van Lynden van Hoeflake, that flattered his vanity. The relationship may have been innocent but it damaged his reputation and Princess Wilhelmina made a scene, calling the situation "ridiculous." William responded angrily, but did not continue the affair.[9]

He refused, however, to turn against Brunswick. Van Bleiswijk, the councilor pensionary chosen for his easy compliance, complained to friends that William would still not act upon anything until he had heard from the duke.[10] William knew that there was widespread antipathy to Brunswick, but he did not want to abandon him as King Charles I had the earl of Strafford: that was an "infamous deed," he told Hardenbroek, and it made Charles a "bad person" (*slegt personaadje*). He was determined not to sacrifice anyone who stood in the breach for him.[11]

William knew that he also needed the collaboration, or at least the assent of Amsterdam, but found it difficult to establish an effective working relationship in which the great city did not simply accept his judgment. Early in January 1779, Huydecooper van Maarseveen of Amsterdam came to William to suggest an end to the dissension between the stadholder and the city. William, as "head of the Republic," should give his judgment on matters to the leaders of the city so that they could act on it. The Prince then complained of the frequent visits to the city by the French ambassador; this was true, Huydecooper admitted, but he visited only merchants, not the members of the municipal government. William thought that his visitor was trying to obtain his approval for the proposed unlimited convoy

5 William V to Van Bleiswijk, 15 Mar. 1778, *Archives*, 5e Sér., I, 509–10.
6 *Ibid.*, 8 Jan. 1779, *Archives*, 5e Sér., I, 651–53.
7 [Derival de Gonicourt], *Lettres Hollandoises, Ou Correspondance politique sur l'état présent de l'Europe, notamment de la République des Sept Provincesi-Unies* (5 vols.; Amsterdam, 1669–1780), II, 126–27.
8 Naber, 48; Hardenbroek, I, 507.   9 Hardenbroek, I, 514–15.   10 *Ibid.*, 486.
11 Hardenbroek, II, 148–51.

for Dutch merchantmen, but this should not be undertaken until the Republic was strongly enough armed for the war with England that might result.[12]

He focused his anger against Amsterdam upon Van Berckel, the Amsterdam burgomaster who led the antistadholderian party in the city. Van Berckel was a scoundrel, William told Hardenbroek; as long as he dominated its government, there could be no confidence in relations with Amsterdam. He was a brutal man, and he (William V) had discovered that brutal men get what they want. (And, we may add, to be brutal was a dream that appealed to the weak man that he actually was.) Hardenbroek admitted Van Berckel was rough and brutal, but said he had always been considered an honorable and incorruptible man. "Yes," the Prince replied, "but it is better for the Republic to be governed by a dozen scoundrels than by an honorable man who brings everything into confusion." What triggered these recriminations was that Holland declined to consent to increased taxation for naval expansion, as William sought.[13]

The appearance of John Paul Jones, the Scots naval captain in the American service, in the Texel roadstead after his capture of an English warship, presented the Prince with new difficulties. Jones was wined and dined by Amsterdam merchants and leaders of the States party, and he became the delight of little Dutch children (who this day sing a pretty ditty in tribute to his heroism); but the English demanded that he be compelled to leave at once (an English squadron was now ready to meet him just off shore). William again attempted to walk both ways at once: condemning Jones, but refusing the English demand as impossible under the Dutch constitution. The English should remember, he told the Dutch ambassador in London, that this country is not Denmark, where the king can do whatever he wants; here the constitution demands more formalities, at least the assent of a majority of the members of the States General.[14] Jones was able to stay safely in Dutch waters because the French ambassador, in a transparent stratagem, declared that the ship was actually French. Since France and England were not yet at war, the English had to permit it to depart and the dispute evaporated.

When, in the aftermath of this episode, the English ambassador, Yorke, suggested to William that he should follow the example the King Gustavus III of Sweden, who had seized full power in a *coup d'état* against the States in Stockholm, the Prince replied that if anyone in the Republic gave him that counsel, he would consider him his worst enemy. He had power enough to do good and did not want a finger's breadth more. If more power

12 William V to van Bleiswijk, 8 Jan. 1779, *Archives*, 5e Sér., I, 651–53.
13 Hardenbroek, II, 51–52.
14 William V to Van Welderen, 23 Nov. 1779, *Archives*, 5e Sér., II, 121–22.

were offered to him, he would refuse, lest his children suffer for his gain.[15] He did not want to be a sovereign; he only wanted to be a "patriot" (*vaderlander*).[16] He prided himself on being a "good citizen."[17]

William was unable to prevent a decision in favor of an unlimited convoy, including timber, which the English insisted must be banned, whatever other concessions they might make. It went out in December 1779 and was met by the English on 31 December. The Dutch convoyers were too few in number to offer more than token resistance, and some merchantmen were taken. William still hoped that peace could be maintained by Dutch entry into the League of Armed Neutrality with Russia, Denmark and Sweden.[18] He was puzzled why the English were forcing his hand. If he conceded to them a ban on all ships carrying timber, he would make himself suspect to a great part of the Dutch nation. He would be compelled (and he repeated a phrase that spoke his strongest feeling) to "ride with the torrent." If the English insisted on again attacking Dutch convoys, war could not be avoided.[19]

The conflict with England was brought to a fever pitch when a copy of a draft treaty between the Dutch and American republics, the work of the American diplomat Henry Laurens and the Amsterdam banker De Neufville and Amsterdam burgomaster Van Berckel on the Dutch side, came into the hands of the English government. They treated it as an official document and laid down an ultimatum: the Dutch authors must be not only disclaimed but also punished, or there would be war. The final crisis was precipitated when the States General joined the League of Armed Neutrality on 10 December 1780, followed almost at once by the English declaration of war. The Prince himself continued to bewail English policy: if the true and permanent interests of the Republic consisted in good relations with England, the truth held the other way round as well. Were the English actually trying to bring the French party into power?[20]

War began with an English declaration on 20 December 1780. Van Berckel became its first political victim. The English singled him out as the villain of the piece because of his participation in the preparation of the draft treaty with Laurens. He ceased to come to The Hague and was replaced in February by Rendorp, a moderate.

Brunswick too became a victim of the war, in which one disaster followed another. Already during 1780, as the relations with England were

15 Hardenbroek, II, 242–43.   16 *Ibid.*, 247–49.
17 William V to Lynden van Blitterswijk, 20 Oct. 1781, [Willem V, Prince of Orange], *Brieven van Prins Willem V aan Baron Van Lijnden van Blitterswijk, Representant van den Eerste Edele van Zeeland*, ed. F. de Bas (The Hague, 1893), 68.
18 William V to Van Bleiswijk, 16 Jan. 1780, *Archives*, 5e Sér., II, 130–31.
19 William V to Van Welderen, 18 Jan. 1780, *Archives*, 5e Sér., II, 131–32.
20 William V to Fagel, 18 Aug. 1780, *Archives*, 5e Sér., II, 250–51.

rapidly turning worse, the public attitude toward him changed. After thirty years of quiet and almost undisturbed residence, with more complaints against him in the inner circles of the Prince's court than in the country at large, he was now made responsible for everything that was going wrong.

Amsterdam initiated the assault upon Brunswick. A delegation consisting of burgomasters De Vrij Temminck and Rendorp and the town pensionary Visscher came from the city to the Prince. Visscher read a lengthy *mémoire* informing William of the proposal of the Amsterdam government in the States of Holland on 18 May calling for the removal of the duke of Brunswick in the interests of the country. It stressed that he was a foreigner who did not love the Republic as his fatherland and did not know its constitution well enough. The duke should be replaced in his role as the stadholder's chief advisor by a small council of native Dutchmen of the highest rank and reputation. The proposal was a revival of one of the key ideas that Bentinck van Rhoon had made to William IV more than three decades earlier. It was the work not of the extreme patriots like Van Berckel but of the moderates led by Rendorp, and it was not directed at William V, with whom Rendorp was on good personal terms, but sought rather to make possible collaboration between the Prince and the city.

William rejected the proposal out of hand as an attack upon his rights. He considered their personal compliments as "foolish" (*gekke*), although no doubt he would have been offended if they had abstained from the courtesies usual on such an occasion. The attempt to separate him from the duke aroused his indignation. Even if the duke had been at fault in any way, and there was no proof that he had been, to dismiss him in this way would be to humiliate himself before the eyes of all Europe. Despite all their asseverations to the contrary, he told the visitors their attack was really directed against him personally. It was the burgomasters of Amsterdam in 1778 who were really the cause of the war. Now they were trying to sacrifice the duke to the people's wrath, as De Witt had been in 1672, and he did not want the duke's blood upon his hands. He preferred to die at once rather than live with such shame; they could kill him at once, but they would never get what they sought. They were not treating with a coward.

The Amsterdammers tried to calm him down. They had nothing, they said, against the duke personally, and they did not demand that he leave the service of the country. It was true that he accepted the duke's advice when it was good, William replied, but he did not follow anyone's advice blindly. They must not think that "they had to do with a child." They offered to take back the *mémoire*, but William said he would keep it to give to Brunswick. To their reiterated assurance that the council would take some of his burden from him, he replied that he would perform his duties as best he could and did not wish to be placed under guardianship. If he was not worthy of performing the duties of his post, rather than take adjuncts he would prefer to put everything down and let the adjuncts govern. His final words were not to expect him to show any cowardice.[21]

William bared his feelings and his ideas even more fully to Hardenbroek. His words were vehement and almost incoherent. The proposal of the Amsterdammers that he accept a council was a revolution, he charged, and they wanted to destroy his reputation. Hardenbroek repeatedly tried to get him to see that Amsterdam no more wanted a revolution than he did, since they would suffer most. "They are all scoundrels, they have deceived me and others," William said with emotion that boiled over. "I consider them to be my worst enemies, and so are all those who take Amsterdam's side." Now he would see who his friends were. Hardenbroek pleaded with him to calm down. If this was what he really believed and he did not change his mind, the Republic was done for. William would not be calmed. The Amsterdammers, he raged on, were trying to put all the guilt for the failures in the war against England upon him. Either he or they would come out on top; one or the other must go under. He would not tolerate being put "under guardianship" (*onder curatele*); he must be in a position to fulfill the duties of his office. "Soon such a council would have a stamp with which they can sign my name for me whenever and as often as they want." Hardenbroek replied soothingly that this was not the purpose of the council. It would only be helping him. The members would be only persons acceptable to him, and he would be its head. William's passion carried him away from the issue toward his frustrations. "I hope that the Republic will outlive me, but things cannot go on in this way. It would be best if I went away and planted cabbages in my own hereditary lands."[22]

It is impossible to read William's own summary of this meeting with the obviously embarrassed Amsterdammers or Hardenbroek's account of the Prince's obsessive anger without a sense that the very vehemence of his protestations revealed a repressed guiltiness that he could not admit, to the visitors or to himself, lest it totally shatter what was left of his self-respect. We see an adult still in psychological dependence protesting against guardianship, demanding to do everything himself when he gave so little time or thought to his work, fearful at the age of forty of still being treated like a child. Wanting his due and unable to perform his duties, he hopes somehow to get away from it all. He was compelling those about him, his wife, his friends, the envoys of England and Prussia, to inure themselves to the thought that they would have to act *for him, in his name, whether he wished it*

21 William V, "Relation," 8 June 1781. *Archives*, 5e Sér., II, 494–98; Brugmans, VI, 355–56; Thulemeyer to Frederick II, June 13, 1781, Thulemeyer, 263.
22 Hardenbroek, II, 568–71. The entry is dated 21 May 1781.

or not, in other words, to put him under a guardianship far more humiliating than a privy council, such as most absolute monarchs had under one name or another, would have been.

William V, in his antipathy to the Patriots, as the antistadholderians began to call themselves, failed to observe the success that they had achieved in winning over to their side a very large fraction of the "people." These were the *burgerij*, the citizenry excluded from participation in government who had formed the solid base of "Orange democracy" and through the burgher guard companies had provided the armed power by which the municipal governments maintained themselves. Their disappointment with William IV in 1748 and 1749 made them ready to collaborate now with that segment of the regents that was itself willing to accept a modicum of "people's influence" (*volksinvloed*), or democracy, in government in order to hamstring the stadholderate.

The Patriot ideology, whether at the level of theoretical tractates or of brandished slogans, combined the traditional republicanism of the "True Freedom" with the egalitarian (or egalitarian-sounding) doctrines of the Englightenment.[23] The Patriot movement was essentially an alliance of disparate and once hostile forces: on the one side the regents who were either opposed in principle to the stadholderate, an attitude that became easier to hold as William V thwarted efforts at conciliation and compromise, or, believing in the system of States-with-stadholder, had lost hope of persuading the Prince to work honestly and effectively within that system; on the other the propertied and educated people who were not accepted as regents. To them government "of the people" meant government that *included* themselves; but in the years to come, when the Patriots succeeded – until the "backwards revolution" of 1787 – in creating forms of participation in rule, they had no actual experience of government.[24]

Yet it was *not* a class antagonism as such at work. Every social stratum was split, some finding refuge in the Orange myth and others in either repetition of the time-worn doctrines of the "True Freedom" or the new notions of the Enlightenment, even in so bold a principle as Rousseau's "sovereignty of the people." "Orange democracy" was therefore increasingly confined to the propertyless wage earners and petty peddlers, as represented in Amsterdam by the famed *Bijltjes*. They continued to look to the Orange prince to defend them against the regents, a profound misunderstanding of the attitude of the stadholders.

---

23 One of the most important recent studies of this development is C. H. E. de Wit, *De Nederlandse Revolutie van de Achttiende Eeuw, 1780–1787* (Oirsbeek, 1974). Idiosyncratic in method and loose in definitions, this work nonetheless argues vigorously the cause of the new "democrats."

24 Brugmans, V, 205–6.

The publication and distribution of Van der Capellen tot den Pol's "To the People of the Netherlands" (*Aan het Volk van Nederland*)[25] was a major political event in the emergence of the Patriot movement. It was published without an author's name, and in Amsterdam it was distributed by someone in gentleman's garb (actually, the Mennonite preacher Francis van der Kemp) who scattered it in the streets.[26] Even so well informed a person as the Utrecht deputy Hardenbroek had not the slightest suspicion that Van der Capellen tot den Pol was the author,[27] and it was not until the twentieth century that the speculations of historians to this effect were confirmed. The little book aroused intense interest and passions. Like earlier Dutch political writings, it argued from historical precedents rather than present needs, and its rhetoric was the florid sentimentality of the eighteenth century. Its proposed reforms did not go deep: a council for the stadholder (as the Amsterdammers had proposed) and elected delegates in the towns, which would provide the burghers not with direct participation in government but with a means of keeping an eye on the governments.[28] But such supervision would mean an end to the closed rule of the regents.[29]

More weighty than such counsels were the "free corps" instituted in 1781. Their publicly announced initial task was to provide additional strength for resisting the demand of the government of Emperor Joseph II in Brussels for the dismantling of the Barrier, the fortress towns in the Austrian Netherlands that were garrisoned by Dutch troops. Their real purpose, however, was to be a counterweight to the burgher guards should these keep their traditional commitment to Orange. One of the last cities to permit their organization was Amsterdam, where the "free corps" was formed only in 1784. The initiative for a national federation of free corps came from Utrecht.[30]

The Prince was very sensitive to the attacks, especially those that were personal in character. Two pamphlets, *The Prayer of the People of the Netherlands* and *Typical Hymn of Praise for the Incorrigible Champions of the English*, were so offensive that he sought prosecution of the authors and disseminators. He found particularly offensive, as well he might, an "utterly abominable" print in the latter, which showed him as Bacchus on a barrel with *freule* van Lynden.[31] We can easily imagine, therefore, what his

---

25 Joan Derk Baron van der Capellen tot den Pol, *Aan het Volk van Nederland: Het Democratisch Manifest (1781)*, ed. W. F. Wertheim and A. H. Wertheim-Gijse Weeninck (Amsterdam, 1966) is the best modern edition. Key passages are translated in Rowen, *Low Countries*, 240–41.

26 Rendorp to Van Bleiswijk, undated (5 Oct. 1781), copy for William V, *Archives*, 5e Sér., II, 637.   27 Hardenbroek, IV, 180.

28 Brugmans, VI, 344.   29 *Ibid.*, 363.   30 *Ibid.*, 368–71.

31 William V to Van Bleiswijk, 9 July 1782, *Archives*, 5e Sér., III, 119–20.

reactions were to a pamphlet called *Letter on the True Cause of the Country's Misfortune*; it purported to be a missive found in the roadway between Utrecht and Amersfoort.[32] Most of it is vituperation and invective, but it includes an amazing allegation. William V, according to the unknown author, was not really the progeny of William IV at all, since Anna of Hanover, after the birth of Caroline, had been judged by professors and doctors to be incapable of bearing another child. She therefore had employed a trick used in other princely hereditary houses (as by William III in the warming-pan tale, which the author does not repeat, about the birth of the son of James II and Mary of Modena in 1688). It was not certain, the pamphlet writer went on, just who the real father was, but it was said he was a barrow-man. To be sure, the son of a barrow-man could very well be noble and virtuous, but this one was a traitor to the country and Anna was a Jezebel.[33] One wonders why Hardenbroek thought it only "as strong as" *To the People of the Netherlands*, which did not descend to such personal filth.[34] Van der Capellen tot den Pol himself found it incredible and a fabrication.[35]

William put his feelings of despair into words that almost drip of tears in a letter to the councilor pensionary. He resented the insulting way in which the States of Holland, in which he knew he had lost all influence, had presented their election lists to him the day before (19 July), and did not think he deserved such contempt. Perhaps he should resign all his offices and return to his lands in Germany; having lost the trust of the "majority of the government," this was probably the best thing for the sake of the country and of himself. Then, he profoundly hoped, the unity, harmony and mutual trust so necessary for the welfare of the country would be restored. He did not see of what use he was any more unless the attitude toward him changed.[36] The note of hysteria that had marked his earlier outbreak when confronted with the demand for the removal of Brunswick is gone now, but the flatness of utter hopelessness has replaced it. There is the same sincere affirmation of his patriotism, but also the same inability to recognize how he himself could be at fault.

He did not seek relief in work, but cursed people constantly, once even at table in the presence of the shocked Princess.[37] He ranted at two men who "now govern the Republic," the publishers of Patriot newpapers.[38] And

---

32 *Brief over de waere oorzaek van 's Lands Ongeval, Gevonden tusschen Utrecht en Amersfoort om deszelfs merkwaerdigen inhoud met den druk gemeen gemaakt* (N.p., 1782) (Kn. 10, 171.)

33 *Brief over de waere oorzaeck*, 5–7.   34 Hardenbroek, IV, 180.

35 Van der Capellen tot den Pol to [De Gijzelaar?], 5 Dec. 1782 [Joan Derk van der Capellen tot den Pol], *Brieven van en aan Joan Derck van der Capellen van de Poll*, W. H. de Beaufort ed. (Utrecht, 1879), 417.

36 Hardenbroek, IV, 103.   37 *Ibid.*, 71.   38 *Ibid.*, 103.

he dwelled upon the Fronde, that French rebellion in the mid-seventeenth century that had put the French monarchy in immense peril.[39]

Late in April, 1782, William V yielded at last to the demands for the removal of the duke of Brunswick from his place at his side, but sent him only to Den Bosch instead of out of the country. William's dependency upon his "second father" was broken, although the Prince's opponents did not believe it, but not his habit of dependency. Van Bleiswijk was too weak a reed to lean on, and Brunswick's role as the Prince's guiding spirit fell to Wilhelmina. She began to take upon herself the task of leadership, at least of the Orangist party if not of the government, that her befuddled and despondent husband did not even attempt to perform any more. Strong-willed, perceptive, intelligent and, if not wholly at home in Dutch institutions, willing to learn, she was as well equipped for the task as anyone in the Prince's circle.[40]

The Princess became the key in efforts to achieve a reconciliation between the House of Orange and the anti-stadholderian party, especially Amsterdam. This became clear when William V and Van Bleiswijk asked Thulemeyer, the Prussian minister, to speak to the leaders of Amsterdam on the Prince's behalf. It was an extraordinary situation – the two top officials of the country, the stadholder and the council pensionary of Holland, appealing to the envoy of a foreign power for assistance in solving purely domestic affairs. But was Prussia "purely foreign" when the king of Prussia was the uncle of the Princess of Orange? For that matter, was the king of Great Britain "purely foreign" when he was the uncle of the Prince of Orange? The request of William and Van Bleiswijk to Thulemeyer was, however, primarily an act of political desperation because there seemed no solution with only domestic forces.

The envoy did as he was asked, but the replies he received were bitter medicine for the Prince. De Vrij Temminck skirted a direct reply, but Rendorp came to the point. There was very little chance that William's personal influence, which was almost destroyed, could be reestablished. The only solution was for him to entrust the leadership to the Princess; her ability, impartiality and patriotism promised much. Thulemeyer agreed but expected difficulty in persuading the Prince. Wilhelmina received Rendorp's proposal favorably but would take part in the government only if her husband asked her. He seemed willing, the envoy reported to Frederick II.[41]

As the end of the year approached, the situation seemed frozen stiff. Astute observers thought that Holland was held back from abolition of the stadholderate by the difficulty of persuading Gelderland, Groningen,

39 *Ibid.*, 73–74.   40 Brugmans, *Geschiedenis van Amsterdam*, VI, 363–64.
41 Thulemeyer to Frederick II, 3 Sept. 1782, Thulemeyer, 331–32.

Overijssel and Utrecht provinces to follow suit.[42] Van der Capellen tot den Pol thought the protectorate placed over the stadholderate by foreign powers was the principal obstacle, and he urged his fellow Patriots to leave the stadholderate as such untouched, while keeping the nation in movement by continuing the campaign, already under way, of "addresses" (petitions) to the States by popular rallies. He had lost all confidence in the regents to carry through the necessary reforms.[43]

The threat of civil war became more visible. Within the Orangist party some in frustration thought the time was near for restoring the Prince to the fullness of his rights by forceful action in the streets, a "little uprising" (*klein oproertje*) as *greffier* Fagel called it. A naval captain was reported to have spoken at table of shutting the mouth of those who shouted for freedom and the privileges of the people when, as would soon happen, the Prince became sovereign.[44] Others warned against such "infamous" means.[45] In his very inaction, William too yearned for an extreme solution. "Let them just drive me out of the Republic," he remarked, "I ask nothing more. Then I will know how I will return."[46]

William held fast to his policy of querulous indignation when prerogatives were taken from him, but went no further.[47] He berated himself for having sent Brunswick away. In outbursts of repressed emotion he shouted that he had lost his sole and truest friend in the world.[48] At a meeting of members of the Council of State with him in February, he frightened those who heard his outbursts, as if he were going out of his mind. He kept repeating, "I will no longer be stadholder," "I will not be allowed to remain stadholder long."[49] That was first reply to any suggestion that he change his policy.[50] The Princess did not conceal her anxiety about the way things were going, and there were reports that the Prince had become very insolent toward her.[51]

A change began with the eruption of demonstrations and riots in December in favor of the Prince. One, in The Hague, was called the "Santa Claus Riot" because of its date, 9 December (St Nicholas Day,

---

42 Hardenbroek, IV, 185–86.
43 Van der Capellen tot den Pol to Driessen, Dec. 1782, Van der Capellen tot den Pol, *Brieven*, 433.
44 *De Post van den Neder-Rhijn*, 4 (1784), 357.
45 Hardenbroek, IV, 369–70, 378; Thulemeyer to Frederick II, 20 June 1783, Thulemeyer, 366–67.
46 Hardenbroek, IV, 604.
47 William V to Members of the States of Holland, 3 Jan., to States of Utrecht, 14 Feb., to the States of the individual provinces, 11 June 1784, C. van der Aa, *Geschiedenis van het Leven, Character, en Lotgevallen van wijlen Willem den Vijfden, Prinse van Oranje en Nassau* (5 vols.; Amsterdam, 1809), V, 20–30, 44–64, 123–26.
48 Thulemeyer to Frederick II, 16 Jan. 1784, Thulemeyer, 385.
49 Hardenbroek, V, 100–1, 118.   50 *Ibid.*, 144, 252–53.   51 *Ibid.*, 119.

when the Dutch have their festive holiday), was marked by shouts of "Long live Orange!" and "The Prince sovereign, the States small!" (*De Prins Souverain, de Staten klein*). Posters appeared on street-corner walls in The Hague directed against the leaders of the Patriot party. In response several deputies in the States of Holland proposed to remove the four regiments of guards in The Hague from the Prince's command and put it directly in the hands of the Delegated Councilors. William considered it a move to deprive him of the hereditary rights of his family. He was if anything even more disturbed when efforts were made to change his commission from the States General as captain-general and to take from him the right of "patents," that is, commands for military movements.

William bared his heart to Frederick II. The enemies of the House by their move to take from him command of the guards in The Hague had raised their masks. It would make his power as captain-general illusory. The parallel proposal to have orders to the navy sent in the name of the States General would destroy entirely his authority as admiral-general. Until now he had been silent when his opponents took away what he had been allowed to do by the complaisance of the States; but this was a change of the constitution that would reduce to an "empty title" (*vain titre*) the prerogatives unanimously bestowed upon his father. He must defend "the legitimate rights of my father's descendants." He hoped therefore that the king would "not see with an indifferent eye" an overthrow of the present Dutch constitution, reducing to naught the post of stadholder and the rights of "someone to whom he was good enough to grant the hand of the Princess his niece." To make him odious to the nation, his foes spread the rumor that he wished to make himself sovereign and become Count of Holland. Nothing was less true. He wanted only to preserve the freedom of the country and its present constitution, according to the oath he took to the state; he would never encroach upon anyone's rights, "least of all those of the States of the United Provinces." He foresaw that the Republic were on the eve of a "general overturn" which would render it useless to all states with which Frederick made common cause. It would help if the king made it evident that he took the maintenance of the present constitution to heart.[52] Frederick replied that he would send a *mémoire* to the States General urging a return to calm, for violence would be "equally baneful" to the stadholderate and the Republic.[53]

There is no reason to doubt William's sincerity in denying any aspiration to sovereignty and the countship; from his childhood it had been inculcated in him that he must be rigidly faithful to the existing constitution. Yet there is either incredible *naïveté* or incredible ignorance if he did

52 William V to Fredrick II, 6 Jan. 1773, *Archives*, 5e Sér., III, 179–83.
53 Fredrick II to William V, 12 Jan. 1783, *Archives*, 5e Sér., III, 184–85.

not know of the talk that went about among *some* of his supporters, within his entourage and in the armed forces. *Their* talk frightened the republican regents and justified to them the measures they took to cut down the stadholdership to safe dimensions.

All these many months, indeed years, the war with England continued. The efforts of the Patriots to win acceptance of the new American Republic met William's dogged opposition. In 1781 the American negotiator John Adams came to Holland from Paris to seek a loan from Dutch bankers and to solicit diplomatic recognition for his country from their High Mightinesses. When he presented a *mémoire* to the president of the States General, it was refused because he was not accredited, and the Prince approved this as meeting the requirements of the constitution.[54] (This was, of course, what in the late twentieth century would be called a "Catch 22" situation: for it was precisely that accreditation that Adams was seeking.) In April 1782 William had to accept unhappily the decision of the States General to recognize the new American Republic and to accept Adams's credentials as its minister. For the Americans the war had been effectively over since the previous October, when Cornwallis had surrendered to Washington at Yorktown.

The English made peace with the Americans with an eye to the restoration of friendship with their former colonies, and with their allies France and Spain, in 1783, but they showed no such good will to the Dutch Republic, the ally that had not lived up to its obligations, worse, had actively assisted the American insurgents although it never became their formal ally. Negotiations with the States General for peace hobbled along until 1784, leaving William V in a dangerously ambiguous position.

The ruling duke of Brunswick, Charles William Ferdinand, who was Duke Louis's nephew, received in June a letter from William V repeating his plaints about the persecution of Duke Louis, his "second father."[55] It was followed by another that was even more passionate. He thought the action against Duke Louis foreshadowed similar efforts to despoil him of the stadholderate and send him into exile, permitting him to receive his "wages" (*mes gages*) if he did not return. His whole cause now depended upon the support of the king of Prussia, for without it the dominant cabal would push things to the extreme. Their aim is to establish an aristocratic tyranny and to enslave the people to their magistrates without the power of the stadholder to protect them, "which is all I want."[56] His capacity for self-deception seems to have been endless. We do not find in this letter the

---

54 William V to Van Bleiswijk, 12 Mar. 1781, *Archives*, 5e Sér., II, 404.
55 William V to Duke Charles William of Brunswick-Lüneburg, 10 June 1784, *Archives*, 5e Sér., III, 278–79.
56 *Ibid.*, 2 July 1784, *Archives*, 5e Sér., III, 281–83.

slightest realization of the disillusionment among the common people in 1747 and 1748 when William IV showed himself to be a friend of the regents, nor that he himself had done nothing specific to make use of the very real powers that he possessed to meet the popular demands. He accepted the Orange myth at face value, but did not see how it had been disrupted by events.

His despondency deepened in July when a delegation of Patriots came to him to ask him to dismiss Brunswick outright. He told Thulemeyer after they left that he was tired of serving a country where a cabal governed. Except for the fact that the country was threatened with war (since peace had just been signed with England, he must have meant the demands of Emperor Joseph II for the opening of the Schelde River to the traffic of the Austrian Netherlands), he would gladly abdicate and withdraw to Dillenburg. The envoy urged him to stay, but to separate his cause from that of the duke. (Reporting to Frederick II, he expressed his own regret that Brunswick did not act on his own to depart and thus help the Prince.)[57] The problem would not go away. Deputies of Dordrecht, Haarlem and Amsterdam presented a written request to William to send Brunswick away as essential to restoration of unity in the country. When William said he would not, they warned that their cities were ready for decisions that would not please the head of the Republic. The deputies from Haarlem even added obscure threats.

William told Hardenbroek the deputies were scoundrels who wished him to perform a scoundrelly act. He would never do it, not even if the whole Republic stood against him. "I used to love this country, but not any more," he said, "for it is an ungrateful fatherland, where it is not enough for them to do injustice but they want to use me to do it too," he said. He wanted to go away, but he did not want to harm the country.

Hardenbroek again endeavored to bring the Prince down from his plane of overwrought emotion. Among the varied classes of people he met in the country, he told William, he had never found any hostility to the Prince's house or children, but on the contrary a general interest in their welfare. True, there was great antagonism against William himself, but that could be overcome by moderation and concessions. His own opinion was precisely the contrary, replied the Prince, and he would not do it. "Aut Caesar aut nihil [Either Caesar or nothing], and I don't care what happens." "They can do with me what they wish," he went on, "they can drive me away, but I will always make up my own mind, and I will not give in." Hardenbroek pleaded with him. If he did not change his policy, then the Republic, the Prince, and "all of us must perish as certainly as there is light

57 Thulemeyer to Frederick II, 9 July 1784, Thulemeyer, 404.

in the sky. Think what responsibility you are taking upon yourself." But the Prince just kept repeating, "I must be stadholder or not at all," and Hardenbroek finally left.[58]

The axe of decision fell on 18 August but it was the States of Holland that acted, not the Prince. Their Noble Great Mightinesses declared the Act of Advisorship, which had come into the hands of the leading Patriot newspaper and had been blazoned to the public in its pages, to be null and void. They ordered Brunswick's deposition. On 14 October Brunswick asked the States General for release from his military posts – the only ones he formally held in the Republic. It was granted at once and the duke departed to Germany. No one expected the Prince to be able to exercise the command on his own, but he stubbornly rejected the notion of a high war council to assist him. He did not want generals imposed on him whom he did not know and had not even heard of, he wrote. They would probably be French, to boot.[59]

The continuing ambiguity of the stadholder's position even among Patriots was clear to see in a long treatise entitled *Constitutional Restoration* ("Grondwettige Herstelling," a word that in Dutch carries strong connotations of physical repairs) that appeared late in December 1784. The work, one of the fundamental documents of the Patriot movement, is anonymous, without even a pen name; a variety of candidates for its author have been suggested, but none has been proved beyond question. It is a statement of complex and not always consistent ideas, often expressed in the overblown sentimental rhetoric so dear to the eighteenth century; historians have therefore debated its precise political coloration without coming to full agreement. It identifies itself as "Patriot" and its choice of heroes makes it clearly moderate.[60]

The essential arguments of the book are that the Dutch government must remain ruled by the States, that those in the country or abroad who condemn efforts to restore such government in its essential points violate the fundamental principles of law and justice, that the "Patriotic restorers" are not moved by a blind, unbounded hatred of the stadholderate and the House of Orange.[61] Its position toward both the stadholder and the people is ambivalent. It does not advocate the abolition of the stadholderate, only severe restriction of its prerogatives, and considers it as an executive institution, as against the legislative character of the States. The stadholdership

58 *Ibid.*, 13, 16 July 1784, Thulemeyer, 405; Hardenbroek, V, 354–58.
59 William V to Van Lynden van Blitterswijk, 2 Dec. 1784, *Archives*, 5e Sér., III, 305.
60 *Grondwettige Herstelling, van Nederlands Staatswezen zo voor het algemeen Bondgenoot-schap, als voor het bestuur van elke byzondere Provincie, geschikt om het voornaam doelwit aan te toonen, waer toe de poogingen van goede regenten en de requesten van vaderlandliev-ende burgers moetgen strekken* (2 vols.; Amsterdam, 1784), I, 39–40.
61 *Ibid.*, 39–40.

is like the governor's post in the United States of America.[62] What is needed is a government of the States with the stadholder as their outstanding servant. At the same time the author recognizes that unless the stadholder and the regents are at odds, there is no guarantee for the rights of the people. He should be a bulwark of the regents against the people and the people against the regents; a remedy against bloody controversies and divisions, restraining ambitious officials and restless popular agitators.[63]

The book denies explicitly that the stadholderate is a kind of monarchy, moderated by an admixture of aristocracy in the form of the Nobles and the urban governments. Those zealots for the stadholderate who have argued this have been "thoughtless," although some stadholders were not without fault in this regard.[64] Because the stadholder, however extensive his authority, possesses none of the essential characteristics of sovereignty, he is not really a quasi-monarch (the author does not use the word, but that is his meaning here), although the temptation to make himself such is very great and lies in "the nature of the human heart."[65] True, the stadholdership is now hereditary, and in that like monarchy, but the stadholder is not above the laws (although William V has on occasion set himslf in such a position).[66] Fortunately, the "recent movement" (the Patriots) has rescued the Republic from the danger of falling under "the power of a single head."[67] The powers of the stadholder are all delegated, and in this "we see the essential difference between a stadholder and a monarch."[68]

The "constitutional restoration" indicated in the title would spare the Prince the unpleasant criticism of which he has been the object in recent years. "He will recognize that in order to make his House great, the Constitution was twisted in precarious times and the Supreme Authority, which cannot be taken from the legitimate rulers of the country without peril, was stripped of power." He must give up the power to fill all offices, for that is beyond the ability of any one person. Acceptance of reform, he must realize, would give him "the respect and love of a FREE PEOPLE."[69] It was a view of the stadholderate within the Republic that was not constitutionally at total variance with the Prince's, but the subtle, flexible policies that it required of him were beyond his capacity.

Events continued to simmer, coming closer to a boil but not at the danger point during 1785. William V held to his pattern of exploding in anger and playing stubborn, only to give in at the end. His own adherents began to organize independently of him. Various projects were brought up in the States General, but everything fell apart when William announced he would leave The Hague and go into a kind of semi-exile in Breda.[70] The

---

62 *Ibid.*, 254–55.   63 *Ibid.*, 248–50, 255.   64 *Ibid.*, 142, 144–46.
65 *Ibid.*, 169–71.   66 *Ibid.*, 146–48.   67 *Ibid.*, 148.   68 *Ibid.*, 149–51.
69 *Ibid.*, xii–xiii.   70 Japikse, "De Staten-Generaal," 136.

sudden decision came when he was at last deprived of his command of the garrison in The Hague and it was put in the hands of the Delegated Councilors. This drastic step was occasioned by a riot in which free corps officers from Leiden were mishandled by the populace. The episode was the culmination of the spread of "free corps" ever since 1784, and they were only the sharp point of a general movement of the more outspoken, more "democratic" Patriots to take effective command of the state.

Thulemeyer tried to dissuade William from leaving The Hague with the Princess and their children, but William insisted. He was afraid of attacks upon his life and he expected that his departure would bring about the defeat of his foes and persuade the nation to call him back with all his prerogatives.[71] With Thulemeyer he was relatively calm, but Rouse, a friend of Hardenbroek's, gives a more shattering picture of what happened. He had ridden off to Huis ten Bosch as if he were a madman, then returned to The Hague to ask Larrey, his secretary, for his commission as stadholder to take to the States of Holland to throw it at them and resign. Larrey delayed him by telling him that a smith would have to be brought in to break open the chest in which it was kept, and then he was calmed down. But not for long. His fury returned. Standing up, he threw his gloves to the floor, banged on the table, ran about the room like a man out of his mind. Cursing, he told the Princess that he was leaving the country. If she wanted to come with him and bring her children, she could, and if she wanted to stay as Gouvernante in his place, she could do that. He knew what the origin of the problem was: ever since he had lost the advice of the duke of Brunswick, he had no more say in what he did. And he stalked out of the room. The scene resumed a quarter of an hour later, and then another time, ending only when word was brought in that the Russian minister had come to speak to him.[72] His good humor returned when he heard that Imperial troops were assembling in Germany. Either there would be a revolution or, putting himself at the head of the army, he could be struck by a bullet.[73] These bleak scenes happened on 12 September.

On 16 September he went to Breda, although he was supposed to be in residence wherever the States General and the Council of State met. From there William and his family went to his country estate at Het Loo, where he continued to think about abdication as the best service he could give his country. On 4 December, William finally made a formal protest to the States of Holland against their resolution of 5 September as a violation of his position as captain-general of the Union. It was soon printed as a pamphlet, so that it was as much directed to public opinion as to the States. He had never, he wrote, claimed a right of military command indepen-

71 Thulemeyer to Frederick II, 10 Sept. 1785, Thulemeyer, 443–44.
72 Hardenbroek, VI, 72–74.   73 *Ibid.*, 75.

dently of or superior to that of the States of Holland. He accepted the sovereignty of Their Noble Great Mightinesses in their province and supported it as strongly as anyone. He acted in military matters on their behalf and in their name. None of this constituted an *imperium in impero*. The stadholdership and the captaincy-general were both inherent in the original constitution of the Republic.[74]

On 2 August, the Patriots in Utrecht wrested power in the city from its Orangist regents. The provincial States withdrew to Amersfoort, the second city of the province, where there was a garrison loyal to the Prince. Meanwhile William V restlessly sought a solution to his problem that would not violate his principles. He began early in 1786 to think of letting events run their course until his eldest son came of age, at which time he could lay down his posts and abdicate the stadholdership. He began to admit, too, that he lacked the skill to govern the Republic and had no chance of regaining the confidence of the nation. He remained gripped by the thought that if he fled to Germany together with the Princess, the people would rise up on his behalf.[75]

The support the Prince received from Frederick of Prussia was equivocal: the king wanted no more than that he be kept "in place," and he was reluctant to send his troops to the frontier in readiness to defend William's cause by arms, as many Orangists wanted. At the moment, Thulemeyer warned the Prussian foreign minister, such a measure would do harm, but it probably would be necessary eventually.[76] This was indeed the king's view too; he saw no one "in Holland or elsewhere" who could direct such an enterprise.[77]

On 22 August came the news that Frederick II had died at Potsdam five days before.[78] To those who knew that he had turned his back on William V, there was a sudden restoration of hope. Thulemeyer went to Amsterdam and then to Het Loo, and on his return to The Hague wrote to the new Prussian king, Frederick William II, who was Princess Wilhelmina's brother, that the "good cause" might soon triumph in Gelderland and perhaps in Utrecht, encouraging the aristocrats in Holland to unite their cause with that of the Orangist party.[79] Even before this dispatch reached him, Frederick William sent reassurances to the Prince of Orange. One of

74 [Willem V], *Missives en Memorie van Consideratien, met Twaalf Bylagen, Van Zyne Doorlugtige Hoogheid den Heer Prins Erfstadhouder Willem den V., omtrent het Commando van 't Guarnisoen van den Haag, door Hoogsderzelven gezonden aan Hun Ed. Groot Mog. de Heeren Staten van Holland en West-Vriesland, en aan de Ed. Groot Acht. Heeren Burgemeesteren en Regeerders der Stem hebbende Steden in Holland* (Rotterdam, 1785), 8–12, 39.
75 Thulemeyer to Hertzberg, 10, 24 Jan. 1786, Thulemeyer, 462–63.
76 *Ibid.*, 10 Jan. 1786, Thulemeyer, 462.
77 Fredrick II to Thulemeyer, 18 Feb. 1786, Thulemeyer, 466 n. 1.
78 Thulemeyer, 495 n. 1.
79 Thulemeyer to Frederick William II, 1 Sept. 1786, Thulemeyer, 499.

his ministers was going to Holland to inform the States General of his deep interest in the Prince and in maintaining his authority.[80]

When news came that the Free Corps in two little Gelderland cities, Hattem and Elburg, had been bloodily crushed by regular army forces at William's command, the States of Holland, Groningen, Overijssel and Zeeland declared William divested of his post as captain-general. Holland took the further step of establishing along its provincial boundaries a military "cordon" of both Free Corps companies and regular troops in its pay as protection against the forces which remained loyal to the Prince.

A more forceful figure than Thulemeyer entered the scene and began to take control of events. This was the new English envoy, Sir James Harris, who had come to The Hague in December 1784, after the conclusion of peace and the resumption of diplomatic relations.[81] It was not long before he began to provide the Orangist party with the leadership which it had missed for so long[82] – Wilhelmina, however ready to act, was inhibited by her unwillingness to clash with her husband. Harris did not speak Thulemeyer's language of moderation and conciliation. He bluntly told his Prussian colleague that the only salvation would be a *coup d'état*.[83]

With William V off in Het Loo and the forthright Sir James taking charge of the opposition to the Patriot-dominated government in The Hague, the Orangist party began to gain coherence. Orange "free companies" – the equivalent of the Patriot "Free Corps" – and Orangist societies were formed. Members of the States and town governments in Zeeland during January and February 1787 bound themselves by an Act of Association (*Acte van Verbintenis*) to maintain the existing government of the republic in general and of the province in particular. It was the "true republican form" that they affirmed they were banding together to defend, with the hereditary stadholdership legally and permanently part of it. They rejected alike monarchical (*eenhoofdige*) and aristocratic regimes, as well as direct democracy.[84]

On New Year's Day, a riot of Orangist democrats broke out in Hoorn. Although Patriots were threatened, the rioters did not feel strong enough to go beyond strong words.[85] Another followed on 10 March, although it had been expected two days before on the Prince's birthday, and it

80 Frederick William II to William V, 3 Sept. 1786, *Archives*, 5e Sér., III, 405.
81 On Harris, see Alfred Cobban, *Ambassadors and Secret Agents: The Diplomacy of the first Earl of Malmesbury at The Hague* (London, 1954).
82 Brugmans, VI, 409.
83 Thulemeyer to Frederick II, 25 Nov. 1785, Thulemeyer, 456.
84 G. W. Vreede, *Mr Laurens Pieter van de Spiegel en zijne tijdgenoten (1737–1800)* (4 vols.; Middelburg, 1874–77), III, 134–37.
85 W. P. Kops, "De Oranje-oproeren te Hoorn 1786 en 1787," *BVGO*, 4e Reeks, 4 (1905), 244–47.

continued for four days.[86] But many Orangists felt there would soon be a direct attack upon the stadholdership, and believed it would be better if the Prince abdicated first.[87] In February William thought the "so-called Patriots" were trying to force the situation to extremes. He was afraid that an army corps under the Rhinegrave, the Count of Salm-Salm, would be sent to The Hague, because, as the oldest colonel in the States army, he would command the garrison, and he is "capable of anything."[88] Only little more than a week before, a mob of democrats, defying the moderates who had just won the municipal elections of 1 February, encircled the city hall and compelled the council to agree to bringing the Rhinegrave to The Hague.[89] This was voted by the States of Holland on 16 February by the barest majority of ten to nine. Greffier Fagel commented scathingly that "governing and constraining The Hague by eight companies of hussars" was "somewhat strange." It was a kind of tyranny.[90]

William, who had moved to Nijmegen, continued to live in a dream world of his own fantasizing. He found the offer brought by Thulemeyer of a guaranty of his status by the courts of Berlin and Versailles repugnant; he did not want his country to become a dependency of foreign powers. This patriotic sentiment (which the Patriots shared if they could find terms of an accord with him which he would accept) did not move Thulemeyer. He replied pungently that dependency had always been and would be the fate of the Republic; and now it alone would give stability to the Dutch constitution, that is, to the hereditary stadholderate.[91]

William was dismayed by what seemed to be in prospect. In May, when Harris was returning to England for a visit, he wrote to King George to "implore" his protection. He feared a revolution wrought not by his own adherents but by the "cabal" (a word that always somehow managed to designate opponents and never one's own side – but this was as true of William's adversaries as of him) that was trying to seize the rudder of state in the province of Holland. Their goal, he said, was not only to overthrow the stadholderate in Holland but also to make themselves masters of the six other provinces, either by promises or by military force. William's duty was to prevent this if he could, and for this he sought the aid of England.[92] George replied with an affirmation of his desire to see no change in the Republic's constitution, and Harris followed up with a letter a few days later that repeated the king's position, adding that serious attention was

---

86 Kops, 247–49.
87 Thulemeyer to Frederick William II, 12 Jan. 1787, Thulemeyer, 517.
88 William V to Fagel, 14 Feb. 1787, *Archives*, 5e Sér., III, 457.
89 Brugmans, VI, 400.
90 Fagel to William V, 16 Feb. 1787, *Archives*, 5e Sér., III, 458.
91 Thulemeyer to Frederick William II, 17 Apr. 1787, Thulemeyer, 536–37.
92 William V to George III, 14 May 1787, *Archives*, 5e Sér., III, 469–70.

being given to finding the best way to prevent the overthrow of the "present constitution."[93]

The break came when Princess Wilhelmina was arrested on 28 June at Goejanverwellesluis near Schoonhoven as she attempted to enter the province of Holland to go to The Hague without the permission of the States. Her captors were first the local Free Corps and then the commission of the States of Holland sent to command the troops that formed the military "cordon" around the province.[94] Once the Hollanders realized that they had caught a tiger (a tigress!) by the tail, they sought to soften the significance of what they had done. She had been detained, they explained, because there was a general order to arrest suspicious persons. For once, William's comment was cool and witty: "they do her the honor to include her in that number."[95] The Hollanders would have had reason to worry more about the observation of the Princess, when she saw with her own eyes the utter lack of training and discipline among the Free Corps, that there was nothing to fear from them.[96]

Events now began to tumble over each other in their rapid sequence. William moved to Amersfoort in Utrecht province, only a few dozen miles from Schoonhoven, where Wilhelmina had been taken while her captors awaited orders from the States of Holland. Once at Amersfoort, he wrote to George III and Frederick William II to assure them that he expected that she would be released but nonetheless imploring their protection in his "cruel situation."[97]

The Prussian king, Frederick William II, replied first with a demand for reparations for the insults to the stadholder and his wife, and assembled a corps of 40,000 troops in the duchy of Cleves, just inside the German frontier from the Netherlands, to show his displeasure. The States of Holland tried to find a way out of the trap in which they had been caught. They sought the mediation of France, and Louis XVI informed the States General on 18 July that he was willing to perform this task, but William refused, for the French king was hardly impartial.[98] Gijselaer, perhaps the most active of the Patriot town pensionaries, told Thulemeyer that his province would gladly treat with the Princess at Nijmegen, provided she openly displayed her disagreement with her husband's principles. Gijselaer was joined by Van Berckel, the equally fervent pensionary of Amsterdam, in assurance that there was a firm

93 George III to William V, 28 May, Harris to William V, 2 June 1787, *Archives*, 5e Sér., III, 479–81.
94 Thulemeyer to Hertzberg, 29 June 1787, Thulemeyer, 561.
95 William V to Van Reede, 11 July 1787, *Archives*, 5e Sér., III, 508.   96 Naber, 112.
97 William V to George III and Frederick William II, 29 June 1787, *Archives*, 5e Sér., III, 489–500.
98 William V to Fagel, 12 July 1787, *Archives*, 5e Sér., III, 509 and footnote.

intention to maintain the stadholderate in the House of Orange and to allow the Princess the exercise of all her prerogatives, but they admitted it would be difficult to keep William, who they said had become odious to the nation.[99]

On 24 August William published a long apology – a defense of his conduct, as that of his ancestor William the Silent had been – addressed to his "Dear Countrymen" (*Waarde Landgenooten*).

The obligations which the notable posts I hold in this country place upon me, [he wrote,] the personal interest that I and my House have in the established Constitution of the Netherlands, the name of ORANGE which I bear, these were sufficient reasons for this turbulent faction to know with certainty that so long as I have effective influence, so long as I was not made suspect to the Nation, it will be impossible for them to achieve their fatal purposes.

He called God to bear witness that the accusations against him were false.

A traitor to the Netherlands does not deserve to live. Now another attempt is beginning to deceive you again, and soon I will be accused of bringing Prussian troops into the country, so as to put upon me another crime of which I am wholly innocent, and where the cause is too well known to have escaped your attention.[100]

This is a striking document. It is utterly sincere and utterly out of touch with reality, indeed a mass of self-justifications so thick that it may well betray the deep uncertainty that beset the Prince as he faced tasks that he could not put down despite all his yearning to be freed of them, and yet was unable to perform. He could write to the kings of Britain and Prussia beseeching their aid and at the same time affirm with not the least sense of self-contradiction that he was not calling in foreign troops. He believed to the letter the principle that the stadholder, hereditary though he was, governed only with the States and as a member of government, not as a quasi-monarch and even less a full-fledged monarch over the country. His purposes were fundamentally misread by the American diplomat in Paris, Thomas Jefferson, who called William a "half king, who would be a whole one."[101]

William V was in fact quite surprised when a Prussian corps under the command of Ferdinand of Brunswick crossed the frontier into the United Provinces on 13 September and began a march of purification across the country. The resistance of the Free Corps, not to speak of the baffled regular soldiery, torn between their traditional commander and their pay-

99 Thulemeyer to Frederick William II, 15 July 1787, Thulemeyer, 568–69.

100 [Willem V], *Aan het Volk van Nederland* (Rotterdam, 1787), 3–7.

101 Thomas Jefferson at Paris to Abigail Adams at London, 1 July 1787, Lester J. Cappon, ed., *The Adams-Jefferson Letters: The Complete Correspondence between Thomas Jefferson and Abigail and John Adams* (2 vols.; Chapel Hill, NC, 1959), I, 180.

masters, was so desultory that one cannot speak of a conquest. The stated purpose of the invasion was to exact satisfaction for the offense to Wilhelmina, but it also expelled the Patriots from power, handing to the Prince of Orange on a platter the victory in what had been until then an incipient and inconclusive civil war.

The end came quickly for the Patriot regimes in the provinces and towns that had turned against the Prince. Amsterdam, where some of the deputies to the States of Holland took refuge, held out a little longer than the others, until 10 October. Any illusion that the amateur soldiery of the Free Corps could match the professionalism of the Prussians was dispelled very quickly. Appeals to France for help were of no avail, for that country was in the grip of fiscal and political crisis, but it did provide a refuge for the numerous Patriots who fled to escape the revenge of the Orangists. On 18 September, the States of Holland had acted to revoke all decisions against the authority of the stadholder, who rode back into the city two days later. The next day he wrote to George III to express his gratitude for the King's support, to which he owed his reestablishment.[102]

Tension between the Prince and the Princess, which had eased somewhat, now revived. His jealousy of his wife's vigor of mind and will were well known, and Thulemeyer saw with concern that those who wanted to regain their own ascendancy over the stadholder worked against her.[103] In any event, she vigorously supported Van de Spiegel, the vigorous and highly intelligent councilor pensionary of Zeeland, as the proper replacement for Van Bleiswijk, the councilor pensionary of Holland, who had attempted to play a mediating role between the Prince and the Patriots and now clearly had to step down. She urged him to accept "for the sake of the public good, our House, and to consolidate this happy revolution." The challenge was too great to be declined, and he accepted, being duly elected by the States of Holland after Van Bleiswijk's resignation in November.

Unlike most of his own supporters, William was reluctant to seek personal vengeance against the fallen Patriots, but this was more a pious wish than an effective barrier for the campaign of repression that ensued. It was noted with some irony that most of the Prussian generals were more favorable to the Patriots than to the Orangists. Nor did they have any respect for the Prince himself. Ferdinand of Brunswick left The Hague for home shortly before year's end, saying, "I put the Prince of Orange in his chair, now it's up to him to stay there."[104]

On 25 January, 1788, the States of Holland adopted a report establishing an oath for regents, ministers, officials, members of the civic guards and

102 William V to George III, 21 Sept. 1787, *Archives*, 5e Sér., III, 537–38.
103 Thulemeyer to Hertzberg, 9 Oct. 1787, Thulemeyer, 605.
104 Hardenbroek, VI, 662–63.

the guilds. It was to the present constitution of Holland, consisting of the free and sovereign government of the States of Holland as it had existed since the foundation of the Republic, with the hereditary stadholdership in the House of Orange, as granted in 1747 and renewed in 1766. The resolution specified the need for an eminent head in other provinces too, and hence a proposal was also made to the States General to seek such a declaration from them.[105] This was done in a mutual Act of Guaranty, after which an amnesty was proclaimed, although with numerous exceptions that did not benefit the refugee Patriots in the Austrian Netherlands and in France. The other provinces were not all enthusiastic for the change. Gelderland and Utrecht in particular wanted the "regulations of government" relaxed, but did not dare to withhold their assent. The "Act of Guaranty" was adopted by the States General on 27 June, with provision for intervention against any province that fell away from its principles.[106]

A co-protectorate over the United Provinces was sufficient for Prussia and England, and was made into a formal treaty in December that gave them the right to intervene in any dispute over the stadholdership. This was followed in April by a measure obviously directed toward France, a defensive treaty with the two powers, and in August by a guarantee of the existing institutions in the Republic.

Van de Spiegel attempted to introduce some reforms in taxation and administration in Holland, but there was no time for them to take root. On 1 February 1793, France declared war upon England and the United Provinces (more precisely, the Prince of Orange as stadholder). French armies, with a Dutch ("Batavian") legion participating, quickly conquered the Austrian Netherlands and then plunged ahead into States Brabant, halting only at the line of the Holland Deep, a broad stretch of the Schelde. A democratic revolution on the French model was introduced, but collapsed when the French lost their grip on their conquests and withdrew. In the United Provinces various Patriots, including both moderates and radicals, formed a secret "revolutionary committee" in Amsterdam. By 1794 the Patriots in exile were seeking not the limitation of the stadholderate but its abolition and the total overthrow of the House of Orange. When the French defeated the allied army in August 1794 at Fleurus, a French army once again occupied States Brabant, as well as Sluis and Nijmegen, but the rivers were only a temporary barrier. They froze hard in December and the French forces crossed them easily. The regular Dutch army performed no better than the "Free Corps" of the Patriots in 1787. The French occupied

---

105 Ageus Jacobus van der Meulen, *Studies over het Ministerie van Van de Spiegel* (Leiden, 1905), 29–31.
106 *Ibid.*, 32–34.

Utrecht on 16 January. Two days later William V and his family took ship for England, while in Amsterdam the revolutionary committee proclaimed a new government, which soon took the name of the Batavian Republic.

On 30 January 1795, William V wrote to Lynden van Blitterswijk to inform him of his arrival in England. "I had never expected to have to leave my country even for a time, but it is a decree of Providence that I cannot resist."[107] His memory was conveniently weak, but it can hardly be expected that he would now remember all the times he had been on the verge, at least in speech, of laying down his offices and going home to the home he had never known, his lands in Germany.

The Republic of the United Provinces was no more, gone forever. So too was the stadholderate. Each had gone down in the débâcle of the other.

The tragedy of William V was the tale of woe of a man too small for a task that birth and history had placed upon him. He longed to put it down and never could, until it was wrested from him. He held a post that he could define down to the last detail, and yet it escaped him that all the prerogatives of his office were nothing without the exercise of leadership. Leadership, indeed, was what the complex, multifarious political system of the Dutch Republic required more than anything else. Over history, it had been the work of either the Princes of Orange or the councilor pensionaries of Holland. William V failed to take the helm of state, but prevented the helmsman who could have guided the ship – for Van de Spiegel, for all the differences of his principles, was a councilor pensionary in the mold of Oldenbarnevelt and De Witt – from doing so. Many of the faults for which William has been berated by historians are anachronisms: he did not seek to create a New Regime of constitutional monarchy, of social equality and nationwide citizenship, the ideals generated by another full century of historical development in his country. Those who built the New Regime worked in terrain cleared of old institutions, old commitments and, yes, old ideas by the whirlwind storm of the Age of Revolution. William V was devoted to those institutions, commitments and ideas but knew neither how to defend them nor how to abandon them.

107 William V to Lynden van Blitterswijk, 30 Jan. 1795, *Brieven van Willem V en Lijnden van Blitterswijk*, 243.

Epilogue: consequences and conclusions

Almost two decades would pass after the departure of William V for England before the House of Orange returned to the Netherlands. During that eventful time the country's political institutions were ripped away and discarded, and in their stead came a variety of forms, democratic, parliamentarian and autocratic. The Batavian Republic was first, installing a new regime on the cleared ground. The historic provinces lost their sovereignty, giving way to a unitary national government. National and local officials were elected, although the range of the electorate varied with shifting political developments. Like citizenry, taxation too became national. The regime was not able to achieve stability. It swung to the left, to the right, and finally had an authoritarian head imposed on it by the Emperor Napoleon. From 1805 to 1810 Napoleon's brother Louis ruled as king of Holland. From 1810 to 1813 the ruler was Napoleon himself, after the country was incorporated into the French Empire. In 1813, as the Empire began to disintegrate, Dutch independence was proclaimed, and William V's son returned, first as Sovereign Prince and then as King William I of the Netherlands. But the old regime did not come back with him. The new institutions were maintained, which over the decades were transformed into the modern constitutional monarchy.

The "Orange myth" was consolidated in the national ideology. It no longer expressed the antagonism between the House of Orange and the regents, however. The stadholderate became a historic memory, studied, discussed, but not part of living experience. For the historian, who "lives" the past by study and discussion, the significance of the stadholderate remains open.

Perhaps the first thing we see is that improvisation in the Dutch Republic was as lasting as deliberate creation. As the French say, "Il n'y a que le provisoire qui dure." The improvised institutions created in Oldenbarnevelt's time lasted for more than two centuries, and the downfall of the Republic was not due to their shortcomings, or even to the inadequacies of the last two stadholders, real as these were, but to the helplessness of the small country in the face of the immense power of revolutionary France.

The two stadholderless intervals demonstrated that the stadholderate was not an integral part of the (unwritten) constitution, unlike the States, provincial and General. The country could be a great power in the seventeenth century, with and without stadholders, and it could become a plaything of the great powers in the eighteenth, with and without stadholders. The stadholderate was maintained, abandoned or restored according to shifting circumstances.

The self-image and the practice of the House of Orange – which in the persons of the stadholders have been the subject of this book – remained caught in an anomalous ground of uncertainties. The Princes of Orange from their first entry into the life of the Netherlands were sovereigns of a tiny distant land, but their real power lay in their status as great nobles in the Low Countries. As the Republic of the United Provinces emerged, they became the servants of the sovereign States, but servants of a new kind, "eminent heads" whose task was to lead. Ambition and pride pointed in one direction, upward into the ranks of European royalty, that is, to becoming sovereigns in place of and over the States; political reality pointed in another direction, to immobility, to remaining fixed in ambiguity, less than kings and more than mere subjects.

The irony of this development was that it resulted from the drumfire of accusations against the Princes from the States party over the decades that they were seeking to become duke and count in the Dutch provinces. It was an accusation that had its foundation in the rhetoric of Orangist preachers and poets and in the less florid but no less outspoken talk of Orangist courtiers. Down to William II the acceptance of their anomalous position by the Princes of Orange may have been a matter of realism rather than of principle. Thereafter, however, they were all taught that to be stadholders was their highest proper ambition, at least within the Netherlands. The exception was William III's quest for the dukedom of Gelderland, and its very failure consolidated that principle. Some of the Patriot leaders during the last decades of the Republic seem to have recognized this development; their exasperation and anger with William V arose from his failure as a leader of the nation.

Leadership became the task and the test of the stadholderate. When the stadholders were the essential source and the principal executors of policy, even if the States remained the bodies that decided it and gave it legal force, the Dutch system worked. But that same role could be played by the councilor pensionary of Holland. The essential "crime" of John de Witt in the eyes of the Orangists had been to prove that there was an alternative to the Princes of Orange. In the eighteenth century, there was a dearth of leadership, whether by councilor pensionary or stadholder. Even Heinsius had been more a foreign minister without the title than a prime minister in the modern sense, a leader of state. William IV and William V possessed the title of stadholders but lacked the force of character and will to impose themselves as leaders. William V in the end had to be rescued from himself by a foreign army as he let power slip into the hands of the Patriots.

The Princes of Orange have been repeatedly berated by historians for not reforming the faulty political institutions of the Republic: the exaggerated provincialism and localism that thwarted the emergence of a full-grown Dutch nationhood in the form of a unitary state under a monarchical head. This is arrant anachronism, for they were not revolutionaries – and neither were most of their critics in their own time. To create such a state then would have had to be the deed of a tyrant, riding roughshod over the existing institutions: the very thing that Philip II was accused of doing. Wiping out the status quo for the sake of an ideal future – revolutionary utopianism – was no one's program in the Netherlands in the age of the Republic of the United Provinces. The Batavian Republic, the work of men formed in the final decades of the old regime, went at that task half-heartedly even though the old institutions had been swept away. Reform – not revolution – would come in its own time, a half-century and more later.

"Orange democracy" was always a puzzle for the stadholders. It was a call upon them to play a role they had no desire to assume, to protect the common folk against the regents. The Princes did not oppose the rule of the regents, only their ruling stadholders or against stadholders. They sought to tame the regents, much as Louis XIV tamed the nobility of France. For the popular forces, the Princes became their hope of redemption from the untrammeled domination of the regents. Yet for modern historians to think that the "people" ought to have developed their own ideology and their own movement, separate from the Princes, is to be as anachronistic as to regret that the Princes were not reformers or modern constitutional monarchs. Democracy in the modern sense developed in the Netherlands in the nineteenth and twentieth centuries apart from and even against the House of Orange, and it was the kings and queens who adapted to it. A queen riding upon her bicycle amid the people would not have been a symbol that would have been understood in the seventeenth and eighteenth centuries.

All in all, the Princes of Orange remained a central presence throughout the history of the Dutch Republic. If the States were its primary political institution, the stadholderate, present or absent, gave it its distinctive coloration. It made the constitution of the United Provinces unique.

Bibliography

PRIMARY SOURCES

A. Pamphlets

The "Knuttel number" – the number of a pamphlet in W. P. C. Knuttel, *Catalogus van de pamflettenverzameling berustende in de Koninklijke Bibliotheek* (9 vols.; The Hague, 1888–1920) – is given after a pamphlet title as "Kn. no."

Amsterdams Buer-praetje. Dat is, Discours tusschen twee Amsterdammers, Claes Torenssen, en Kees Vries, over de doot van Syn Hoogheydt. Amsterdam, 1650. Kn. 6,868.

Apologie Of Verded--iginge, van 't gene by de Gemeente in Zeelandt gedaen, tot herstellinge van Sijn Hoogheyt den Heere Prince van Oranjen Willem-Hendrick. In alle 't gesagh ende digniteyten van sijne Voor-Ouders Hoog-l. Mem. Door een Voorstander des Vaderlandts. N.p., n.d. (1672). Kn. 10,261

Bedenckinge Op de Deductie Van de Ed. Gr. Mog. Staten van Hollant, Noopende den Artickel van Seclusie Van den Heere Prince van Oraenjen; Ingesteld door een Patriot van 't Vaderlant. N.p., 1654. Kn. 7,550.

Berg, A. van den, *Verdediging, of Antwoort op het schandeleuze en monstrueuse Boek, Genaamt Hollandts Intrest.* Dordrecht, 1663. Kn. 8,808.

[Blasius, Johan], *Stok in 't Hondert, Op 't Burgerlyk Versoek.* (Amsterdam), 1672. Kn. 10,554.

Brief over de waere oorzaeck van 's Lands Ongeval, Gevonden tusschen Utrecht en Amersfoort om deszelfs merkwaerdigen inhoud met den druk gemeen gemaakt. N.p., 1782. Kn. 20,171.

Brief van Claudius Civilis Aan de Heer Justus Batavus. Wegens de noodzakelijkheid en de Redenen van de Burgeren van Gouda, om by Request te verzoeken, dat alle Ampten verkocht worden tot nutte van det gemeene Landt. N.p., 1747.

[Brunswick-Wolfenbüttel, Louis, Duke of], *Kort Vorstel van het geene omtrent den overgang van Zyne Hoogheid den Heere L. Hertog van Brunswyk, in den Dienst van de Republicq der Vereenigde Nederlanden den deszelfs Conservatie in den gemelden Dienst is voorgevallen, en vervolgens aanleiding heeft gegeeven tot het passeeren van Zeekere Acte Tusschen Zyne Hoogheid den Heere Prince van Orange en Nassau, en gemelde Zyne Hoogheid den Heere L. Hertog van Brunswyk, Op den 3. Mey 1766 aangegaan.* The Hague, n.d. (1781?)

Christelijcke en Politique Redenen, Waer om dat Nederlandt en Engelandt tegens malcanderen niet moghen Oorloghen. Rotterdam, 1652. Kn. 7,204.

Bibliography

Conditien ende Verbintenissen; Extract uyt de Resolutie van de Ed. Mog. Heeren Staten van Uytrecht, aen Sijn Hoogheyt de Prince van Oranjen, Weegens d'Opdracht van Hartog van Geldre en Grave van Zutphen. En Sijn Hoogheydts Antwoordt... Arnhem, 1675. Kn. 11,323.

Conditien ende Verbintenissen, Waer op Sijne Hoogheydt is opgedragen de Hooge Overicheyt over de Provincie van Gelderlandt ende Sutphen... Arnhem, 1675. Kn. 11,321.

Copie van een Brief, geschreven uyt Rotterdam aan NN. Licentiaet in de Rechten tot Dantzich: Behelsende in 't korte 't Geene in de Vereenigde Nederlanden sedert den Jare 1648, tot den Jare 1672 voorgevallen is, raeckende de Manieren en Maximen van Regeringe en Oorspronck der tegenwoordige Onheylen, de selvige in desen Jare door de verderffelijcken Oorlogh der Koningen van Vranckrijck en Engelandt overgekomen. In 't Eerste Iaer der Herstellinge van de Stadhouderlijcke Regeeringe, Pro Populo Principifico. Rotterdam, 1672. Kn. 10,479.

Deductie ende Debat tegens de Consideratiën vam de Heeren Gecommitterde Raden van Zeeland, op eenige voorname Poincten ende Ingredienten van de Propositie in Februari laestleden, 1668, van de Heeren Gedeputeerden van haer Ho. Mo. de Heeren Staten Generael der Vereenigde Nederlanden, in de Vergaderingh van de Heeren Staten van Zeeland gedaen. Amsterdam, 1668.

Den Bedrogen Engelsman met de handen in 't Hair. Of t'Samenspraeck tusschen drie Persoonen, Daniel, een Fransman, Robbert, een Engelsman, en Jan, een Hollander. Nevens een vergelijckinge tusschen den Marquis d'Ancre, en Cornelis en Ian de Wit. N.p., 1672.

Den Herstelden Prins Tot Stadt-houder en Capiteyn Generael vande Vereenighde Nederlanden,... tegens de boekjens onlangs uytgegeven met den naem van Interest van Hollandt, ende Stadt-houderlycke Regeeringe in Hollandt, &c. Amsterdam, 1663. Kn. 8806a.

Den rechten ommeganck. Kn. 6,781.

De oog-geopende Zeeuw, Gestelt in maniere van een t'samensprekinge Tusschen een Hollander Ende een Zeeuw, Aengaende de seclusie van sijn Hoogheydt den Prince van Oranjen. N.p., n.d. (1654) Kn. 7,565.

De rechte ondeckinge Vande Hollantsche Regeerende Loevensteynsche Heeren. Dordrecht, 1652. Kn. 7,302.

d'Ontdeckte Ambassade van de Groot, Ambassadeur in Vranckrijck. Waer in 't geheym van sijn secrete Handelingh met sijn Complicen vertoont wert. In 't licht gegeven door een Liefhebber der waerheyt. N.p., 1672.

d'Ontroerde Leeuw: Behelsende Een Historisch Relaes van de merkweerdigste Geschiedenisse van tijt tot tijt voorgevallen sint de beginselen van desen Oorlog, tot nu toe. Amsterdam, 1672. Kn. 10,526.

Een Placcaet tot Aenwas der Schepen, ende Moet-ghevinge aen de Zeevaert van dese Natie. Donderdag den 9 Octob. 1651. Gheordonneert by het Parliament dat dese Acte terstont ghedruckt ende ghepulibicert sy. Translated from the English. The Hague, 1651. Kn. 6, 955.

Eenvoudigh advis. Kn. 7,257.

Fransch Praetie. Sic vos non vobis. Münster, 1646, Kn. 5,297.

Hagius, G., *Afgeparste Waerheyt ofte Nodige en Naeckte aenwijsinge: Hoe dankbaer-*

Bibliography

lijk de Magistraet, eenige uyt de Vroedtschap, ende alle de praesente Bevelhebbers van Leeuwarden tracteren hare Gecommitteerden, die sy, tot het instellen en bevordren van de Reformatoire Poincten, op den 27sten. September 1672, by d'Ed. Mog. *Heeren Staten van Friesland gearresteert, hebben genomineert ende versocht..* N.p. (Leeuwarden), n.d. (1673).

Hoe veel den Vereenigde Provintien Gehoort gelegen te zijn, de her-stellinge van den Coninck van Groot-Britangie. Uytgegeven op de tegenwoordige gelegenheyt van Oorlog tusschen Hen, en de Engelsche Rebellen. The Hague, 1653. Kn. 7,426.

Hollants praatjen, Tusschen vier personen, Een Geldersman, een Hollander, een Vries, en een Brabander, Aangaande de Souverainiteyt van Syn Hoogheyt... Antwerp, 1650. Kn. 6,824.

Invallende Gedagten, by het Overdenken der tegenwoordige Tyds Omstandigheden. Groningen, n.d. (1748).

[Johnston, James], *Verdedigende Redenvoering Voor de Ere van den Doorluchtigen, Getrouwen en Doorsightigen Grondlegger der Vaderlandsche Vryheid Willem den Eersten.* By een Edelman uyt Middlesex. Translated from the English. Leiden, 1779.

Koffy-Huis-Praatje, Tusschen een oud Amsterdamsch Koopman, een Fries, en eenige anderen Gehouden, des Nagts van den 4 May. 1747 in het Koffyhuis van Monsieur N. te Amsterdam. Amsterdam, 1747. Kn. 17,612.

Korte Vragen en Antwoorden, Over de Deductie ofte Declaratie van de Staten van Holland ende West-Vrieslandt.... Amsterdam, 1654, Kn. 7,552.

Le Chasse du Prince ou Relation de la Reception faite à S.A. Monsieur le Prince d'Orange Guillaume III, en la Province de Zelande. Et de son Installation là méme en la dignité de Premier Noble. arrivèes [sic] *les 18. et 19. Septembre 1668.* N.p., 1668. Kn. 9,668.

Leeven en Bedrijf Van sijn Hoogheyt Willem Hendrick de Derde, Prince van Orangien, En Nassau, &c. Door een Liefhebber der Historien. Amsterdam, 1675.

Missive Aen den Heere &c. Behelsende eenige Consideratien over de Resolution door de Ed: Mog: Heeren Staten van Zeelant Genomen den 24. Maant February 1675. Middelburg, 1675. Kn. 11,328.

Ontdeckinghe, Van den tegenwoordigen standt onses Vaderlandts, waer het hapert, en hoe de In-ghesetenenen, uyt haer groot verstel, spoedelijck souden connen verlost worden, en uyt de Enghelsche Oorlog gereddet. Middelburg, 1653. Kn. 7,462.

Politique Aenmerckinge over den Oorlogh, Tusschen Engelandt en de Vereenigde Nederlanden. N.p., 1665. Kn. 9,128.

Presentatie van de Ridderschap ende Steden der Quartieren van Nimmeghen, Zutphen ende Arnhem, aen syn Hoogheyt den Heere Prince van Orangien. N.p., 1675. Kn. 11, 320.

Rechtsgeleerde Verhandeling over eene Gewigtige Preëminentie, den Heeren Stadhouderen omtrent de Regering der Steden eigen. Door Mr de ★★★. Rotterdam, 1747. Kn. 17,606.

Redenen Waerom het oorbaerder is Dat de Vereenichde Nederlanden Haer met de Republyq van Engelandt Verbinen, om t'samen eenderley ende gemeenen Vrienden en Vyanden te hebben, als met eenige andere Naeburige Princen... Rotterdam, 1651. Kn. 6,978.

Bibliography

Resolutie Van de E: Mog: Heeren Staten van Zeelandt, Rakende het Hertoghdom van Gelder en het Graefschap van Zutphen. Middelburg, 1675. Kn. 11,324.

[Rooy, J. de], Stadhouders Eerste Geboorte-Galon. N.p., 1672. Kn. 10,635.

Tegvlarivs, Hermannvs, Inhvldings-Predicatie, Op de Vermaerde Intrede van Syn Hoogheyt, Den Doorluchtigsten ende Hoogh-Gebooren Vorst ende Heere Wilhelm, By den gratie Godts Prince van Orangien &c., Gedaen op den Bede-dagh, den 8. Mey, Anno 1647. Delft, 1647. Kn. 5,579.

The Present State of Holland, or a Description of the United Provinces. London, 1745.

t' Leven van Willem den IV. Prins van Oranje en Nassau. Amsterdam, 1752.

Tweede Deel van 't Wacht-Praetje, Over de oude Privilegien en Voor-Rechten der Amsterdamsche Burgers, gehouden in der selver Wacht-huys aen de Weesper-Poort den 10. September 1672. Tusschen een Sarjant, Adelborst, en Schutter. N.p., 1672. Kn. 10,565.

Verklaringen van de respective Provincien gedaen ter Vergaderinge van haer Hoogh Mog., tot onderhoudinge van Eendracht, tot beschherminge van den Staet, ende tot handthavinge van de Gemeene sake. The Hague, 1702 (misprinted 1792). Kn. 14,748.

Vrymoedige Aenspraek Aen alle Oprechte Liefhebbers van zijn Hoogheyt den Heere Prince van Oranje. haer wettelijcke Overigheyt, Ende Vaderlandt. Ofte een 't Samenspraeck, Tusschen een Oprecht Hollander, Soldaat, Bootsgesel. En In-woonder van desen Staet. The Hague, n.d. (1672?) Kn. 10,291.

"Wel-hem Recht-hert van Vry-land." Brief Rakende het vangen der Ses Leden Van de Groot-Mogende Heeren Staten van Hollandt en West-Vrieslandt, en 't beleg-eren van Amsterdam. "In 't Vrije Hollandt: Meenrecht Vredericxson Stavast, 1650." N.p., 1650, Kn. 6,771.

[William III, Prince of Orange], Missive van syn Hoogheyt, Den Heere Prince van Orangie, Geschreven aen de Heeren Staten van Zeelant, Rescriberende op haer Ed. Mog. Missive van den 16. der voorleden Maant February 1675. N.p., 1675. Kn. 11,330.

William V, Prince of Orange, Aan het Volk van Nederland. Rotterdam, n.d. (1787).

Missives en Memorie van Consideration, met Twaalf Bylagen, Van Zyne Doorlug-tige Hoogheid den Heer Prins Erfstadhouder Willem den V., omtrent het Com-mando van 't Guarnisoen van den Haag, door Hoogstdenzelven gezonden aan Hun Ed. Groot Mog. de Heeren Staaten van Hollandt en West-Vriesland, en aan de Ed. Groot Achtb. Heeren Burgemeesteren en Regeerders der Stem hebbende Steden in Holland. Rotterdam, 1785.

Zeeuwse Ratel, geroert Tusschen dry Persoonen, Een Hollander, Zeeuvv en Hagenaar, over Het Uitsluiten en deporteren van een Stadthouder Generaal. Middelburg, 1654. Kn. 7,564.

B. Other works

[Adams, Abigail, John Adams and Thomas Jefferson], The Adams–Jefferson Let-ters: The Complete Correspondence between Thomas Jefferson and Abigail and John Adams, ed. Lester J. Cappon. 2 vols. Chapel Hill, NC. 1959.

Bibliography

Aitzema, Lieuwe van, *Saken van Staet en Oorlogh, in, ende omtrent de Vereenighde Nederlanden*. 2nd edn, 6 vols. in 7 parts. The Hague, 1669–72.

Archives ou correspondance inédite de la Maison d'Orange–Nassau, eds. G. Groen van Prinsterer *et al.* 5 series; 25 vols. Leiden and Utrecht, 1835–1915.

[Avaux, Claudes de Mesmes, Comte d'] *Négociations de Monsieur le Comte d'Avaux en Hollande*. 6 vols. Paris, 1752–53.

[Baerle, Caspar], *Poezy van Caspar van Baerle*, ed. P. S. Schull. N.p., 1835.

[Bentinck van Rhoon, Willem], *Briefwisseling en Aantekeningen van Willem Bentinck, Heer van Rhoon (tot aan de dood van Willem IV 22 October 1751) Hoofdzakelijk naar de Bescheiden in het Britsch Museum*, eds. C. Gerretson and P. Geyl. One vol. (all published). Utrecht, 1934.

Blok, P. J., ed., *Relazioni Veneziani: Venetiaansche berichten over de Vereenigde Nederlanden van 1600–1795*. The Hague, 1900.

[Capellen, Alexander van der, Heer van Aartsbergen], *Gedenkschriften van Jonkheer Alexander van der Capellen, Heere van Aartsbergen, Boedelhoff, en Mervelt*, ed. Robert Jaspar van der Capellen. 2 vols. Utrecht, 1772–3.

Capellen tot den Pol, Joan Derk Baron van der, *Aan het Volk van Nederland: Het Democratisch Manifest (1781)*, eds. W. F. Wertheim and A. H. Wertheim-Gijse Weeninck. Amsterdam, 1966.

Cats, Jacob. *Alle de Werken*. Amsterdam, 1712.

[Court, Pieter de la], V. D. H., *Interest van Holland, ofte Grond van Hollandswelvaren*. Amsterdam, 1662.

Dekker, R. M., ed., *Oproeren in Holland gezien door de tijdgenoten. Ooggetuigeverslagen van oproeren in de provincie Holland ten tijde van de Republiek (1650–1750)*. Assen, 1979.

[Dohna, Friedrich von], *Les Mémoires du Burgrave et Comte Frédéric de Dohna, 1621–1688*, ed. H. Borkowski. Königsberg i. Pr., 1898.

[Gonicourt, Derival de], *Lettres Hollandoises, Ou Correspondance politique sur l'état présent de l'Europe, notamment de la République des Sept Provinces-Unies* 5 vols. Amsterdam, 1779–80.

Grondwettige Herstelling, van Nederlands Staatswezen zo voor het algemeen Bondgenootschap, als voor het bestuur van elke byzondere Provincie. 2 vols. 1784–85.

[Guiche, Antoine de Gramont, Comte de], *Mémoires du comte de Guiche, concernant les Provinces-Unies des Pais-Bas*. London, 1744.

[Hardenbroek, Gijsbert Jan van], *Gedenkschrifdten van Gijsbert Jan van Hardenbroek, Heer van Bergestein, Lockhorst, 's Heeraartsberg, Bergambacht en Ammerstol, President der Utrechtse Ridderschap, Gedeputeerde ter Generaliteits–Vergadering enz.*, eds. F. J. L. Krämer and A. J. van der Meulen. 6 vols. Amsterdam, 1901–18.

[Heinsius, Anthonie], *De Briefwisseling van Anthonie Heinsius, 1702–1720*, ed. A. J. Veenendaal, Jr, 3 vols. The Hague, 1976–1980.

Hollantse Mercurius. 41 vols. Haarlem, 1651–1691.

[Huygens, Constantijn, Sr], *De Briefwisseling van Constantijn Huygens (1608–1687)*, ed. J. A. Worp. 6 vols. The Hague, 1911–17.

[Huygens, Constantijn, Jr], *Journaal van Constantijn Huygens, den zoon, gedurende de veldtochten der jaren 1673, 1675, 1676, 1677 en 1678.* 4 vols. Utrecht, 1876–88.

Idema, P., *De plegtelyke Intreede Van Syn Doorlugtige Hoogheydt den Heere Johan Wilhelm Friso, Door de gratie Gods Prins van Oranje en Nassau, &c. &c. &c. En Syn Dierbare Gemalinne, Maria Louisa, Gebooren Princesse van Hessen-Cassel. Binnen Groningen den 13. Martius 1710.* Groningen, 1710.

Kossmann [misprinted Kossman], E. H., and A. F. Mellink, eds., *Texts concerning the Revolt of the Netherlands.* Cambridge, 1974.

Krämer, F. J. L., *"Mémoires de Monsieur de B.... ou anecdotes tant de la cour du Prince d'Orange Guillaume III, que des principaux seigneurs de la république de ce temps,"* Bijdragen voor Vaderlandsche Geschiedenis, 19 (1898), 62–124.

[Maurice, Prince of Orange], "Prins Maurits, Fragment," ed. P. J. Blok, *Bijdragen voor Vaderlandsche Geschiedenis,* 6de Reeks, 9 (1930), 161–76.

[Michiel, Francesco], "Verslag van den Ambassadeur in Den Haag, Francesco Michiel, aan Doge en Senaat, 27 Mei, 1638," W. G. Brill, ed. and trans., *Bijdragen en Mededeelingen van het Historisch Genootschap,* 7 (1884), 67–88.

Rowen, Herbert H., ed., *The Low Countries in Early Modern Times: A Documentary History.* New York, 1972.

[Slingelandt, Simon van, and Sicco van Goslinga], *Briefwisseling tusssen Simon van Slingelandt en Sicco van Goslinga, 1697–1731,* ed. W. A. van Rappard. The Hague, 1978.

[Thulemeyer, F. W. von], *Dépêches van Thulemeyer, 1763–1788,* eds. Robert Fruin and H. T. Colenbrander. Amsterdam, 1912.

Waeragtig Verhaal van de Muiterij binnen de stad Rotterdam, die tegens de regeering ontstaan is. Ter goeder Trouw beschreeven door iemand, die van gemelde Muiterij kennis gehad heeft. N.p., 1785.

Wicquefort, Abraham de, *"Mémoire sur la guerre faite aux Provinces-Unies en l'année 1672,"* ed. J. A. Wijnne, *Bijdragen en Mededeelingen van het Historisch Genootschap,* 11 (1888), 70–344.

[William I, Prince of Orange], *The Apologie of Prince William of Orange against the Proclamation of the King of Spaine: edited after the English edition of 1581,* ed. H. Wansink. Leiden, 1969.

Correspondance de Guillaume le Taciturne, Prince d'Orange, ed. M. Gachard, 6 vols. Brussels, Leipzig, Ghent, 1850–66.

[William III, King of England and Prince of Orange, and Hans Willem Bentinck, first Earl of Portland], *Correspondentie van Willem en van Hans Willem Bentinck, eersten Graaf van Portland,* ed. N. Japikse. 5 vols. The Hague, 1927–37.

[William V, Prince of Orange], *Brieven van Prins Willem V aan Baron Van Lijnden van Blitterswijk, Representant van de Eerste Edele van Zeeland,* ed. F. de Bas. The Hague, 1893.

[Woertman, Dirk], "Korte notitie van 't geene gebeurt is bij occasie van 't afsterven van de Heer Boudaen, Raad in de Vroedschap der stad Utrecht, en mijne bevordering in desselfs plaats, met het geene van tijd tot tijd daerop is gevolgd." *Bijdragen en Mededeelingen van het Historisch Genootschap,* 5 (1882), 251–306.

Bibliography

SECONDARY SOURCES

Aa, C. van der, *Geschiedenis van het Leven, Character, en Lotgevallen van wijlen Willem den Vijfden, Prinse van Oranje en Nassau.* Amsterdam, 1809.

Algemene Geschiedenis der Nederlanden. New edn, 15 vols. Haarlem, 1977–83.

Arend, J. P., *Algemeene Geschiedenis des Vaderlands, van de vroegste tijden tot op heden.* Continued by O. van Rees, W. G. Brill, and J. van Vloten. 15 vols. Amsterdam, 1840–82.

Arntzen, G., "Waren Willem IV en Frederik de Grote vrienden?," *Tijdschrift voor Geschiedenis,* 64 (1951), 315–32.

Baelde, M. E. J., "De Orde van het Gulden Vlies," *Spiegel Historiael,* 19 (1984), 169–73.

[Baillet, A. de, pseud. Balt. Hezeneil de la Neuville], *Histoire de la Hollande, depuis la tréve de 1609, où finit Grotius, jusqu'à nôtre temps.* 4 vols. Paris, 1698.

Barendrecht, S., *François van Aerssen: Diplomaat aan het Franse Hof (1598–1613).* Leiden, 1965.

Bax, J., *Prins Maurits in de volksmening der 16e en 17e eeuw.* Amsterdam, 1940.

Baxter, Stephen B., *William III and the Defense of European Liberty, 1650–1702,* New York, 1966.

Blok, P. J., *Frederik Hendrik, Prins van Oranje.* Amsterdam, 1924.

Geschiedenis van het Nederlandsche Volk. 8 vols. Groningen, 1892–1908.

Willem de Eerste, Prins van Oranje. 2 vols. Amsterdam, 1919–20.

Boogman, J. C., "The Union of Utrecht: its Genesis and Consequences." *Bijdragen en Mededelingen betreffende de Geschiedenis der Nederlanden,* 94 (1979), 277–407.

Bootsma, N. A., *De Hertog van Brunswijk, 1750–1759.* Assen, 1962.

"Prinses Anna van Hannover," in: *Voor Rogier,* 127–46.

Brants, Antoni, *Bijdrage tot de geschiedenis der Geldersche Plooierijen.* Leiden, 1874.

Brugmans, H., *Geschiedenis van Amsterdam van den oorsprong af tot heden.* 8 vols. Amsterdam. 1930–34.

Cobban, Alfred, *Ambassadors and Secret Agents,: The Diplomacy of the first Earl of Malmesbury at The Hague.* London, 1954.

Crew, Phyllis Mack, *Calvinist Preaching and Iconoclasm in the Netherlands, 1544–1569.* Cambridge, 1978.

Darnton, Robert, *The Business of Enlightenment: A Publishing History of the Encyclopédie, 1775–1800.* Cambridge, Mass., 1979.

Decavele, J., "De edelman Oranje en de Calvinisten," *Spiegel Historiael,* 19 (1984), 201–6.

"De mislukking van Oranjes 'democratische' politiek in Vlaanderen," *Bijdragen en Mededelingen betreffende de Geschiedenis der Nederlanden,* 99 (1984), 626–51.

Delfos, Leo, *Die Anfänge der Utrechter Union, 1577–1587: Ein Beitrag zur Geschichte der niederländischen Erhebung, insbesondere zu deren Verfassungsgeschichte.* Berlin, 1941; reprint edn, Vaduz, 1965.

Deursen, A. Th. van, *Bavianen en Slijkgeuzen: Kerk en kerkvolk ten tijde van Maurits en Oldenbarnevelt.* Assen, 1974.

Het kopergeld van de Gouden Eeuw. 4 vols. Assen and Amsterdam, 1978.

Bibliography

"De raadpensionaris Jacob Cats," *Tijdschrift voor Geschiedenis*, 92 (1979), 149–61.

"Staatsinstellingen in de Noordelijke Nederlanden, 1579–1780," in: *Algemene Geschiedenis der Nederlanden*, V, 350–87.

Ekberg, Carl J., "From the Dutch War to European War," *French Historical Studies*, 8, no. 2 (Spring 1974), 393–408.

The Failure of Louis XIV's Dutch War. Chapel Hill, 1979.

Eysinga, W. J. M., *De Wording van het Twaalfjarig Bestand van 9 April 1609*. Amsterdam, 1959.

Eysten, J., *Het leven van Prins Willem II (1626–1650)*. Amsterdam, 1916.

Fockema Andreae, S. J., and H. Hardenberg, eds., *500 jaren Staten-Generaal in de Nederlanden: Van Statenvergadering tot volksvertegenwordiging*. Assen, 1964.

Franken, M. A. M., *Coenraad van Beuningen's Politieke en Diplomatieke Aktiviteiten in de Jaren 1667–1684*. Groningen, 1966.

Fruin, R., "De bemiddeling tusschen de kronen van Frankrijk en Spanje door de Staten der Vereenigde Nederlanden in 1650 aangeboden," *Bijdragen voor Vaderlandsche Geschiedenis*, 3e Reeks, 10 (1897), 197–234.

"Over de oorlogsplannen van Prins Willem II na zijn aanslag op Amsterdam in 1650," *Bijdragen voor Vaderlandsche Geschiedenis*, 3e Reeks, 9 (1896), 1–40.

Tien Jaren uit den Tachtigjarigen Oorlog, 1588–1598. 5th edn, The Hague, 1924.

Gebhard, J. F. Jr, *Het Leven van Mr Nicholaas Cornelisz. Witsen (1641–1717)*. 2 vols. Utrecht, 1881–82.

Gerlach, H., "Het bestand in de Noordelijke Nederlanden, 1609–1621", in: *Algemene Geschiedenis der Nederlanden*, VI, 198–314.

Geyl, P., *Democratische Tendenties in 1672*. Amsterdam, 1950.

De Patriottenbeweging. Amsterdam, 1947.

Geschiedenis van de Nederlandse Stam. Paperback reprint edn, 6 vols. Amsterdam, 1961–62.

Het stadhouderschap in de partij-literatuur onder De Witt. Amsterdam, 1947.

Oranje en Stuart, 1641–1672. Utrecht, 1939.

Willem IV en Engeland tot 1748 (Vrede van Aken). The Hague, 1924.

Groen van Prinsterer, G., *Handboek der Geschiedenis van het Vaderland*. 3rd edn, 2 vols. Amsterdam, 1863–65.

Groenveld, S. *De Prins voor Amsterdam*. Bussum, 1967.

"Natie en nationaal gevoel in de zestiende-eeuwse Nederlanden," in: *Scrinium en Scriptura: Opstellen, aangeboden aan J. R. van der Gouw*. Groningen, 1980, 372–87.

"Ter Inleiding: Willem van Oranje. Een hoog edelman in opstand," *Spiegel Historiael*, 19 (1984), 158–62.

Groenveld, S., and H. L. Ph. Leeuwenberg, eds., *De Unie van Utrecht: Wording en werking van een verbond en een verbondsacte*. The Hague, 1979.

Haak, S. P., "De wording van het conflict tusschen Maurits en Oldenbarnevelt," *Bijdragen voor Vaderlandsche Geschiedenis*, 5e Reeks, 3 (1916), 177–226, 6 (1919), 10 (1923), 177–248.

Haitsma Mulier, E. O. G., and A. E. M. Jensen, eds., *Willem van Oranje in de Historie: Vier eeuwen beeldvorming en geschiedschrijving*. Utrecht, 1984.

Bibliography

Haley, K. H. D., *William of Orange and the English Opposition, 1672–4*. Oxford, 1953.

Hallema, A., *Prins Maurits, 1567–1625: Veertig jaren strijder voor 's lands vrijheid*. Assen, 1949.

Harding, Robert R., *The Anatomy of a Power Elite: The Provincial Governors of Early Modern France*. New Haven and London, 1978.

Heeres, J. E., "Stad en Lande tijdens het erfstadhouderschap van Willem IV," *Bijdragen voor Vaderlandsche Geschiedenis*, 3e Reeks, 4 (1888), 252–344.

Hibben, C. C., *Gouda in Revolt: Particularism and Pacifism in the Revolt of the Netherlands, 1572–1588*. Utrecht, 1983.

Histoire de Guillaume III. Roi de la Grande Bretagne. 2 vols. Amsterdam, 1692.

Holt, Mack P., *The Duke of Anjou and the Politique Struggle During the Wars of Religion*. Cambridge, 1986.

Huges, J., *Het leven en bedrijf van Mr. Francois Vranck*. The Hague, 1909.

Hutton, R., "The Making of the Secret Treaty of Dover," *The Historical Journal*, 29 (1986), 197–318.

Israel, Jonathan, I., *The Dutch Republic and the Hispanic World, 1606–1661*. Oxford, 1982.

Jacob, Margaret C., *The Radical Enlightenment: Pantheists, Freemasons and Republicans*. London, 1981.

Janssens, P., "Willem van Oranje aan het Brussels Hof 1549–1559," *Spiegel Historiael*, 19 (1984), 174–81.

Japikse, N., *De Geschiedenis van het Huis van Orange-Nassau*. 2 vols. The Hague, 1937–38.

"De Staten–Generaal in de achttiende eeuw (1717–1795)," in: Fockema Andreae and Hardenberg, *500 jaren Staten–Generaal*, 99–141.

"Onafhankelijksheidsdag (26 Juli 1581)," *Bijdragen voor Vaderlandsche Geschiedenis*, 5e Reeks, 1 (1913), 213–40.

Prins Willem III: De Stadhouder-Koning. 2 vols. Amsterdam, 1930–33.

Jongkees, A. G., "Vorming van de Bourgondische staat," in: *Algemene Geschiedenis der Nederlanden*, III, 184–200.

Jongste, J. A. F. de, "Een bewind op zijn smalst. Het politiek bedrijf in de jaren 1727–1747," in: *Algemene Geschiedenis der Nederlanden*, IX, 44–59.

"De Republiek onder het erfstadhouderschap," in: *Algemene Geschiedenis der Nederlanden*, IX, 73–91.

Kalshoven, Arnoldina, *De diplomatieke verhouding tusschen Engeland en de Republiek der Vereen. Nederlanden, 1747–1756*. The Hague, 1915.

Kernkamp, G. W., *Prins Willem II, 1626–1650*. 2nd edn, Rotterdam, 1977.

Kikkert, J. G., "Geen standbeeld voor Maurits," *Spiegel Historiael*, 20 (1985), 418–23.

Willem van Oranje, Weesp, 1983.

Kluit, A., *Historie der Hollandsche Staatsregering, tot aan het jaar 1795*. 5 vols. Amsterdam, 1802–5.

Kluiver, J. H., "De Republiek na het bestand, 1621–1650," in: *Algemene Geschiedenis der Nederlanden*, VI, 352–71.

Bibliography

Koenigsberger, Helmut Georg, "Fürst und Generalstaaten: Maximilian I. in den Niederlanden (1477–1493)," *Historische Zeitschrift*, 242 (1986), 557–79.

"Orange, Granvelle and Philip II," *Bijdragen en Mededelingen betreffende de Geschiedenis der Nederlanden*, 89 (1984), 573–95 (reprinted in *Politicians and Virtuosi*, below).

Politicians and Virtuosi: Essays in Early Modern History (London and Ronceverte, W. Va., 1985).

Kops, W. P., "De Oranje-oproeren te Hoorn 1786 en 1787," *Bijdragen voor Vaderlandsche Geschiedenis*, 4e Reeks, 4 (1905), 222–88.

Kossmann, E. H., "The Low Countries," in: *The New Cambridge Modern History* 14 vols. 1957–79. IV, 359–84.

Lademacher, Horst, *Die Stellung des Prinzen von Oranien als Statthalter in den Niederlanden van 1572 bis 1584: Ein Beitrag zur Verfassungsgeschichte der Niederlande*. Bonn, 1958.

Maltby, William S., *Alba: A Biography of Fernando Alvarez de Toledo, Third Duke of Alba, 1507–1582*. Berkeley, Los Angeles and London, 1983.

Meulen, Ageus Jacobus van der, *Studies over het Ministerie van Van de Spiegel*. Leiden, 1905.

Mollema, J. C., *Geschiedenis van Nederland ter Zee*. 4 vols. Amsterdam, 1939–42.

Mout, M. E. H. N., "Het intellectuele milieu van Willem van Oranje," *Bijdragen en Mededelingen betreffende de Geschiedenis der Nederlanden*, 99 (1984), 596–625.

Muller, P. L., *De staat der Vereenigde Nederlanden in de jaren zijner wording, 1572–1594*. Haarlem, 1872.

Naber, Johanna, W. A., *Prinses Wilhelmina, Gemalin van Willem V, Prins van Oranje*. Amsterdam, 1908.

Nierop, H. F. K. van, "De adel in de 16de-eeuwse Nederlanden," *Spiegel Historiael*, 19 (1984), 163–68.

Van ridders tot regenten: De Hollandse adel in de zestiende en de eerste helft van de zeventiende eeuw. Dieren, 1984.

"Willem van Oranje als hoog edelman: patronage in de Habsburgse Nederlanden?", *Bijdragen en Mededelingen betreffende de Geschiedenis der Nederlanden*, 99 (1984), 651–76.

Parival, J. N. de, *Abregé de l'histoire de ce siècle de fer*. Leiden, 1653.

Parker, Geoffrey, *The Dutch Revolt*. Revised edn, Harmondsworth, 1979.

Pater, J. C. H. de, *Maurits en Oldenbarnevelt in den Strijd om het Twaalfjarig Bestand*. Amsterdam, 1940.

The Peace of Nijmegen 1676–1678/1679. La Paix de Nimègue: International Congress of the Tricentennial, Nijmegen, 14–16 September, 1978. Amsterdam, 1980.

Poelhekke, J. J., *De Vrede van Munster*. The Hague, 1948.

"Een gefrustreerd Antwerpenaar: Frederik Hendrik, Prins van Oranje. 1584–1647," in: Poelhekke, *Met Pen, Tongriem en Rapier*, 47–56.

"Frederik Hendrik en Willem II," in: Tamse, *Nassau en Oranje*, 111–52.

Frederik Hendrik, Prins van Oranje: Een Biografisch Drieluik. Zutphen, 1978.

Geen Blijder Maer in Tachtig Jaer. Zutphen, 1973.

Bibliography

Met Pen, Tongriem en Rapier: Figuren uit een ver en nabij verleden. Amsterdam, 1976.

Porta, A., *Joan and Gerrit Corver: De politieke macht van Amsterdam (1702–1748).* Assen and Amsterdam, 1975.

Press, Volker, "Wilhelm von Oranien, die deutschen Reichsstände und der Niederländische Aufstand," *Bijdragen en Mededelingen betreffende de Geschiedenis der Nederlanden*, 99 (1984), 677–707.

Raa, F. G. J ten, and F. de Bas, *Het Staatsche Leger*. 8 vols. (all published). Breda, 1911–64.

Ridder-Symoens, Hilde de, "Vrouwen rond Willem van Oranje," *Spiegel Historiael*, 19 (1984), 181–86.

Riley, James C., *International Government Finance and the Amsterdam Capital Market, 1740–1815*. Cambridge, 1980.

Rosenfeld, Paul, "The Provincial Governors from the Minority of Charles V to the Revolt," *Anciens Pays et Assemblées d'états*, 17 (1959), 1–63.

Rowen, Herbert H., *John de Witt, Grand Pensionary of Holland, 1625–1672*. Princeton, 1978.

John de Witt, Statesman of the "True Freedom". Cambridge, 1986.

"Neither Fish nor Fowl: The Stadholderate in the Dutch Republic," in: Rowen and Lossky, *Political Ideas and Institutions*, 1–31.

The King's State: Proprietary Dynasticism in Early Modern France. New Brunswick, NJ, 1980.

"The Revolution that Wasn't: The *Coup d'Etat* of 1650 in Holland," *European Studies Review*, 4 (1974), 99–117.

Rowen, Herbert H., and Andrew Lossky. *Political Ideas & Institutions in the Dutch Republic: Papers Presented at a Clark Library Seminar 27 March 1982*. Los Angeles, 1985.

Samson, P. A., *Histoire de Guillaume III. Roi d'Angleterre, d'Ecosse, de France, et d'Irlande, &c.* 3 vols. The Hague, 1703.

Schama, Simon, *Patriots and Liberators: Revolution in the Netherlands, 1780–1813*. New York, 1977.

Schelven, A. A. van, *Willem van Oranje: Een boek ter gedachtenis van idealen en teleurstellingen*. 4th edn Amsterdam, 1948.

Schepper, H. de, "De burgerlijke overheden en hun permanente kaders." in: *Algemene Geschiedenis der Nederlanden*, v, 312–49.

Schöffer, I., "De opstand in de Nederlanden, 1566–1609," in: *Winkler Prins Geschiedenis*, ii, 75–118.

"De Republiek der Verenigde Nederlanden," in: *Winkler Prins Geschiedenis*, ii, 119–246.

"Naar consolidatie en behoud onder Hollands leiding (1593–1717)," in: Fockema Andreae and Hardenberg, *500 jaren*, pp. 64–98.

Schulte Nordholt, J. W., *Voorbeeld in de Verte: De invloed van de Amerikaanse revolutie in Nederland*. Baarn, 1979. Translated into English as *The Dutch Republic and American Independence*. Chapel Hill, NC, 1982.

Schutte, G. J., "De Republiek der Verenigde Nederlanden, 1702–1780," in: *Winkler Prins Geschiedenis*, ii, 203–46.

243

Bibliography

Scrinium en Scriptura: Opstellen, aangeboden aan J. B. van der Gouw. Groningen, 1980.

Slothouwer, F. G., "Friesche troebelen gedurende het jaar 1748," *Bijdragen voor Vaderlandsche Geschiedenis*, 3e Reeks, 2 (1885), 402–29.

Swart, K. W., "Oranje en de opkomst van het Statenbewind," *Spiegel Historiael*, 19 (1984), 195–200.

"Wat bewoog Willem van Oranje de strijd tegen de Spaanse overheersing aan te binden?", *Bijdragen en Mededelingen betreffende de Geschiedenis der Nederlanden*, 99 (1984), 554–72.

"Willem de Zwijger," in: Tamse, *Nassau en Oranje*, 45–80.

William the Silent and the Revolt of the Netherlands. London, 1978.

Tamse, C. A., ed., *Nassau en Oranje in de Nederlandse Geschiedenis*. Alphen aan den Rijn, 1979.

Tex, Jan den, *Oldenbarnevelt*. 5 vols. Haarlem, 1960–72.

Theissen, J. S., "Iets over de verhoudingen in de Republiek in 1684," *Bijdragen voor Vaderlandsche Geschiedenis*, 5e Reeks, 7 (1920), 188–216, 8 (1921), 81–97.

The New Cambridge Modern History. 14 vols. Cambridge, 1957–70.

Vaughan, Richard, *John the Fearless: The Growth of Burgundian Power*. New York, 1966.

Philip the Bold: The Formation of the Burgundian State. Cambridge, Mass., 1962.

Voor Rogier: Een bundel Opstellen van oud-leerlingen de Hoogleraar bij zin afschied aangeboden, eds. F. F. J. M. van Eerenbeemt, A. F. Manning and P. H. Winkelman. Hilversum, 1974.

Vrankrijker, A. C. J. de, *De Motiveering van onzen Opstand: De theorieën van het verzet der Nederlandsche opstandelingen tegen Spanje in de jaren 1565–1581*. Nijmegen, 1933. Reprint edn, Utrecht, 1979.

Vreede, G. W., *Mr. Laurens Pieter van de Spiegel en zijne tijdgenoten (1737–1800)*. 4 vols. Middelburg, 1874–77.

Waddington, A., *La République des Provinces-Unies, la France et les Pays-Bas espagnols de 1630 à 1650*. 2 vols. Paris, 1895–97.

Wagenaar, Jan, *Vaderlandsche Historie, vervattende de geschiedenissen der nu Vereenigde Nederlanden, inzonderheid die van Holland, van de vroegste tijden af*. 21 vols. Amsterdam, 1790–96.

Wertheim, W. F., and A. H. Wertheim-Gijse Weeninck, *Burgers in verzet tegen regentgen-heerschappij: Onrust in Sticht en Oversticht (1703–1706)*. Amsterdam, 1976.

Wertheim-Gijse Weeninck, Annie Henriëtte, *Democratische Bewegingen in Gelderland, 1672–1795*. Amsterdam, 1973.

Weststrate, H. A., *Gelderland in den Patriottentijd*. Arnhem, 1903.

Wijn, Jan Willem, *Het krijgswezen in den tijd van Prins Maurits*. Utrecht, 1934.

Wilson, Charles, "Arbiter of the Republic" (review of Herbert H. Rowen, *John de Witt, Grand Pensionary of Holland*), in *The Times Literary Supplement*, 20 Sept. 1978, pp. 1069–70.

Winkler Prins Geschiedenis der Nederlanden, eds. J. A. Bornewasser et al. 3 vols. Amsterdam and Brussels, 1977.

Wit, C. H. E. de, *De Nederlandse Revolutie van de Achttiende Eeuw, 1780–1787: Oligarchie en Proletariaat*. Oirsbeek, 1974.

Index

245

Index

CAMBRIDGE STUDIES IN EARLY MODERN HISTORY

Titles formerly published in the series but no longer in print:

For list of current titles please see front of book